The
Man-Made
City

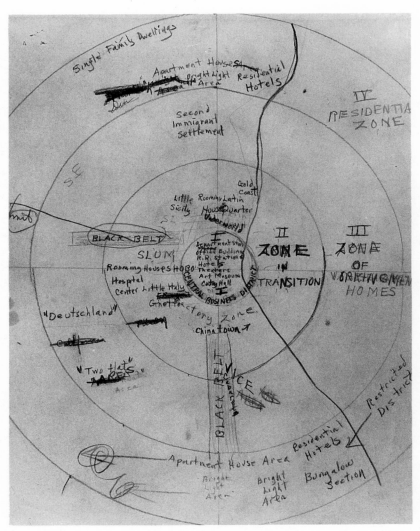

Ernest W. Burgess's first sketch of the natural areas of Chicago.

GERALD D. SUTTLES

THE MAN-MADE CITY

THE LAND-USE CONFIDENCE GAME IN CHICAGO

THE UNIVERSITY OF CHICAGO PRESS

CHICAGO & LONDON

Gerald D. Suttles, professor in the Department of Sociology and the Committee on Geographical Studies at the University of Chicago, is author of the widely acclaimed *The Social Order of the Slum* and *The Social Construction of Communities* and is coauthor of *Poverty and Social Change,* all published by the University of Chicago Press.

The University of Chicago Press, Chicago 60637
The University of Chicago Press, Ltd., London
© 1990 by The University of Chicago
All rights reserved. Published 1990
Printed in the United States of America

99 98 97 96 95 94 93 92 91 90   5 4 3 2 1

Library of Congress Cataloging-in-Publication Data

Suttles, Gerald D.
    The man-made city : The land-use confidence game in Chicago / Gerald D. Suttles.
        p.   cm.
    Includes bibliographical references.
    ISBN 0-226-78193-3
    1. Chicago (Ill.)—Social conditions.   2. City planning—Illinois—Chicago.   3. Urban renewal—Illinois—Chicago.   4. Neighborhood—Illinois—Chicago.   I. Title.
HN80.C5S965   1990
307.3′4′0977311—dc20   89-20161
                                                                              CIP

∞The paper used in this publication meets
the minimum requirements of the American National
Standard for Information Sciences—Permanence of
Paper for Printed Library Materials, ANSI Z39.48–1984.

For my father,
Berlin

CONTENTS

Contents

ILLUSTRATIONS

Illustrations

Maps

Plates

ACKNOWLEDGMENTS

This is an old-fashioned book. It aims less to advance sociology than to improve Chicago as a place to live. There is no modesty in this claim for the latter is far more difficult than the former. Unabashedly reformist as I am, my message is aimed at the general reader. Thus, I have avoided the disciplinary practice of writing the book twice, once as theory and again as findings. Those who know about such things will immediately recognize my debt to Robert E. Park and George Herbert Mead. I would find it hard to condense their work beyond what they have done themselves.

Some will find the book harsh and unrelenting in its criticism of Chicago. I can only say that I think that such self-examination is warranted and in the best Chicago tradition. I write as a Chicago loyalist, but I like Chicago because it is like me—transparently imperfect. It is a book for adults.

The bulk of this manuscript is a descriptive account of brick and mortar projects on Chicago's North Side and in its Central Business District. Another investigator might have called this "urban planning," perhaps "process planning." Some Chicagoans do take this view, persistently reconfiguring what has been done into something intended. I have taken rather lightly this deliberative view, seeing it more as a satisfying retrospective account than one of rational design. This study, then, focuses as much on what is not done or what is done badly as what is done intentionally. So many plans are made that those which survive to completion seem almost fortuitous: projects that somehow stumble past the obstacles to serve political claimants.

Readers may find it easier to believe this of Chicago than of other places. Chicago is the media model of civic corruption, and readers may get impatient as they encounter one foible after another. What is so obviously wanted is a bit of professionalism, more individual integrity, and at least an approximation of bureaucratic procedure. But as readers wend their way through these case studies, I hope they will begin to see that these kinds of reforms are a local industry in Chicago. It is not from lack of effort, intelligence, and good intentions that the city's defects of management are so evident. Rather it is the lack of any standards for comparative judgment which throw project after project into indeterminate dispute. Documenting this claim takes up the better part of this book, and it is only in the last chapter than one can begin to see the kind of urban information system that might better inform Chicago's reformers and politicians alike. I apologize for the delay, but I did not see my way there until I got there. The impatient reader may want to read the Methodological Appendix to more briefly follow me in how one gets from the first chapter to the last.

For Chicagoans, a more rational planning process is not simply a question of civic beautification. The city has failed to keep pace with other cities, and the costs of political predation and uncertainty have already prompted a sense of backwardness. Broad-shouldered boosterism and reforms alone cannot meet the competition, and the city still lacks any comparative standards against which to evaluate its performance. It remains mired in debates over distributive equity that easily dissolve into contests over patronage. The only thing remarkable about these contests is the moralism that fails to disguise them.

Nonetheless, Chicago can still be looked at with an unveiled eye not usually directed at other places. Max Weber once likened it to "a man whose skin has been peeled off and whose intestines are seen to work" (1975, p. 286). What Weber had in mind was not the sheer physical presence of the place (and least of all the slogan "the city that works") but the lack of dissimulation by its residents. Chicago's skeletons go rattling down the streets, uncloseted. In the absence of any basis for convincing, collective examination, every Chicagoan is a privileged individual critic.

Several generations of sociologists have been advantaged by this transparency, and I am one of them. I cannot begin to thank all those people whose frankness and encouragement kept me going over the years. I am especially indebted to Marion Faldet and the Spencer Foundation who supported me for a year's leave of absence, although my study did not fit into their program and had no obvious, immediate application. I am grateful to members of the Metropolitan Planning Council, the Department of City Planning, and numerous civic and community groups only some of whose names appear in this study. I am grateful to them not only because they told me what was "really happening" but because they argued with me about what it "really meant."

Some individuals played especially important roles in data collection and analysis. Priscilla Kyros did much of the coding with extraordinary exactitude and patience. Ramola Joseph and Michael Emerson helped me chase down fugitive documents and sources that I would have given up on except for their resourcefulness.

Field studies take an enormous amount of time and disorder one's domestic life. My wife was more than patient. She selected the right times to ignore me and the right times to be a critical audience.

Regrettably, my appreciation for Morris Janowitz's encouragement and advice must be posthumous. But somewhere, up there in the Great University of the Sky, I can see him comparing his view of Chicago with my more terrestrial one. I hope he is not too disappointed.

The
Man-Made
City

ONE

THE MAN-MADE CITY

Chicago must be one of the most planned cities of the modern era. An extraordinarily uniform street grid conveys this impression, and it is repeated by numerous other features of the man-made landscape. A magnificent lakeside park runs the entire length of the city, and it comes as no surprise that this parkland is constructed almost entirely from fill. A system of boulevards connects a series of pleasure garden parks, each arrayed in a geometric pattern about the city center. The Chicago River, its flow reversed from its natural course, runs like an arrow to join a pair of clearly excavated channels, one north, one south. Museums, a planetarium, a zoo, and several other public edifices are sited almost as if on a landscape architect's renderings. Full city blocks are uniformly eight to the mile, five to the kilometer. The rail focus takes on almost the exact appearance of a cellular diagram. Nearly everywhere there is geometric certainty: in the office towers, in the statues flanking major streets, even in the elaborated facades designed by Sullivan, by Burnham, by Le Baron Jenny.

It is of some puzzlement that many of Chicago's most articulate observers have sought to find the source of all this order in the cumulative accomplishments of individuals going their separate ways. The Chicago School of Sociology more than any other part of that discipline has extended this view to the point that it remains a foil for more collectivist or conspiratorial approaches (Bulmer 1984). An equally prominent Chicago School of Economics is widely known for its contention that the unregulated marketplace is or should be the ultimate arbiter which selects among human intentions. There is even a homegrown political science that purports to have found a "behavioral theory of democracy" in which votes are treated as token purchases in the political marketplace. And, of course, there are the Chicago novelists—legions of them—who have found in the city itself a metaphor for chaos and unyielding individualism (Smith 1984).

The idea that some sort of selective process might produce

order out of diversity did not originate in Chicago, but it certainly has become entrenched in that city's vocabulary for self-examination. There are exceptions. A locally grown journalism is so notorious for its ability to find conspiracies that those who aspire to dispassionate explanations are apt to lean in the opposite direction. But even here, collusion is seen less as the realization of public purpose than as the cabals of little groups. It must be said that the city's historians have followed a more diverse course, often finding evidence for concerted action, but here too the ecological metaphor has found frequent use. Local architects—yet another Chicago school—are still more diverse in outlook, tending, on the one hand, to repeat Burnham's command to "make no little plans" while, on the other hand, defending their separate projects as unavoidable responses to "the market" (Condit 1973, 1974).

This ecological metaphor has become so embedded in Chicago's language for self-examination that one sometimes wonders if it does not feed upon itself. For scholars who want to follow this approach, there are reams of quotations and footnotes to assist their case. For every article, novel, or statistical compilation that suggests a man-made city, there must be a dozen that confidently assert the blind power of market forces, of demographic trends, of driving subsistence needs, or of narrow political gains. Yet if one suspends belief for a moment and allows that doubt some license, one begins to see a very uneven pattern of development. There are reasonably clear periods of robust economic and cultural development in Chicago, and there are also rather dreary periods of disunity, indecision, and economic and cultural stagnation. Perhaps it is only now, after 150 years, that Chicago can be said to have a history in the fuller sense of a time span sufficient to reveal the variety of human endeavors it took to shape it. Park and Burgess began their studies of Chicago when it was barely eighty years old. They followed a period of unified growth but drew their empirical observations from a time of growing disunity, corruption, and frustrated reforms. If one now looks over their work and the older city that informed it, the question arises as to when and in what cases is the ecological metaphor an apt characterization and when does it fall short. Is it just that entrepreneurs, politicians, elites, and citizens get on the subsocial bandwagon when there is one and fall into quarrelsome isolation when there is a downturn in the business cycle? Or is something more complicated involved: the social contrivance of such popular bandwagons, the uneven role of leadership, and the mixed results of efforts to overcome mutual suspicion and the overhead costs of corruption?

One can draw some tentative conclusions to these questions from the abbreviated historical survey that follows. But the main burden of this study is entirely contemporaneous. Chicagoans live in exciting times, which is to say that their present may be informative if not altogether pleasant. A very wide array of trail bandwagons are out there now, and the results are still uncertain. We will turn to a number of these social experiments after some initial effort to situate the city both in historical and comparative context.

The Port City of the Prairie

From its settlement in the 1830s until the 1860s Chicago was dominated by an elite of exceptional energy and uniformity in background. These men, most of them from small-town New England, engaged in real estate development, merchandising, and especially the transhipment of raw or partially processed goods (Mayer and Wade 1969; Jaher 1982). Almost all could be said to have an abiding interest in Chicago as the great transportation center of the "American West," even though multiple sources of income was the rule.

But if they avidly pursued their separate interests—and practically all were successful in doing so—they were also heavily engaged in public life and the collective enthusiasms of the period. A small number of them simply circulated the office of mayor among themselves for the first thirty-two years of the city's incorporation. Others went off to the national congress where they unwaveringly pressed for federal grants and legislation to assist the Port City of the Prairie. Reading the history of these men, it is difficult to avoid the impression that they were caught up in a vision of municipal growth that transcended their personal fortunes. Some of them rotated in and out of public life with a regularity that defies contemporary example. Having occupied high public office for one term, they would take a lower office for a subsequent term. Out of office or in office, they were active petitioners for grand public projects, for new federal expenditures, and novel ways of solving the young city's awesome problems of sanitation and construction.

Native born, New Englanders to the core, they scarcely resembled the remaining population who quickly become heavily foreign and Catholic. Having arrived early with modest means, they

The Man-Made City

certainly got in on the ground floor of investment opportunity, but they were also magnets in the fuller sense of that word, attracting to themselves a following of diverse origin.

In the span of thirty years, these magnets set in motion most of the great projects that were to preoccupy Chicagoans until the Great Fire of 1871 and some others to follow that are still incomplete. Chicago had one of the poorest ports on the southern end of Lake Michigan (Mayer and Wade 1969, p. 20). With federal assistance it was made into the best port in the region. The grid pattern (essentially an extension of the Federal Land Survey) with its uniformity of access was imposed with remarkably few exceptions. The Illinois-Michigan canal was completed (with state financial assistance) ten years after the city's incorporation. Within no more than six years (1845–1854) Chicago (again with federal help) became the rail capital of the nation. In the 1850s, the entire grade of the existing city was raised by jacking up buildings so that fill could remove them from the muck that had been tolerated for the previous twenty years. Then the roads were paved with the novel device of wooden blocks soaked in pitch and topped with a covering of gravel.

All these accomplishments may be what one would expect of a *unified* elite whose fortunes rested on the transhipment of goods and rising land values. Moreover, a close look at many of these projects shows that civic leaders were able to cover much of the cost with public sources and that they were constantly active in seeking still more favorable legislation from the state and federal governments. Indeed, the first convention (1850) ever held in the city—there were 20,000 conventioneers and only 16,000 residents—was a gathering to protest federal neglect of the Western region. But the ambition of these leaders extended much wider than obvious class advantage. In 1859, the first University of Chicago opened its doors; a historical society had been established three years earlier. A public school system was organized by the 1850s and drew widespread admiration (Parton 1867). Perhaps the most notable accomplishment, the one that was to distinguish Chicago from all the other Great Lakes cities, was the commitment to a vast lakeside park system and another that would ring the city to the west. Still incomplete, this parkland was to become a continuous object of controversy which remains so to this day. Nonetheless, the rallying cries of those who saw the general value of the parks—*Urbs in horto* and "Forever Open, Clear and Free"—were coined in a city Gustaf Unonius called a "vast mud puddle" in 1842.

The Man-Made City

The Windy City

By the beginning of the 1860s, the union of commercial and official leadership came to an end in widespread charges of corruption and ineptitude. Despite the wartime boom and postwar prosperity, dissention was everywhere; over land grabs by the railways, the Sunday closings of saloons, "grantism," and the general disbursement of "boodle." After 1861, several years of drift and uncertainty prevailed. The Great Fire in 1871, however, prompted a popular call for unity and a great show of boosterism. But civic leadership during this period never really established itself, and one mayor after another failed to attract a durable following. The spasm of energy that went into recovery from the fire was quickly spent by the depression of 1873 (Nord 1985). Looking back over the 1869–1875 period, Bradley and Zald (1965) refer to the mayors as "transitional" figures, and the term is appropriate if we mean that they only presided over a time of change. A mixture of reformers and populists, they shared little in common other than their lack of resemblance to their predecessors. Not until the first term of Monroe Heath (1876) was confidence in local government gradually strengthened. Even so, the transition he presided over was not a revitalized political leadership but the emergence of a new economic elite that chose to "influence rather than rule."

From 1880 to 1892, however, Chicago enjoyed yet another extravagant period of economic and cultural growth. The central figures this time were the big industrialists like Armour, Swift, McCormick, and Pullman, or the great merchants like Field and Leiter. By all accounts it was a time of enormous development although only barely able to survive the currents of labor unrest. Still the packinghouses boomed, the mail-order houses found their market, and Chicago came to rank just behind Pittsburgh in the production of steel. This economic growth was paralleled by impressive cultural edifices: the Art Institute, the Auditorium Theater, and the new University of Chicago. Both a Chicago School of Architecture and of Literature took on their distinctive shapes, and by the time of the Columbian Exposition Chicago had become the "Windy City."[1]

During all this growth and innovation it is hard to find in the city's political leadership much of a positive role other than the willingness to let businessmen take the initiative. Indeed, Harrison

---

1. Which at the time referred to the boastful claims of its leaders, not the weather.

Carter—five times mayor—seems to have taken this as his official charge. By the time of the 1893 Columbian Exposition, the city could almost be said to have a private government. Many new men of wealth (Armour, Swift, Pullman, Yerkes) were drawn into public life, and still others from established families (Palmer, Field) were aroused to greater participation.

But the Columbian Exposition seems to have been the high watermark of this mobilized elite. A brief depression followed, and thereafter political graft and labor unrest become more and more intense. Also, investment took a more selective turn, flowing heavily into local utilities (Yerkes's traction system, Insull's electrification of the city), the Sanitary Canal, or already established industries like the mail-order business. Most would seem to be industries that had to bear the overhead costs of political corruption and labor racketeering, either because they could not move or because embedded capital made movement very expensive. The clothing industry did not grow, at least not until 1914. In addition, the industrial districts the city had pioneered in the 1880s were increasingly being located outside the city, many of them in Indiana. The new electrical industry and the expansion of the steel industry moved almost entirely in this direction after 1900, and suburban growth began to outdistance that of the city at this time. The annexations, which proceeded so rapidly before 1893, were now drastically slowed by self-conscious suburban communities which sought to establish themselves as "model communities" directly in contrast to Chicago.[2]

Still, population growth within the city continued at an impressive rate, although increasingly it was viewed with alarm as massive slums spread and a black ghetto of unusual confinement appeared. Within ten years (1897–1906) Pullman, Swift, Palmer, and Yerkes died or left town (Lewis and Smith 1929). The new leaders who rose to prominence in their place are probably better remembered for their frustrated efforts at reform than for any new industrial or cultural accomplishments. Alarmed by the city's disorder and terrible living conditions, the Commercial Club commissioned Burnham and Bennett's *Plan of Chicago* (1909), but little of this plan was acted on until after the First World War. The city lost its movie industry at about the same time. In the years just before the First World War, Chicago's chief growth industries seem to have been patronage politics, labor racketeering, vice, social reform, and

2. Some were "sobriety" communities.

The Man-Made City

a refinement of the novel as social criticism. Only the vice and the novels might be considered "export industries."

The Second City

Despite the race riots of 1919, Chicago entered another decade of economic and cultural growth. There was, of course, a national postwar "boom," but Chicago rode it out with extravagant accomplishments. The lakeside and river-edge improvements were especially impressive, leading Carl Condit to call the area around the Field Museum the "architecturally most impressive 'cultural center' in the United States" (1974). But almost equally impressive was the proliferation of downtown office buildings and the creation of an industrial design especially suited to the growing use of electricity. A huge municipal pier, the Civic Opera building, the Merchandise Mart, Midway Airport, and Soldier Field all date from this period.

Looking back it is a little difficult to identify the basis for such extravagant growth. The printing and electrical industries did experience strong growth, the former located largely within the central city. But there is also reason to think that after years of wrangling, reform leaders like Charles Wacker, Montgomery Ward, and Julius Rosenwald were able to seize upon the improved business climate and to prevail with the Chicago Plan (i.e., Burnham's plan) despite an obstreperous and unpredictable mayor, "Big Bill" Thompson. Thompson, of course, also liked to call himself "Bill the Builder," and he did not invariably oppose these reformers. The reform administration of Dever also provided some relief from Thompson's obstructionism. Corruption and vice, however, were not effectively reduced, and gangsterism reached a high point of notoriety with the St. Valentine's Day massacre. Even after the close of the decade, Thompson sought reelection (unsuccessfully) by openly inflaming ethnic hostilities.

Much as one may admire the results of this construction boom, it does seem to have outstripped the local economic base which was to have supported it. Acknowledged (Mayer and Wade 1969, p. 342) as a period of excessive optimism, the 1920s left the city and its suburbs with a vastly overdeveloped infrastructure (overextended industrial districts, overzoning of commercial strips) that was not to be put into use until the 1950s. The depression of 1929 did see a sys-

The Man-Made City

tematization of patronage politics and the emergence of the career politician who had "come up through the ranks." The Great Depression was an overpowering experience throughout the country, but in Chicago it lingered on in the form of exceptional caution and pessimism into the early 1950s. A. J. Liebling's *Chicago: The Second City* (1952) was a telling and painful portrait (Berry et al. 1976). A city that had probably overreached itself in one postwar boom turned very cautious when faced with another. Not until well into the first of Richard J. Daley's six terms as mayor was there a rekindling of optimism and a new period of economic and cultural expansion.

The City That Works

When Richard J. Daley came into the mayor's office in 1955, it had been over fifty-five years since anyone in the office had become a chief magnet to draw around himself the proponents of new investment and innovation. Up from the ranks of the Eleventh Ward Regular Democratic Organization, first a "stockyard cowboy" and then a night school lawyer, there was little reason to expect great accomplishments from him as mayor. The previous mayor and a member of the party that Daley now headed so opposed him that he contested Daley in open election. Yet, as the early literature on Daley shows (Banfield 1961; Wilson 1962; Banfield and Wilson 1963; Bradley and Zald 1965), he did three things that inspired confidence in his administration and gave him a progressively stronger hand in mobilizing support for public projects. First, he made a number of appointments, bringing into his administration several acknowledged "experts," people like Ira Bach, Donald Mackelman, Lewis Hill, Edward Marciniak, and Orlando Wilson. He sought and obtained the advice of prominent business leaders of what were then the city's "sunrise industries": James Downs (real estate development), William Holabird (architecture), Joel Goldblatt (retailing), and Arthur Rubloff (real estate development). Well-known urban experts (Philip Hauser, Anthony Downs, Harold Mayer) were drawn into city planning as consultants.

Second, during the early period of his administration, Daley appears to have been very cautious in taking initiative, but equally responsive once various interest groups had thrashed out some agreement and presented him with a "project" (Banfield 1961). In this way he seemed invariably to succeed, while at the same time

The Man-Made City

avoiding involvement in the debates that almost always preceded such proposals. He was described as acting only on the basis of existing consensus rather than throwing his weight around (Bradley and Zald 1965): a "facilitator" rather than a "boss."

Finally, and again earlier in his six terms, Daley maintained good relations with "downstate" Republicans, always a difficult relationship but one Daley openly supported as a part of his pragmatic approach of "good government is good politics." Party ideologies were avoided, and gubernatorial elections were subdued so that "upstate-downstate" relations were easy to repair after each contest.

Investor confidence and local ambition, which had reached such a low point at the time of Liebling's "second city," responded quickly to Daley, and a flurry of building commenced. The world's largest airport was constructed and cleverly included within the city's boundaries. A giant exposition hall was constructed along the lakefront and helped the city capture much of the convention trade. Both the Illinois Institute of Technology and the University of Chicago were persuaded to stay in the city by the measures of extensive urban renewal. The construction of Carl Sandburg Village on the North Side probably helped to promote that area before the term "gentrification" came into use. The city's skyline, almost unchanged since the 1930s, erupted with new skyscrapers.

Daley attracted a great deal of attention from very able social scientists (e.g., Banfield, Myerson, Bradley, Zald, Wilson), and a literature that had once drawn upon Chicago politics only for caricature (Lewis and Smith 1929, Liebling 1952, Stead 1894, Wendt 1934) now turned ambivalent or, sometimes, downright positive. Patronage, vote buying, and scandals still occurred, of course, but Daley's own willingness to compromise—to get the best deal—was applauded. Chicago was "the city that worked." This impression fit his public image. Never a rhetorician,[3] he was still able to stage great shows of party unity with himself as the object of wholesale acclaim. When he entered a party gathering, the crowd separated for him like the Red Sea.[4] A family man, intensely loyal to neighborhood and church, he was able to convey his affection for Chicago with a kind of pugnacious defensiveness that even Norman Mailer conceded was "the very face of Chicago" (1968, p. 90).

3. Daley took elocution lessons which improved his speeches, although not so much as to relieve him from frequent satire.
4. The audience was cued by the playing of "When Irish Eyes Are Smiling."

The Man-Made City

And, of course, it was this defensiveness that made him unable to control his outrage at the Yippies, black militants, and cosmopolitans who confronted him at the 1968 Democratic convention. Daley's humiliation at that convention and the subsequent riots in the city are frequently seen as the main cause for his subsequent weaknesses. But after 1968, very few social scientists returned to reexamine the Daley administration, and most of the accounts, especially those widely read, were written by journalists (Mailer 1968; Royko 1971; O'Conner 1975; and Kennedy 1978). If one looks closely at the period after 1968, however, it would appear that Daley reversed many of his previous practices and that he did so at a time when the city itself was changing its demands upon leadership.[5] Many of the people he had drawn into office had aged and become the subject of scandal or widespread opposition (see Chap. 7). They were not replaced or were replaced only after exhausting public demonstrations (e.g., Benjamin Willis, school superintendent). In the one notable instance where Daley did replace the head of the scandal-ridden Metropolitan Sanitary District, the new head of the district was fired by the trustees a few years later. Subsequently, several of the trustees were indicted. Many of those who had been "bright young businessmen" when Daley first drew upon their advice began to preside over sunset rather than sunrise industries. Daley himself began to take the initiative and proposed several projects that met stiff public opposition or became the object of dissatisfaction. The crosstown expressway was defeated by a citywide coalition that brought Alinsky tactics into familiar use by middle-income neighborhood groups (Emmons 1986). A third airport to

5. Practically all those who observed the pre-1968 Daley administration were very able social scientists (Banfield 1961; Wilson 1962; Banfield and Wilson 1963; Myerson and Banfield 1955; Bradley and Zald 1965; Greenstone and Peterson 1973) while nearly all those who wrote subsequent accounts were journalists (Mailer 1968; Royko 1971; O'Conner 1975, 1977; and Kennedy 1978). The former give a very uniform description of the Daley political process, but only Greenstone and Peterson (1973) reach barely beyond the 1968 period. They do comment on the puzzling difference between Banfield's facilitator and what they observed in a short footnote (p. 274). The journalists seem simply to have assumed a continuity of political process or, more likely, to have ignored such a distinction.

Milton Rakove's work (1975) might be considered an exception to this, but his observations were gained almost entirely from ward politics. Guterbock's study (1980) also focuses on ward politics, but the central finding of his study is a change in the political process stressing the importance of public confidence rather than patronage in that process. Rakove's work was frequently mentioned in the Chicago mass media. Indeed, he has been frequently featured as a guest writer. Guterbock was scantily reviewed by the local press.

The Man-Made City

be located in Lake Michigan drew so much criticism that it was quickly abandoned. City engineers and planners were unable to present a satisfactory design for the Franklin Street subway and connector, and federal criticism added fuel to local opposition. A new hockey stadium was equally unsuccessful in obtaining federal funding, and Daley also failed in his bid to renovate Soldier Field. Daley did succeed in clearing Place du Sable just west of the Loop, but the site remained vacant for the remainder of his administration as well as that of two succeeding mayors. Illinois Center, to the east of the Loop, did become the location for extensive office development, but the design of the center is widely regarded as a lost opportunity to attract a wider range of visitors to the city's downtown.

Progressively, Daley's insistence on the large downtown project was juxtaposed to the neighborhood developments supported by community groups. Both parties to this dispute became entrapped in a rhetoric that equated downtown development with investment and neighborhood renewal with redistribution. As each side embraced this language, their proposals narrowed to subscribe to this formula. Downtown projects were defended almost entirely on the basis of how many jobs or how much tax revenues they would produce. Neighborhood developments were described equally as a public benefit for low-income groups or "minorities." People seemed simply to loose sight of a growing need to retain some residential areas for a highly skilled labor force and to create a "twenty-four-hour" downtown to capture the growth of urban tourism.

In the midst of this, a strong public critic and personal enemy[6] was elected governor of Illinois. If Daley was indifferent to party ideologies, he was not insensitive to personal attacks. "Upstate-downstate" relations deteriorated, and a Democratic mayor and Democratic governor could not unite to face a federal government increasingly dominated by Republicans. Daley's posture seemed to harden as he was locked into this defensive position. Unwilling to replace many of his appointees, he was unable to restrain them. The number of scandals and indictments multiplied. When he had entered office, Daley was identified with the "little guy," the hyphenated American and the blue-collar worker. Now he was seen as the defender of entrenched ethnic groups and downtown businessmen

6. Daniel Walker who had presided over the very critical report on the riots during the 1968 Democratic convention.

and against blacks and the new minorities, since the former rallied to his defense while the latter stayed on the offensive. Status politics replaced investment politics.

The local media did record—often gleefully—many of Daley's failures and embarrassments. But these were blow-by-blow accounts treated as exceptions within a trend line of unbroken success. Compared to Cleveland and New York, Chicago was still "the city that works." Those who were apprehensive about public investment and alarmed by the clamor for redistribution to the neighborhoods lined up behind Daley with renewed resolution. Except for a brief period when William Singer appeared to be a credible alternative for mayor, Daley remained the one man widely believed to be able to overcome the decentralized baronies that had preceded him. Daley's own endorsement became almost the sole basis for project support, and the city's in-house capacity for planning decayed, fossilized, or became irrelevant. Indeed, Daley farmed out much of the planning effort (e.g., the Chicago 21 Plan) to exactly those businessmen and architects who would benefit from new public investments. Despite his heart attack in 1974, Daley was prevailed upon to run for a sixth term. A weakened man, he died a year later leaving a public administration that would poorly serve three successors.

At the height of Daley's power, in 1965, Bradley and Zald (1965) thought they could detect in him and his immediate predecessors a series of incremental steps toward the new urban chief administrator. He was Banfield's (1961) facilitator who assembled talent, sorted among supportable options, and acted as gatekeeper within the limits of local consensus. Whether a reformer or a boss, the chief city administrator had come to a common destination where a "new ethos of 'the good of the community' becomes dominant and shapes the administration of the mayor" (Bradley and Zald 1965, p. 167). With vastly improved hindsight, one might say instead that even very successful urban administrations go through a kind of natural history in which they are progressively scarred by scandal, in which what were once "new men" age into being "the same old crowd." Even successful public investment strategies will eventually elicit an enlarged claim for redistribution as new inequities appear to demarcate comparative winners and losers.[7] One

7. Even Mayor Kevin White seems to have been unable to escape this cycle in the booming Boston economy.

should not expect, then, a linear progression of urban administration shaped simply by the imperatives of effective decision making.

But even with hindsight this seems too simple. The Chicago that existed after 1968 was very different than the one that faced Daley in 1955. By 1968 Chicago was as much Hugh Hefner's city as it was Mayor Daley's. The Second City was its best-known theater. There was a growing and more outspoken gay community. Feminism had become a social movement. Manufacturing and mass retailing might still be the dominant industries, but the growth sector had moved very much in the direction of "market-driven" firms in entertainment, conventions, services, and above all the futures market, which had come to resemble organized gambling. These are piloted by a very different breed of individuals than the businessmen Daley drew into his administration. College educated in the postwar period and unconventional in their careers, they are often willing to explore very experimental life-styles. Even today they are not being heavily recruited into public life.

Daley's winning strategy, like that of many other mayors, had been to piece together federal funds and private investments into large-scale brick and mortar projects. While this responded to one part of the local economy, it ignored the part that was occurring by the 1960s in small firms, in warehouse lofts, or in run-down shopping strips. Many of these experiments did not even look like businesses in the way Chicagoans were accustomed to think of them. Often they made nothing tangible like metal barrels or ball bearings. They handled paperwork or provided ill-defined information and services. Sometimes they were run by hustlers who had been in and out of bankruptcy more than once. Scarcely visible and highly experimental, the leading edge of the growth sector was not easily recognized. It was especially difficult to recognize when a proven strategy moved Chicago in another direction.

Challenge and Response

Sixty years ago J. Paul Goode delivered a lecture titled, "Chicago: A City of Destiny" (1923). To overstate his position: the city site was a great regional economy that had only to wait for the bodies to appear. Twenty years later Harold Mayer delivered an equally well-known lecture, "Chicago: City of Decisions" (1955).[8] The main point

8. Both lectures were presented to the Geographic Society of Chicago.

of Mayer's remarks was to say that once decisions are made it is more difficult to unmake them. Nonetheless, he prevailed upon Chicagoans to face a number of decisions no longer obviously guided by the natural landscape. There was much to unify the approaches of Goode and Mayer. Both regarded the city site and region as the chief determinants of further decisions and growth. Those who responded "accurately" to make the "best use" of locations and space would rise to positions of power and leadership. Others would imitate them. Thus, there was a kind of self--correcting pattern of leadership selection which, in the long run, should work to the advantage of each community.

Nonetheless, Mayer obviously felt some uneasiness about the efficiency of this process and thought that more informed guidance might speed things along in a city that had been marking time for twenty-five years. One reason for his unease was the view that land-use decisions are self-correcting only in the long run. The very uneven pace of Chicago's development was now visible, and the interludes of indecision were of impressive length. Certainly one could point to the periodic emergence of "new men" to provide leadership and build confidence. But they had not emerged with the regularity of the tides. There also appears to have been a peculiar coincidence between new economic development and the erection of new cultural institutions, as if the latter were as essential as the former in capturing public enthusiasm and confidence. At times, great plans do seem to have almost "entrapped" public commitment so as to override ethnic and racial divisions. And, in each of these more favorable episodes, one could usually point to the exceptional cooperation of all levels of government: federal, state, and city.

If one is simply looking for an explanation, then, I suppose there is a sense in which the ecological metaphor applies, but it does so only if we do not ask much of it. All the detail is lost, and so long as there is some "adaptation" in the long run, falsification is impossible. The only guide to policy seems to be "to wait." Such theoretical opportunism, however, is unsatisfying, and what I find more appealing is a brief section from Wilbur Thompson's *A Preface to Urban Economics* (1965, p. 18).

> If the rich always did get richer (and the poor poorer) in interregional competition, long range forecasting would be much easier than it actually is. But victories can bring complacency and defeats can be challenges. We might postulate a crises theory of human behavior in regional economic de-

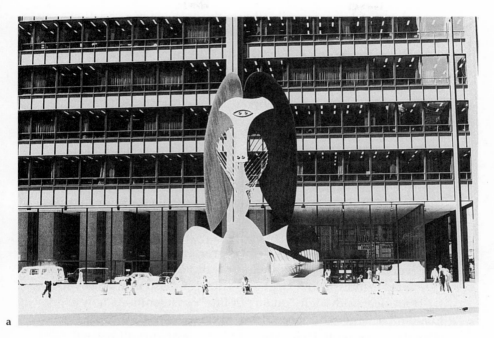

Memorials to Richard J. Daley, mayor: (a) Daley Center in Daley Plaza; (b) plaque at Daley Bicentennial Plaza.

velopment: a community rises to the occasion in a variation on the Toynbee theme of "challenge and response."

What Thompson suggests is that urban information systems are extremely imperfect and that only failure, often glaring failure, can sometimes provide the corrective in the search for some avenue to success. In the three cases Thompson briefly reviews (Boston, Detroit, and Pittsburgh), he estimates that "as much as two decades may elapse between shifts from one economic base to a substantially new one" (p. 21). But he quickly adds, "Of course, this is the very kind of knowledge which, once revealed, might effect changes in the developmental pattern and might even shorten the period of response." Thus, an even more nearly "man-made" city may be possible and desirable.

In the contemporary setting, it is fairly clear to urban leaders that the era of the smokestack city is over. In turn, practically every city seems to be making an effort to attract a new generation of "knowledge industries." The means to accomplish this, however, is far from clear, although "quality-of-life" considerations now seem to loom far larger and go contrary to the received idea that if you provide the location, technology, and infrastructure all else will follow: clean neighborhoods, good schools, fine cultural institutions, and a rich civic life. Of course, it never quite worked that way. Carl Condit (1973) has forcefully reminded us that the Chicago "that emerged in mid-century presented a perfect paradox of brilliant technological and architectural achievement standing beside the failure to produce a decent human environment for the majority of its citizens" (p. xi). There are many who would agree with Condit, and it is precisely this failing, they would add, that hampers Chicago's bid for recovery. A unified and self-conscious effort to improve the city's human environment, however, will itself present new challenges. The old ecological metaphor obscured a great deal of planful direction, making it appear a response to necessity. A more thoroughly man-made city heightens our awareness of choice and responsibility and requires a political process that is more than simply permissive.

TWO

THE THIRD CITY

In 1980, when the Census Bureau finally announced that Chicago had become the nation's third city, Mayor Jane Byrne threatened to take the matter to court.[1] Both daily newspapers found it newsworthy and presented it as a watershed in local history.[2] Of course, this change in city rank was not entirely unforeseen, but it did seem to bring to the surface a new level of journalistic alarm and completed a transition in the popular conceptions of Chicago's future. In the 1960s the urban crises could be seen as a widely shared predicament, all boats floundering in the same ebb tide. If Chicago differed, it was in its stronger showing as "the city that works." Until 1976 they could even enjoy the spectacle of Lindsey, Beame, Perk, and Rizzo struggling for popular support while their own mayor was a symbol of continuity. By the mid-1970s the relative growth rate of the "sunbelt" was widely noted, but Chicago's condition was not singled out from that of the "frostbelt" in general. Just before 1980, the dramatic shift from smokestack industries to high-tech industries had created some signs of alarm. But it was the Census Bureau's announcement that aggregated all these increments of bad news into a qualitative sense of local backwardness. Progressively, the term "rustbelt" replaced "frostbelt."

This rather delayed response is not exactly striking because it lagged that of the sociologists by only a short margin. Throughout the late 1960s and early 1970s the demographic reports of Pierre de Vise dwelled primarily on the flight to the suburbs and the growing dependent population in Chicago, but the general picture was one

1. Bernard Carey, Illinois state's attorney, did bring suit against the Census Bureau but withdrew it pending the outcome of a failed Detroit suit. Obviously, some were concerned with the federal money depending on headcounts, but city pride was also at stake. Mike Royko defended that pride by declaring Chicago "a first-rate third," and the *Sun-Times* headlined, "It's not heaven in the City of Angels" (7 September 1980).

2. The *Sun-Times* editorialized a "Plan for a smaller city" (2 September 1980), and the *Tribune* editorialized, "Chicago gets smaller" (7 September 1980). Later, when a corrected census count reestablished the city's second rank, the margin was too small and temporary to be front-page news.

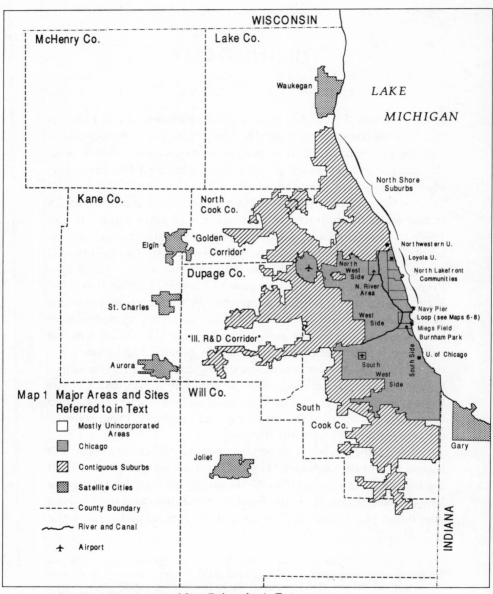

Map 2.1. Major Areas and Sites Referred to in Text

of regional growth.[3] It was not until the Census Bureau report that a host of urbanologists suddenly became the bearers of bad news (Sternlieb et al. 1982; Vining 1982; Brown and Wardwell 1980; Peterson 1981, 1985).[4] In the time since then, regional decline has become something that can be openly recognized.

None of this, however, provides Chicago leaders with obvious remedies or avenues of intervention. There is some discussion of a "national industrial policy," but when this is mentioned to businessmen, many of them wince at the thought of a national policy of protectionism with investment credits going to the highest vote getters. There is also a call for local mobilization, and the Commercial Club has produced a timetable for economic investment and growth. The Illinois congressional delegation is pointed to with faint hope. The Central Area committee has produced yet another plan for Chicago's downtown, although it is mainly one that calls for the completion of an earlier, 1973 plan. Mayor Byrne produced several plans during the period just before her failed effort at reelection. The governor has developed an investment program called "Build Illinois," but it is already being challenged for its neglect of the City of Chicago and is so underfunded that the program scarcely exists. All these bandwagons, then, seem to be stranded. To understand why, we must look closely, first, at what kind of evidence people take for local assessment and direction and, second, how the rhetoric of public debate both shapes and obscures the alternative to be taken.

Population and the Rhetoric of Mobilization

Population figures are extremely important to Chicago's decision making and debates over what course to take. The census counts themselves seem to have a kind of decisive summary authority which overcomes all the interdecennial uncertainty that otherwise

3. Berry et al. (1976) and Hauser (1964, 1968) had authored similar reports; like de Vise's theirs were noted by the local press.

4. The report that focused most exclusively on Chicago was a 1982 symposium at the University of Chicago ("The Future of Our City") organized by Paul Peterson and subsequently published as *The New Urban Reality* (1985). Although the symposium was well attended by civic leaders and academicians, it drew little local news coverage. As the city's crises deepened, the 1985 publication drew front-page attention from the *Tribune* (23 April 1985). A few weeks earlier, civic leaders were willing to pay $150 each to attend a conference ("Bright New City" series) to hear a social scientist lambast them for lack of effort and foresight.

permits a range of contested optimism and pessimism.[5] However, population figures are probably equally important in the day-to-day life of countless businesses, nonprofit organizations, and governmental units. Investment bankers, charitable organizations, marketing firms, and regional planners all make decisions based on simple gravity models or multipliers that are driven by the number of inhabitants (or their incomes). Governmental units know that head counts equal federal dollars. Population figures and the components of population dominate much of their thinking and produce a kind of determinacy or the appearance of certainty when it would otherwise be lacking. For many people, population figures seem to serve somewhat the same function as profit does in a business place; it is the "bottom line."

At public hearings, one can be very impressed with these figures even when they seem to bear only a very tangential relationship to pending decisions (e.g., the debate over the continuance of Meigs Field which serves mainly nonpaying commuters between Springfield and Chicago). "Costing out" various public-private projects carries with it some of the same numerical persuasiveness, but here too the figures are apt to be driven by population estimate (number of customers, residents, visitors, etc.). Generally, then, the person "with the numbers" is listened to. But, in public debate, he is often listened to with a selective ear: Which way is up?

Until recently the population figures for Chicago had not looked that bad. The city was losing population, but the suburbs were growing. The notion that the metropolitan region was a single, highly mobile marketplace seemed to have taken a firm hold, and, in any case, most of the models being used worked best (i.e., reduce error) at very high levels of aggregation.[6] Interdecennial projections

5. The general "knowledge" that Chicago grew more rapidly than any previous American city seems to have given this sign of "progress" a heightened value in local assessments. This knowledge seems also to include the assumption that population growth was closely connected with economic and cultural growth and that each form of growth had been rather uniform until recent decades. Actually, the rate of population growth was quite uneven up to 1900. After 1890, however, the rate of population growth steadily declined until it became negative in 1950.

6. By 1970, population data for small areas was less available because the Census Bureau shifted heavily to user tapes. Thus, for the first time in forty years the *Chicago Metropolitan Fact Book*, which provides census data on small areas, was not published. Only through the heroic efforts of David Street was one (Erbe et al. 1984) published for the 1980 Census. Even so, local government and local business groups were unwilling to support the 1980 *Factbook*. Its editors were fortunate to receive the support of the Joyce Foundation and the MacArthur Foundation.

often overshot the mark, and during the 1970s the Northeastern Illinois Planning Commission felt itself justified in using the "Adelphi Technique" (the use of "expert" informants) to project regional population. "Expert agreement" seems, in this instance, to have fed on shared hopes, because the projections badly overshot the mark. Here, as elsewhere, one does not want to be a "merchant of doom." Or, as some might put it, "Doing business here in Chicago is a game of positives."

If Chicago observers had relied more on comparative figures, they would have seen a somewhat different picture, although not one that would have provided an especially early warning of decline. In figure 2.1, I have assembled the 1950–1960 population gains

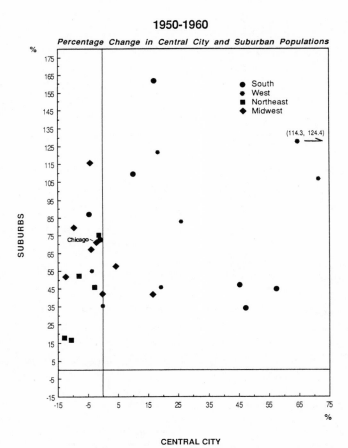

1950-1960

Percentage Change in Central City and Suburban Populations

Fig. 2.1. Population Gains and Losses in the Central Cities and Suburbs of the Twenty-Seven Regional Capitals of the United States, 1950–1960

The Third City

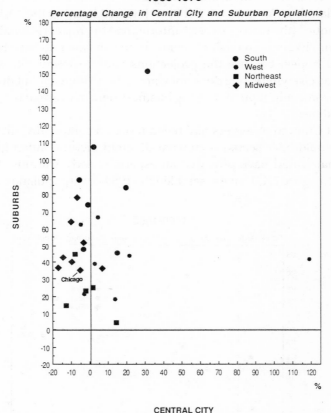

Fig. 2.2. Population Gains and Losses in the Central Cities and Suburbs of the Twenty-Seven Regional Capitals of the United States, 1960–1970

and losses for the twenty-seven largest U.S. metropolitan areas.[7] Figures 2.2 and 2.3 present the same findings for the two subsequent decades. The population growth of the suburbs is given along the ordinate while the growth or loss of population in the central cities is given along the abscissa. In the first period, Chicago is very near the center of the pack, losing some population in the central city, gaining more in the suburbs. One might say that it is close to the

7. What Berry and Horton (1970) call third- or higher-order cities in the United States. These cities perform similar regional functions; they compete with one another and would seem to be the appropriate units for such a comparison. The same cities are used later in this chapter to evaluate the relationship between black migration and general population change in these central cities and their suburbs. See the "Methodological Appendix" for further discussion.

1970-1980

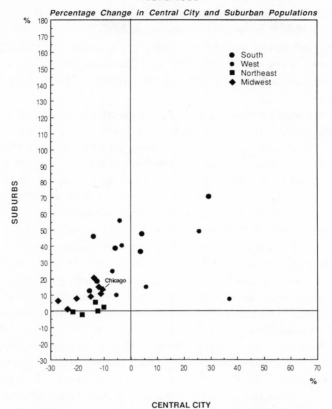

Fig. 2.3. Population Gains and Losses in the Central Cities and Suburbs of the Twenty-Seven Regional Capitals of the United States, 1970–1980

national average among such cities or, expressed differently, holding its own among competitors. A few sunbelt cities were experiencing inordinate growth, but that could be easily dismissed because of their appeal to limited populations (e.g., retirees) or because they began with such a low population base in 1950.

By the 1960–1970 decade, however, a more definite pattern emerges (fig. 2.2). All the larger Northeastern cities are crowded together in the lower left-hand quadrant because their central cities are losing population and their suburbs are growing very little or not at all. The Midwestern cities are just above them, almost as tightly grouped, losing slightly less in the central cities, gaining somewhat more in their suburbs. Almost every Southern and Western city is

The Third City

experiencing sustained growth in their central cities and suburbs. Regional differences and the sign of things to come for the Midwestern cities is here almost unmistakable. The 1970–1980 period (fig. 2.3) continues this trend, showing the regional distribution of cities even more tightly grouped. By this time, of course, the bad news for Chicagoans was out in a more dramatic form: a change in city rank.

One might think that such figures would have been heeded at an earlier date, say by 1970. Indeed, to some extent they may have been noticed, and often similar figures do grind away in the data banks of investment houses, consulting firms, or, for that matter, institutions like the Federal Reserve bank. But these are low-profile moments in city decision making, and when the stage shifts to public announcements the tone changes and bad news is often resisted. Without any apparent sign or prompting, the mood changes to a declarative one: we are coming back, it is just the business cycle, we've been through the worst, it's time for an upturn, every trough has a bottom.[8] Not everyone, of course, makes such statements, and some community groups and civic associations can be especially challenging.[9] Their marginal positions, however, often lead only to a kind of indulgent patience followed by a polite silence. "We listened them out," it is said, perhaps with greater honesty than was intended. Political leaders and especially businessmen must usually put a better face on things. The reason is very simple. Their job is to mobilize people, not to search for truth. As one business leader put it to me: "Look, I've always been up on Chicago and I still am. You have to be on the upside to be in this business. All this gloom and doom doesn't do anything. You can make money when everybody is making money." Or a successful political hopeful: "Who's going to work with you if you are always a downer, putting the city down, saying that we're only in it for our own? Politics is a game of positives."

So if population figures are very important in private decisions, a rather different construction must be placed on them in public. As it turns out, this is true of most other indications that we

8. From 1975 to 1978, the Continental Bank's quarterly surveys showed a steady increase in local consumer confidence (*Sun-Times*, 22 May 1978).

9. There is also an ill-defined mockery of this boosterism prevalent along the north lakefront where the losing ways of the Cubs are championed as an alternative to this sort of hype.

might want to use to more finely tune city responses to economic challenges. Of course, it is not always true. When the Census Bureau has spoken and a city changes its relative rank, it does seem to provoke a good deal of soul searching.

The Newsworthiness of Decline

Between the beginning of 1978 and the end of 1983, the *Chicago Tribune* and the *Chicago Sun-Times* ran sixty-one articles explicitly concerned with the comparative performance of American cities or the lessons they might provide Chicago in improving its performance.[10] As can be seen in table 2.1, local interest in the city's relative standing peaked in 1980, the year of the Census Bureau's announcement. It should be added, however, that some of these articles started before the April announcement when the change of the city's rank was more nearly a rumor than attested fact. Indeed, apprehension about the forthcoming population figures seems to have kicked off a modest news war in which both dailies ran a series that makes up the bulk of the articles published in 1980.

Sometimes combative and sometimes defensive, most of these articles (72 percent) still emphasize the positive lesson other places can provide to Chicago. Accounts of New York are often (five out of eight articles) critical, especially before 1980, but that seems an established journalistic pattern in "the second city." One article on Houston so roundly condemned that city that a number of Houston businessmen met publicly to defend it's "uniqueness" (McComb 1981) by declaring Houston "incomparable." Still, the general pattern of news coverage seems to be like the more general one of "looking on the upside." Indeed, most of the journalists I talked to felt that they had a responsibility to "find solutions" rather than to "dwell on the negatives."

Obviously there is a strong sense of being in the "big city

10. All these articles were written by local journalists or guest writers invited to contribute to the newspapers. I did not include promotional articles from the travel section, wire service news releases or articles reprinted from other newspapers. All purported to provide a serious analysis; thus human interest stories and articles aimed only at entertainment were excluded. This involved some close calls, but I believe the general distribution in table 2.1 is fairly representative of the "serious coverage" of Chicago's comparative position.

The Third City

Table 2.1. Feature Articles Describing Cities Other Than Chicago
for the Lesson They Provide

Year	Local Journalist Or Guest Writer	Focus of Article	
1978	9	Atlanta +	Cleveland − −
		Baltimore + +	New York − − −
		Boston +	
1979	15	Atlantic City +	Las Vegas −
		Baltimore +	New York −
		Boston + + +	Philadelphia + +
		Detroit +	San Diego +
		Houston +	Washington, D.C. +
		Kansas City +	
1980	21	Atlanta + +	Houston − +
		Baltimore, Boston, Houston, Phila-delphia, and New York +	Kansas City +
			Knoxville +
			Los Angeles − +
		Boston +	Milwaukee +
		Columbus +	Minneapolis +
		Denver + +	New York ±
		Detroit −	Portland + +
			Salt Lake City +
			Seattle +
1981	5	Bath, Me. +	San Francisco +
		New York +	St. Louis ±
		Philadelphia +	
1982	5	Los Angeles −	Pittsburgh −
		Minneapolis +	St. Louis ±
		New York −	
1983	6	Baltimore + +	Kansas City +
		Detroit −	Milwaukee +
		Houston +	
Total	61		

Note: + Generally positive lesson. − Generally negative lesson. ± Mixed lesson.

league," although it is entirely an American league. Articles on foreign cities remain on the travel pages. It cannot be shown in this
table, but most of the articles focus heavily on specific economic initiatives (aggressive promotion, downtown renewal, tax increment
financing) and political or private sector leadership. Over the entire
period, however, there does seem to have been a growing awareness of "quality-of-life" considerations (cultural institutions,
amenities, neighborhood improvement). From a close reading of
these articles and many others, one could detect a shift away from

very specific efforts to create jobs to more general ones to attract tourists and residents. Boston's Faneuil Hall, for example, was universally praised and attracted a remarkable amount of coverage. Many of the articles seem to have been prompted or guided by very specific projects or proposals in Chicago: the World's Fair, a Rouse project for Navy Pier, Mayor Byrne's proposed casino, the expansion of O'Hare Airport, a foreign trade zone, etc. In this respect, evidence is mobilized to support or oppose local proposals.

After 1980, attention to the comparative performance of other cities fell off sharply, but by that time the daily press was much more preoccupied with Chicago itself, and both papers ran an extensive series analyzing and describing the shortcomings of the city. While most of these articles expressed a conditional optimism for the long run, their description of the present was definitely on the "downside."

It is hard to judge the adequacy of journalistic coverage, but after reviewing the daily Chicago press for five years it is difficult to avoid certain impressions. First, the press is very much a part of the "confidence game" of project promotion, and most journalists see their responsibility as one of finding solutions. One does not sound the alarm until some dramatic watershed has been passed, and only then do views converge on "the problem." Second, if one includes the full range of reporting, the variation in judgments and proposals is simply astounding. The newspapers, then, seem only to reflect broader public disagreements rather than a separate evaluation of them. Once again, journalists are likely to see the expression of all points of view as a professional responsibility. They may be gatekeepers, but the gate is so wide that the evidence falls in all directions. This is not for lack of critical reporting; the Chicago press has a long tradition of investigative journalism and a group of columnists who write withering articles on political corruption and private business deals. But, like the remainder of the responsible press, they adhere to the norms of being constructive and allowing for the expression of all views.

In the mass marketing of news, then, forecasters agree only after the event. Still, I have no reason to say that Chicago's press was exceptionally slow in recognizing the city's long-term decline. They did no worse than the *New York Times* in anticipating that city's near fiscal collapse. In the mass marketing of news, indecision and disagreement are news, sometimes the only news.

The Third City

Walking on Water

One reason that urban information systems are so imperfect is that there is no single balance sheet. Economic indicators are usually mixed, and often there is some good news along with the bad news. Lead articles in the Chicago Association of Commerce and Industry's *Chicagoland*, for example, normally present their case within a short time frame (one to three years) within which changes are easily attributed to the business cycle (e.g., "The industrial vacancy rate was down 8 percent over last year"). Lengthy time series like the one in figure 2.4 would seem to show a disastrous drop in industrial investment with diminished "recoveries" following each down cycle. These data, however, were never presented this way despite the fact that they come directly from the above-mentioned publication. A number of national business organizations (e.g., Alexander Grant and Co.) and local ones (e.g., Illinois Chamber of Commerce) do routinely include the Chicago region in their assessments of business climates, but even businessmen are likely to dismiss them as

INDUSTRIAL INVESTMENT IN CHICAGO & SUBURBS

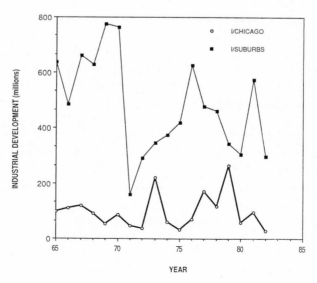

Source: Chicago Association of Commerce and Industry

Fig. 2.4. Industrial Investment in Chicago and Suburbs

"lobbying efforts" to lower tax rates or avoid government regulation.

The general quality of information, then, tends to be low, and it is often suspect. This is probably true of most urban centers, but Chicago seems to be exceptionally slow in using the available regional econometric models that might give a more detached evaluation of local investment. It was not until 1984 that the Northeastern Illinois Planning Commission purchased such a regional model (from Batelle). Local business groups have expressed some interest in supporting a more ambitious effort at forecasting and the evaluation of alternative investments, but they remain apprehensive about how such methods might be politicized. Several of the local universities have a strong technical capacity for developing such models, but there are no centers for doing so like those at the Kennedy School in Boston or the University of California in Los Angeles.[11] Ironically when the Northeastern Illinois Planning Commission and some business leaders wanted to explore closer connections with the local universities, they singled me out as the most available contact. The State of Illinois has begun to use such models for special purposes (e.g., environmental impact), but it is a very low-profile operation. When the Northeastern Illinois Planning Commission did purchase its model, the City of Chicago became a copurchaser. But this kind of forecasting has not made the news.

This sort of selective vision is only partly due to the low quality of information and fears about its manipulation. If one regularly attends the public announcements of some new venture—a new office building, a library, or sports arena—one cannot help but be struck by the peculiar mix of hardbeaded business talk and visionary zeal. There will be extensive references to "the bottom line," "residuals," and "end uses." Someone may even invoke "multipliers," and on occasion some real numbers may be mentioned (most often the number of jobs created). But there will also be a host of references which go beyond this appearance of calculated certainty. Almost invariably "this great city" will be mentioned. The high

11. Ironically, such a center may be developing at Northern Illinois University some fifty miles from Chicago. This kind of "applied work" seems to have relatively low prestige and to be carried out in business schools or in institutions not at the very top of the academic hierarchy.

points of aesthetic design will be pointed to. "Posterity," "future generations," and the commemoration of heroes[12] may contribute to this enlarged vocabulary of appeal and proof. Those making the presentation will not be just architects and businessmen but politicians and civic leaders, and some of the latter may be "just there" to add their presence. Scale models with miniature trees, green spaces, and statues will be presented even when it is admitted that "this is just a concept. We don't know what it will look like in detail." Large renderings will bring summer, crowds, color, and newness to the anticipated project. It is like an unveiling, which combines the presentation of a work of art, a commemoration of civic heroism, a statement of faith in the future, and an assurance that it is all "sound business practice."

At such unveilings, one can almost see the audience hover between uncertainty and optimism, between reality and fantasy, as each eyes the other and waits to see if someone will ask a deflationary question[13] or offer inflationary support. Eyes are especially likely to turn to someone with an unblemished reputation as a large developer: someone, it is said, "who can walk on water."[14] Such people are very rare, but when present their enthusiasm or coolness can outweigh all the other evidentiary support. All the statements

12. Perhaps the most obvious instance of this was the naming of a giant exposition hall as "McCormick Place." Despite widespread opposition to the location on lakeside parkland, the *Tribune* unfailingly supported this site. Even after the first building burned down and the faults of the site were well known, similar support was forthcoming for its reconstruction on the same site. Thus, current expansion of the exhibition hall faces the formidable problem of connecting it with an annex across an eight-lane highway.

Mayor Bilandic sought to revive the cross-town expressway by renaming it the "Burnham Corridor" but with less success. Similar instances could be pointed to along with a number of cases where some new public space or amenity (parkland, a sculpture, a plaza) serves as a trade-off to mollify opposition.

13. Usually such questions are very mild and seldom directly critical. But, however mild, they can "suspend" support just at the point where it might otherwise be forthcoming. Sometimes representatives of local community groups are outright critical, and others may be made uncomfortable by this breech of etiquette, although they may voice equally harsh criticisms in private. Nonetheless, there are a few people, those with an unblemished record as investors, who can offer abrupt criticism, often consisting of no more than one sentence. When the first version of Dearborn Park was "unveiled," Philip Klutznik, a major Chicago builder and later President Carter's secretary of commerce, said simply, "It looks like the Kremlin." That killed it.

14. The phrase is used in a narrow sense to describe someone who can get public commitment without first getting financing. But it can also be used in a more general sense to describe someone whose reputation alone can carry a project.

on job creation, on tax revenues, and on multipliers just seem to become irrelevant. Thus, the most important information is who will support it rather than some more or less detached and mechanical method of calculation.

In a way I think that this is almost inevitable, not only because such faith in individual reputations may be justified but because most of the methods of projecting costs and benefits in Chicago are too crude to inspire high confidence. Completion dates are almost never met, cost overruns are nearly universal, and political scandals are as likely as not. None of these things are in the equations. But even if they were, one wonders if there is not a deeper sense in which some diminished uncertainties would prevail. As soon as one introduces social benefits as against only private profit, the ledger really becomes unfathomable and the list of possible beneficiaries and losers unlimited. One might be able to say that project A is better than project B, but there may be a dozen other projects competitive with project A but with rather different beneficiaries. Individual reputations, then, provide determinacy where none may be forthcoming in such a prolonged and thorough calculation of costs and benefits.

One of the problems at the current time is that Chicago today does not have many of these magnets who can "walk on water." Many of those who came to be recognized during the Daley years have aged or been tarnished by scandal or failure, and new political or business leaders have not taken their place. The earlier industries that produced such magnets—construction, banking, and heavy manufacturing—are in decline, and their decline has meant a decline in public confidence. One needs only to mention U.S. Steel, the Continental Bank, Commonwealth Edison, or International Harvester to get some impression of this erosion in public confidence.

Nor have new political leaders risen to take their place. Mayor Daley, of course, loved scale models of large projects and almost always presided at their unveiling. Mayor Bilandic started his failed effort at reelection with a quote from Burnham, "Make no little plans," and the rest of his election speech consisted of a slide show of brick and mortar projects underway or on the drawing board. Mayor Byrne also presided over many unveilings, and she demanded a new city plan on what others thought extremely short notice. But only Daley could "walk on water."

The Third City

Make No Little Plans

The "big project" seems to have a special place in Chicago. Burnham recommended it,[15] and he is quoted with frequency and authority. Not only does it fit the city's image as a blustering adolescent ("that toddling town," "the windy city," "the city of big shoulders"), the big project seems also to overcome the doubts and apprehensions that are equally embedded in the image of hustlers, payrollers, and grafters ("city on the make," "city on the take"). The big project, then, is above all an instrument to establish public pride and commitment. The biggest skyscraper, the busiest airport, even the world's largest parking lot are all positive proof that routine, honest government is not the only means to civic accomplishment. It may not be the "city of brotherly love" or the "city of roses," but it is said to be "the city that works."

Chicagoans, and especially its journalists, love to talk about their city's corruption, wheeling and dealing and opportunism. But even the most critical accounts are likely to include a special appreciation for the irony of big projects that succeeded despite of, or because of, these departures from civic virtue. In his 1980 study of political support, Guterbock refers to this pattern as "defended venality," and he would lead us to believe that such an outlook penetrates right down to the average voter. What counts is what is done—not how it is done. Big projects are newsworthy in any city, but in Chicago they seem unusually essential to building public confidence. It is rather like the beginning swimmer who throws himself into the deep end of the pool in the belief that some desperate commitment is necessary to overcome his misgivings and inabilities. Incrementalism is not easily accepted in a population only too aware of the fragility of public consensus. Chicagoans seem to "go in over their heads" so that they cannot "back out."

Burnham's precedent has imposed itself on the practice of city planning. Four major city plans or portions of them were published between 1966 and 1983. The first and most ambitious was the 1966 *Comprehensive Plan of Chicago*, a summation and extension

15. The most frequent quote being "Chicago has two dominant features: the expanse of Lake Michigan, which stretches, unbroken by islands or peninsulas, to the horizon; and a corresponding area of land extending north, west, and south without hills or any marked elevation. These two features, each immeasurable by the senses, give the scale. Whatever man undertakes here should be either actually or seemingly without limit" (Burnham and Bennett 1909, p. 79).

of the aspirations of the Daley administration.[16] It projected a quarter-million population increase by 1980 (rather than the half-million decrease that occurred). Land devoted to manufacturing was to be increased by 60 percent. High-density housing was to prevail along the entire lakefront and, west of the Central Business District, all the way to the city limits. Transportation lines and industrial strips were to be consolidated along common corridors with residential areas lying between them like islands, each of which would include a complement of community facilities (schools, greenways, institutions, shopping centers). Strip shopping was to be virtually eliminated and replaced by regional, community, and neighborhood retail centers. There was to be a 20 percent increase in the land devoted to business (i.e., office space). Preservation is mentioned, but the color plates give the impression of "the Bright New City."[17] The document stressed very much the improvement of family life, economic opportunity and the rational allocation of transportation, and employment. But the overpowering impression is simply one of scale and magnitude. If little plans have no "magic to stir men's blood" (Burnham, again), this one should have quickened the civic pulse.

And to some extent it did. These were peak years for the Daley administration, and the amount of office space in the city more than doubled between 1965–1972. The expressway system—nearly 500 miles of it—was almost completed in the same period. But the bright new islands of family life did not take shape. In the same year as the publication of the *Comprehensive Plan,* the *Gautreaux* decision halted the further construction of public housing. By 1973, the demolition of dwelling units outnumbered the construction of new ones. Ironically, where unplanned and private redevelopment was occurring on the North Side, land reclassification permitted builders

16. This was the first comprehensive plan since the 1909 Burnham and Bennett *Plan of Chicago.* A *Preliminary Comprehensive Plan* had been published in 1946 and *Recommended Policies for Redevelopment* had been published in 1954. The last two plans seem not to have captured the enthusiasm of Liebling's "second city." A 1958 *Development Plan for the Central Area of Chicago* caught some of the enthusiasm surrounding the Daley administration.

17. A slogan that came into wider use during the late 1970s when it was promoted by Mayor Jane Byrne. In fairness to Ira Bach, the 1964 *Basic Policies for the Comprehensive Plan of Chicago,* a "discussion document" that preceded the 1966 *Comprehensive Plan,* had more substance to its aim at preservation. Bach was held in high confidence by many Chicagoans, and he worked very hard to encourage preservation. Standing alone, however, he could not "walk on water."

to concentrate high-rise housing on a massive scale (e.g., a 44 percent increase in dwelling units in southeast Lake View [Berry et al. 1976]). Indeed, private developers in Chicago seem to have been extremely timid in advancing the frontiers of redevelopment. Usually they have waited until homeowners or small investors created a "hot" spot and then deluged it with high-rises.

Sensing in 1970 that the *Comprehensive Plan* could no longer move men's souls, the Central Area committee commissioned the *Chicago 21* plan (1973)[18] to guide further development in the eleven-square-mile Central Area. The plan was presented as a continuation of the 1966 *Comprehensive Plan*, and it does resemble the plan in several ways. Photographic plates feature much new construction. In the scale models, new buildings are white, the old ones are gray. Over a million jobs (a 40 percent gain) in the Central Area are projected for the year 2000. There is to be an equal growth in retail sales. And families are prominently and repeatedly mentioned as the primary beneficiaries. There are, however, also noticeable differences. For the first time, the Central Area is described as a residential "community," and half of the document is devoted to community development. Preservation is not just mentioned: there is a mapping of historic structures. Cultural and recreational centers are seen as anchors comparable to the major department stores or large office towers. Although the most costly items remain transportational ones, the overriding impression is that of creating a new residential population to replace the decline in suburban shoppers and the restoration of a white presence in the Loop during the evening hours.

In reviewing this plan in 1980, Cafferty and McCreedy continued the image of Chicago as a city where big businessmen act unilaterally and with effectiveness. It is true that business groups annually have a public meeting where they provide a positive "scorecard" on the achievements of the "21" plan. But it is also true that there is private disappointment. So, in the early 1980s another Central Area plan (published in 1984) was commissioned by the

18. Although the plan was attributed to the Chicago Plan Commission, and encouraged by Daley, it was devised largely by Skidmore, Owings and Merrill. In Chicago there is nothing unusual about the commission of a city plan to a private business. Burnham and Bennett's *Plan of Chicago* was commissioned in just this way. Indeed, some informants indicated a much higher confidence in a plan developed in this way rather than by "politicians." As some pointed out, when developers make a plan, they do so with backers already in mind.

The Third City

Central Area committee.[19] While it affirmed the previous "21" plan, it was also occasioned by the hope that the 1992 International Exposition would provide a dateline that would finally mobilize the city to complete the 1973 plan. Still, a number of features distinguish the second Central Area plan. A mix of office space, service industries, tourism, retailing, cultural centers, and housing are seen as complementary. High-tech, hospitals, and universities are seen as a part of this mix, but manufacturing is scarcely mentioned. Visual elements, landmarks, and amenities are treated as investments rather than luxuries. Renderings far outnumber photographic plates, and they are reproduced with a patina suggestive of Burnham and Bennett's *Plan of Chicago* (1909). Families are not mentioned at all but loft dwellers are. At the time of its publication, I asked a prominent real estate businessman what he thought of it. "Well," he said, "I think that they will be lucky if they complete as much of it as the 21 plan. And you know how that went." Mayor Washington did accept the plan, prefacing it with a letter of pride and encouragement. But some felt his heart was not in it.

But even before the Central Area committee could get their plan off the drawing board, Mayor Byrne had produced yet another preliminary *Comprehensive Plan* (1981). Hastily assembled before the 1982 campaign, it was a slim document listing only goals and policies. Some of the priorities are interesting. On the lead page, leisure-time activities are mentioned first, cultural institutions second, office space next, and manufacturing last. Households rather than families are mentioned. There is a heavy emphasis on equal opportunity "for all Chicagoans." And culture and the arts are given a strong role in promoting the city. The plan was meant only to prompt discussion. There was a little discussion, and people were surprisingly polite.[20]

Looking over the first three of these plans (the 1966 *Comprehensive Plan* and the two Central Area plans), one cannot escape the impression that any of them might have been a good plan for the previous decade. By "good" I mean that they might have been inspirational if not inspired. In the 1950s there was lots of enthusiasm for the sort of newness, bigness, and broad-shouldered growth em-

19. Also prepared largely by Skidmore, Owings and Merrill.
20. See the written testimonies of the Metropolitan Housing and Planning Council, Chicago Urban League, League of Women Voters of Chicago, Greater North Michigan Avenue Association, Northeastern Illinois Planning Commission, Friends of the Chicago River, and Hull House Association, (9 November 1982).

The Third City

braced by the 1966 plan. In the 1960s it probably would have been much easier to attract families from *within* the city to live in areas peripheral to the Loop. Certainly federal transit funds were more available to the first of the Central Area plans. The second Central Area plan finally made a strong effort to adapt to a growing black middle class and its incorporation into the Central Area "community." But this plan appeared just at that point when an empowered black leadership could insist on something more.

The people who formulated these three plans were talented people.[21] They are aware that plans are as much confidence builders as they are rational instruments to shape a knowable future. But since the city was changing so fast and in ways that were not easily expressed in this promotional *genre,* an undercurrent of doubt plagued all of the plans, especially the more recent ones. The most important of these changes was a steady decline in the city's white population and a growing sense that the doubts of the black population could not be disarmed no matter how much these plans might stir the civic pulse of current planners.

The Rhetoric of Racial Etiquette

One of the most sensitive issues in Chicago is its racial mix. The city is now (1980) about 40 percent black, 20 percent Hispanic, with the remainder mostly white, although there is a sizable Oriental population. Among much of the nonblack population there is a very general concern that blacks are displacing the other populations, that many of the blacks are permanently dependent on welfare, and that civil rights legislation has made it all but impossible to deal with blacks as employees, as clients, or as tenants. What more than anything else seems to confound nonblacks is the absence of any sign of self-imposed social control within the black community itself. The rates of illegitimacy, homicide, burglary, and school dropouts among blacks are unprecedented even in Chicago's history (Wilson 1985). And all this comes after a period of substantial public investment in assistance, training, and housing. None of this goes

---

21. Some of the plans won national awards. Sociologists were consulted on all three of the plans: Philip Hauser on the 1966 plan, Morris Janowitz on the 21 plan, and myself on the last of the Central Area plans.

unnoticed either in the press or in visible public meetings. But one is not supposed to state it quite as baldly as I just have.[22]

Instead, the current rhetoric of racial etiquette requires a highly evasive language loaded with words of superior abstraction that avoid invidious comparisons and denies that blacks (and increasingly everyone else) possess human agency. Even if blacks are the main object of discussion, it is preferable to speak of "minorities." Some positive features of the black community (music, soul food) can be called "black culture," but the less flattering ones are "historical discrimination." Institutions rather than individuals are "racist." Low-paying jobs that go begging are "dead-end" jobs rather than "entry-level" jobs. The black poor are not "lower class" but an "underclass." Welfare dependency is "structural unemployment." Individual attributions of responsibility are "blaming the victim." New and disembodied entities prowl the landscape of this vocabulary; "the system," and "social reality." School "dropouts" are "push outs." The "uneducated" are the "miseducated." Where a new word is lacking, an older one can be discredited or inverted by the prefix "so-called" ("the so-called American system"). An early assertion that one is "telling it like it is" counters the strong claim that one is describing "social reality" while all other categories are obfuscation. The exceptions are "tokens."

Increasingly, this rhetoric is being extended beyond the black community, to illegal aliens ("undocumented workers"), refugees ("the new minorities"), and nationality groups ("the white ethnics") as other groups attempt to portray themselves as victims while also laying some residual claim to "achievement." In private, of course, attributions range from outright bigotry to bewilderment or sympathy. Yet despite its reputation as a "racist city," public discussion of race in Chicago seems to be just about as purified of human agency as it is elsewhere.[23] Only infrequently do individuals in high public

22. There are exceptions. Both Bill Granger and Mike Royko occasionally assert the responsibility of blacks for their own behavior. But their comments seem to be taken as their own and to achieve the status of "humor" precisely because they openly reveal what it is presumed many others are "thinking" but not saying. Representatives of groups, even rather parochial community groups, tend to adhere to the rhetoric of racial etiquette referred to above.

23. Following the recent mayoral election, Ralph Whitehead observed that the highly selective pattern of news coverage that focused only on the candidates may have given people the impression that overt bigotry was more acceptable (1983). *The Chicago Reporter* (January 1985) did show a sharp increase in racial incidents in the period *following* the election.

office slip up by singling out "your people" or "project people." It is done, but it is done to achieve specific effects, that is, to challenge blacks or, occasionally, some other "minority."

The difficulty with such a rhetoric, of course, is that it is part of "the system." Since human agency, group responsibility, and invidious comparisons cannot be assigned, the arsenal of social control is empty. Understandably, people on either side of the racial divide are reluctant to remonstrate with one another, and the tendency is one of withdrawal rather than contest or engagement. This kind of withdrawal is especially difficult to overcome because it is guiltless and blameless. Essentially it accepts blacks on their own self-definition as a wronged people who are too damaged to be expected to impose self-control.

Not the least attraction of this rhetoric is the ability of whites to extend it so as to exonerate themselves from any direct responsibility for creating the condition of blacks.[24] Social causality seems to be lodged completely in "social classes," "interests," "institutions," "elites," or "social structure." Ordinary people are simply excluded from responsibility, and, as Prager (1985) argues, this may be one reason that further public discussion of the reciprocal responsibilities of whites and blacks has become progressively muted by a tendency toward an exclusive concern with personal self-improvement. Whites should not impose their ways on blacks. Blacks should not be expected to change their ways. Tolerance has been achieved, but the price seems to be a new kind of avoidance and privatization.

Undoubtedly one can overemphasize the importance of this public rhetoric, for despite its pervasiveness in secondary relations one still frequently hears the older rhetoric of bigotry in taverns, on street corners, in households, or in backyards.[25] But in churches, community meetings, ceremonies, and places of public entertainment, the rhetoric of racial etiquette is unpracticed language. While

24. Indeed, some whites on Chicago's Southwest Side have formed a movement ("Save Our Neighborhoods, Save Our City") in which they have declared themselves equally the victims of "institutional discrimination" (Boylan 1985). They are only another wronged minority.

25. The term "black," however, seems almost entirely to have replaced the words "nigger" or "Negro." The first of these terms is still used occasionally to provoke outright conflict or to "test" strangers whose racial views are uncertain. In this last instance, this usage can be quite disconcerting when someone tests you by using the term "nigger" and, despite your response, falls back into the usage of "black" because it is habitual.

this language may not quickly penetrate primary relations, I do believe that it has a powerful influence upon the confidence whites feel either in their ability to resist residential displacement or in the prospects for a renewed effort at social control within the black underclass. Also, public accounts are about all that whites and blacks have of each other as social collectivities. Cross-racial friendships, of course, are quite frequent, and in private members of either group may deplore the disengagement of whites and the failures of social control among blacks. But these private conversations take the form of confessionals, and it is hazardous to go public with the same statements.[26]

In a number of conversations I have had with investors, the general outlook seems to be one of puzzlement or resignation.[27] "What's with those people?" "Why can't they get their act together?" Recently, the demographer de Vise[28] summed up a widespread conviction when he was quoted in the *Chicago Sun-Times* (3 April 1985) as saying: "Most so-called underclass young blacks are 'unemployable.' In increasing numbers [they are] poorly schooled black youths, indoctrinated in black pride [who] face potential employers in Afro hairstyle and dress—unskilled, untrusted and unwilling to take dead-end jobs." Outside the business community, the general white outlook toward these blacks seems to be one of progressive disengagement or disguised resistance in the claim to be only "another minority themselves." As one woman put it, "Now even the priests talk like Jesse Jackson."[29]

In Chicago and elsewhere there is evidence of this pattern of disengagement between blacks and whites. If one takes the percentage gain in the black population among the twenty-seven largest U.S. central cities in one decade and the percentage of total population change in the following decade, there is a pervasive pattern of exodus from the central cities experiencing the highest levels of black in-migration ($r = -.46$, $p < .007$ for 1950–1960; $r = -.39$, $p < .02$

26. See, for example, the uproar following William J. Wilson's *The Declining Significance of Race* (1980).

27. Not all were white, and one black businessman told me, "I've got lots of entry level jobs but I can't get these [black] kids to take them. I don't know what you can do with them."

28. De Vise often breaks ranks with the other local social scientists, and his pronouncements often provoke outrage. For that reason, they are widely publicized.

29. The statement was made in reference to Monsignor Egan's criticism of a "white ethnic" conference which had described some of the maladies of the black community as self-imposed.

The Third City

for 1960–1970; $r=-.58$, $p<.0007$ for 1970–1980). There is no indication that this retreat has diminished over time or that it is simply the
result of disproportionate white movement to the suburbs in those
cities experiencing increasing black in-migration. The correlation
between black in-migration and the population growth of the suburbs of these cities is also negative ($r=-.29$, $p<.07$ for 1950–1960;
$r=-.18$, $p<.18$ for 1960–1970; $r=-.33$, $p<.04$ for 1970–1980). Either
black migrants managed to pick those metropolitan centers most
likely to decline in population or their presence was the occasion for
a more general exodus. And there is no sign that the exodus has diminished in the most recent decade.[30]

This general picture of disengagement is continued if we look
at investor choices in the six-county area including and extending
around Chicago (map 2.2). As can be seen from the bar graphs in
each spatial unit, industrial investor choices in the period 1970–1983
are progressively oriented away from the region's black community
which is concentrated on Chicago's West and South Sides and in the
northern portion of Lake County, Indiana. These are shares of investor decisions rather than dollar amounts or jobs created, but for
that reason they probably better reflect the climate of investor opinion. The reorientation of investor preference to the north and west is
especially notable since South and West Cook County and Lake
County, Indiana, have in the past been the areas of most concentrated industrial development. One might argue that this older
development has run its course, but as early as 1972 the area had the
highest industrial vacancy rate, and there is ample vacant land available. Transportation facilities (especially lake access, highways, and
railroads) are as good as elsewhere in the region, with the possible
exception of O'Hare Airport which benefits the northern and western sectors. However, Midway Airport, once the nation's busiest,
and located very close to the southern sector and the black community, became a depressed area during the 1970s. Only after the
capacity of O'Hare was saturated in the last few years has there been
an increase in traffic at Midway.

It should be pointed out and emphasized that the decline in
investors in the southern sector occurs convincingly only after 1975,
when the region's steel industry experienced a sharp downturn and
much of the decline must be due to a drop-off in the number of in-

---

30. White's (1984) study would seem to show that ethnic whites have been leaving
cities more readily in the 1970–1980 decade than in previous ones.

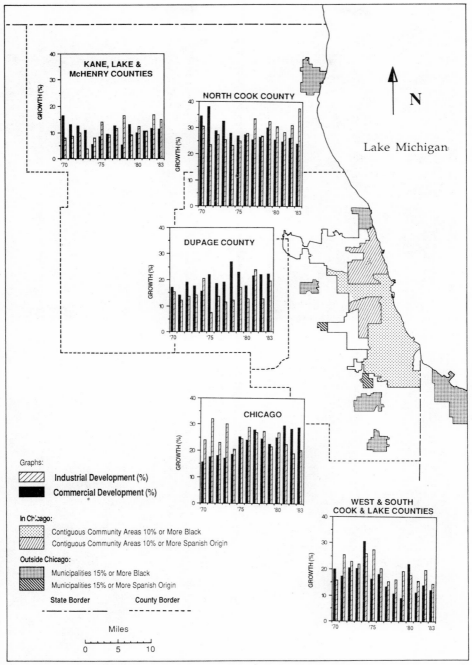

Map 2.2. Shares of Industrial and Commercial Investment in the Chicago Region, 1970–1983

a

b

Suburban and Central City development: (a) new industrial buildings in north Cook County; (b) new residential buildings in Chicago.

The Third City

vestors whose operation complemented that of the steel industry. But at the same time one must emphasize that the region is building a new industrial base, only now it is not much linked to the steel industry and is very much oriented toward white residential areas at a greater distance from the city.

Shares of commercial investors were looked at separately for each spatial unit on the assumption that commercial investment might more nearly reflect the growth of the region's "sunrise" businesses (office buildings, financing, futures, upscale retailing) as against its "sunset" businesses (heavy manufacturing). Clearly the southern sector, the one closest to the black population, has undergone a substantial decline in the number of commercial investors, and this decline precedes that of the steel industry. The City of Chicago is experiencing a steady increase in its share of commercial investors, and it does include the largest proportion of the region's blacks. If one looks closely at these investments, however, they are heavily concentrated in the city's Central Area[31] or on the North Side, areas well away from the black belts on the South and West Sides. Somewhat surprisingly, North Cook is experiencing a declining share of commercial investors despite its favorable showing in terms of industrial investors. However, North Cook, sometimes called "the Golden Corridor," starts with the highest share of commercial investors (about a third of the total), and throughout the 1960s it is said to have attracted heavy commercial investment. Some observers thought that the area was now saturated with commercial establishments or that industrial firms were outbidding them for the remaining sites. One investment banker added, "It's very well situated for industrial investors. They like to get close to all that Hispanic labor [on the Chicago North Side]."[32]

These data are crude, they are probably underreported, and they do not include measures of disinvestment. But better data or data on disinvestment, I think, would only amplify the orientation

31. A somewhat larger area than the Loop now that Chicago has two CBDs like many other large cities: one for mass marketing to a diverse clientele (the Loop), and another "upscale" CBD (Michigan Avenue) which caters to a less risky clientele. Actually, the Loop has undergone some disinvestment in retailing at its southern (and blackest) extremity. Three major department stores (Sears, Montgomery Wards, and Goldblatts) have closed. Unfortunately, data on disinvestment is not available. Perhaps this is another way of looking on the "upside."

32. One marketing executive made the contrast between Hispanic and black labor much more explicit: "If you go to Mexico City you can see it. Those kids are out there on the streets hustling to wash your windshield or do anything else. It's almost ideal training for working here. With blacks it's almost the opposite."

The Third City

of investment away from the region's black population. A member of the city's Department of Planning recently observed: "The black community is drastically underserved by even routine shopping services. Even grocery stores are leaving them. The only ones opening grocery stores in the black community are Arabs or middle easterners." One is struck by the growing presence of these Lebanese and Palestinian merchants who apparently cannot compete with established chain stores in most other areas but are willing or desperate enough to take risks that the chains avoid. Certainly there is no lack of available plant space or land. The director of city planning questioned at a recent meeting: "What are we going to do with all this vacant land? Land that no one is going to build on during the life time of anyone here. Hydroponic agriculture?"

Even a brief visit to the region's black belts and adjacent areas is more convincing than these data, and I present them mainly to cast some doubts on competing arguments that emphasize technology or plant obsolescence to the exclusion of race. But the racial significance of these data seem immediately obvious to most investors or consultants to whom I have talked. Some will emphasize a technological explanation ("It's the decline of the steel industry"), but for most race figures more directly into their "confidential" construction of the problem. "Look," one businessman told me:

> I don't have anything against blacks. I have a lot of them here. But to hire one probationary black employee, I have to interview eighteen. And I don't care what they say, work absences are worse. It's not always their fault. Things just seem to be always happening to them. The house is broken into. Someone has to be taken to the hospital. They just seem trouble prone. You can't help feel for them but you can't let your feelings run away with you.

A number of other reasons are frequently mentioned. Retailers who cater to both blacks and whites say they have to increase shelf space.[33] If you expand your services to blacks you may drive out the upper end of the white clientele.[34] There are the headaches of affir-

33. To provide specialty items for blacks but also to increase the price range.
34. Retail stores at the north end of State Street are now "upscaling" their product lines. Apparently, many "top of the line" department stores are downsizing their outlets and leaving the lower end of the market to discount stores. The lack of shelf space in these smaller outlets moves them toward a more homogeneous (and whiter) clientele. The highly publicized efforts of Reverend Jesse Jackson's Operation Push to force firms in black communities to hire blacks was often mentioned as a drawback to locating near these areas. One businessman was more blunt than others: "Its just extortion. But you have to put up with it only if you can't move. Mostly distributors."

mative action, the danger or litigation, an enlarged grievance backlog. "They bring in drugs. It's bad enough with whites." "You have to worry more about security. Somehow it's harder to know who goes in or out." "Pilferage? Yeah, there's more pilferage."

Detail by detail, all this seems to add up to a pattern of statistical discrimination very much like that described by Gary Becker (1971). Unable to be highly accurate and selective in their black clients and employees, businessmen and investors take the lower-risk strategy of reducing or eliminating their contact with them. But, while Becker's analysis seems closely to coincide with my observations, I would like to add here one further observation that seems to compound this kind of "discrimination without 'gut level' prejudice." During the last two decades, many white businessmen seem to have gone through a learning experience in which they have lost patience with blacks. "Look, I tried with blacks, but eventually I got tired of being called a racist" (an ex-Vista worker turned rehabber). "They have as good a chance as the Mexicans. What have they done with it?"(A laundromat operator who recently got himself a doberman pinscher). Often this learning experience is articulated by accounts of direct experiences such as the ones above. But it can also be articulated in the rhetoric of racial etiquette which itself seems to provide a moral rationale for disengagement. "They want their culture? Boom boxes, love children, and Afros. OK. I want mine." "I know you can't blame them. But what can you do?" "It's a game. They try to get what they want. We try to get what we want." The older claims of moral responsibility, of course, were always lightly felt, and many of the earlier experiments at affirmative action were only for public relations. But, at least they were *good* " PR" then, whereas now these experiments are only a legal requirement.

All this has the obvious effects of aggregate avoidance of blacks as employees and clients. It has a far more pervasive and subtle effect on what urban initiatives can be voiced, what kinds of deals can be cut, and on the general climate of public confidence. Affirmative integration is "unmentionable." Shared classroom time (rather than full integration) is "tokenism." A strict enforcement of housing codes (or auto insurance and licensing) is "racism." A widespread use of illegal aliens in preference to blacks goes undebated. New housing in border areas must be high priced or must increasingly take the form of the "community under glass" (see below, Chap. 6). But probably the most general result is an internecine war of words in which ulterior motives are believed far more than publicly stated objectives. While most people feel compelled to use the rhetoric of racial etiquette, most of them do not seem to believe in it. The "real social reality" (I have heard it referred to that way) is thought to lie outside public discourse. Two housing developers put it this way: "Anymore I wouldn't try to publicize the social goals of a project. They won't believe you and it will just get you in trouble. You're better off if you just say you want to make money." Yet very shortly after making this statement, one of these developers did emphasize the social goals of a project during the public announcement of its completion. Why? "Well on those occasions you have to say something about how it is going to benefit the city, everybody." In the last instance, the project was financed by both public and private funds. Increasingly, at least in Chicago, urban projects are public-private partnerships, and, as I hope to show in the next chapter, these partnerships are almost invariably scripted in the rhetoric of racial etiquette.

Urban Development as a Confidence Game

Urban development takes place in a sea of mistrust and ambiguity where ulterior motives are often more plausible than either publicly announced objectives or what sociologists call "group interests." Information is scarce, it is often of poor quality, and sometimes it is a "deep secret" or downright "unmentionable." Ignorance and error, then, are more nearly the typical case than the exception. As a result, the sort of "means-ends" paradigm of collective rationality that plays so large a part in "public policy analysis" seems not so much wrong as irrelevant. What one is struck with, instead, is the marked resemblance to a confidence game. First, there is the need for a "front man" or a series of front men who can exude a sense of confidence themselves as well as leave the strong impression that they have "better" or "inside" information. In city development this takes the enlarged form of enlisting reputable consultants, the incidental presence of elites, and where possible the endorsement of someone known to be able to "walk on water." These people (the "shills") need not be known for the purity of their motives, but they must give the impression of an entrepreneurial capacity for wheeling and dealing. Indeed, a certain shadiness or marginal legality may be part of what helps convince people (the "mark") that some enlarged windfall is possible. Business as usual suggests only "passbook interest."

Second, elaborated props and stages must be incorporated into the unveiling of new projects. Thus, it is common to use rather palatial settings (the "store" is often a bank building with a magnificent view of the city) for announcements or ribbon cuttings (the "come on"). Expensive props, renderings, scale models, and photographs give the impression of accomplished reality, as if only by taking the first step everything else would follow. The quotation of "numbers," the language of the "bottom line," and even the nodding agreement of others present (the "stooges") give credence to the inevitability of the project with the only question being whether or not one will get aboard.

Third, there must be a belief that the "mark" himself is somewhat venal, or in other terms that there must be some "cush" (patronage, jobs, favored contractors, "affirmative" hiring). What this conveys is not simply the conviction that the general public will "go along" but that important people (the unions, the aldermen, public employees) will do so and that one is not simply taking lambs to the slaughter. "They" are not in it just for their health either.

Fourth, there must be some kind of "convincer," often a bit more promissory than the ones that real confidence men allow their marks to win. But the inclusion of public goods—some parkland, public access, plazas, distinguished design elements—all seem to provide a kind of "gift" or "windfall" which would be lost if one did not go through with the rest of the project. Thus, tax increment financing is often billed as "not costing you a cent." While such "convincers" may be only on the drawing board, it is still possible to point to other cities or instances where "it worked." To do so often involves a very selective history or choice of examples, so that time is compressed and a restricted "psychological" field is created.

Fifth, there must be commitment, indeed "overcommitment" to the extent that the "mark" sees himself as already having gone beyond the point of no return. The "big" plan aims to accomplish this not only because its payoff is irresistible but because the sheer scale of it "seals" the participation of others into the same "deal." The big plan is presented as if it had already been agreed to, and a long list of notables is sure to decorate the front or after pages. The plan will include many projects already accomplished as if "it"—the plan—were already underway and is now being reviewed only in early or late passage. Money has already been spent, contracts let, governmental agreements ironed out, and RFP's announced. One is already in too deep water to back out.

Finally, there are "inside men" who must act quickly but without panic to give the impression of steady progress so that no one gets cold feet or "blows" the operation. "Breaking ground" as early as possible is essential, even if it means starting in the worst weather and before all the financing is in place. Progress reports are regularly scheduled, and they may involve some "inventiveness" in expanding a "report card." Celebrations, topping-off ceremonies, ribbon cuttings, or a finishing touch of statuary all give evidence of regular progress. "Hitches" (delays, cost overruns, scandals) must be managed, minimized, explained, or put outside the "plan" so that they do not contaminate the next step. Occasionally, someone must be "cooled out," by "listening them out," by the "silent treatment," or by alluding to their ulterior motives and opportunism. An emphasis on polite exchange, a reluctance to meet criticism head-on, an agreeable and positive willingness to "iron things out" make passionate objection appear as obstructionism.

Up to a point, the confidence game metaphor is revealing and even useful. There is always a large element of persuasion in urban development. But after this point, persuasion alone cannot work. The parties to urban development must engage one another in repeated games, and their confidence in one another must rest on some signs of accomplishment as well as effective theater. Otherwise, the theatrics, essential as they are, become transparent and unconvincing.

In Chicago this sense of theater is overpowering—in the statewide programs with no funding, in the elaborate renderings that are "only a plan," in the lofty language of social goals for private projects, in the poorly disguised efforts at affirmative patronage, or in the rhetoric that evades social responsibility and the need for social control. People sense this, for they have developed another language of the "so-called" to cast doubt unselectively in every direction. When the social construction of confidence is this flimsy, it verges on comedy. We can see this best in the public theater of neighborhood development.

THREE

NEIGHBORHOOD REDEVELOPMENT FROM ABOVE

Between the beginning of 1978 to the end of 1982 I was able to single out 119 proposed land-use changes in various parts of the central city of Chicago. Some of these land-use changes had advanced scarcely beyond an announcement while others were very near completion. A substantial minority were multipurpose "site improvements" with price tags of several million dollars. A few were expected to cost over a billion dollars. Most of these larger projects will be familiar to Chicagoans for they have been widely reviewed in the press. Nearly all the remaining projects are much smaller in scale and, typically, would be considered local community projects, while the large multipurpose ones are intended to serve a much broader population, often said to be the entire city or region.

This is not a representative sample of Chicago's land-use changes for this five-year period. Rather it is an effort to gather information on a wide range of such changes with the aim of constructing a natural history of some of the more frequent forms of urban redevelopment or, in rare instances, urban "preservation." They were selected largely from news reports, from the records of the Metropolitan Housing and Planning Council,[1] from interviews with community-based informants, from a number of planning committees on which I served, and from living and doing part-time research in two community areas (the North River area and Rogers Park) over the five-year period. Thus, these cases tend to be the better publicized either because of their sheer size or because they were especially subject to public debate. What is most obviously missing from this list is a large number of office and residential towers which were sited in or near the city's Central Area. Except where these towers required extensive zoning changes or special tax provisions, they tended to be less problematic. Nevertheless, I have included a

---

1. Now the Metropolitan Planning Council, a private group that monitors land-use decisions. During the 1978–1982 period, I served on its local planning committee. It bears no responsibility for any of my conclusions.

few of these high-rise developments (in Chaps. 5 and 6) for illustrative purposes although fewer than a representative sample would contain.

On some of these projects I have only the sketchiest information, mostly what is available from published sources and only one informant. On others I have very detailed data, including direct participant observation and the descriptions provided by several informants. Despite the unevenness of the data and the selectivity of the sample, there are a number of observations worth making. The most obvious is that the overwhelming majority of these projects are concentrated in the community areas that flank the north lakeshore (see maps 3.1–3.3) or in the city's Central Area (see maps 6.1–6.3). The Central Area still attracts high investor confidence, a concerted public-private program of construction, and somewhat weaker opposition to "displacement."

Following the riots in the late 1960s, portions of the Loop lost most of their white night-time trade. A number of movie houses shifted to "black exploitation" or porno films, and the surrounding street-level businesses oriented themselves to this trade. The value and volume of this trade was low, and some of the large theaters (3,000+ seats) began to fail or could maintain only a marginal operation. The construction of a number of office towers did little to help matters because they included no retail space at ground level. Quite early, by 1970, a variety of proposals were made to create a nearby, well-to-do residential population which could help revive the area's entertainment zone. Many of the projects focused in or around the Loop are geared to this aim, but, as we will see, the office or residential tower remains the most likely to move off the planning boards.

Directly to the south and about a mile to the west, the city's two "black belts" begin and reach almost to the city limits. They are contiguous areas of black residence broken only by the integrated community around the University of Chicago and a couple of integrated islands near the northern boundary. Aside from the university community, investor confidence in these areas is extremely low, and since the Supreme Court's *Gautreaux* decision even subsidized housing is only rarely placed in these communities. The university community did undergo substantial reinvestment during the 1950s and early 1960s (Rossi and Dentler 1961), but that revival is now nearly complete. In the 1960s, a few large-scale housing projects were undertaken at the northern extremity of the black belt, but that effort exhausted itself when it became obvious that white families

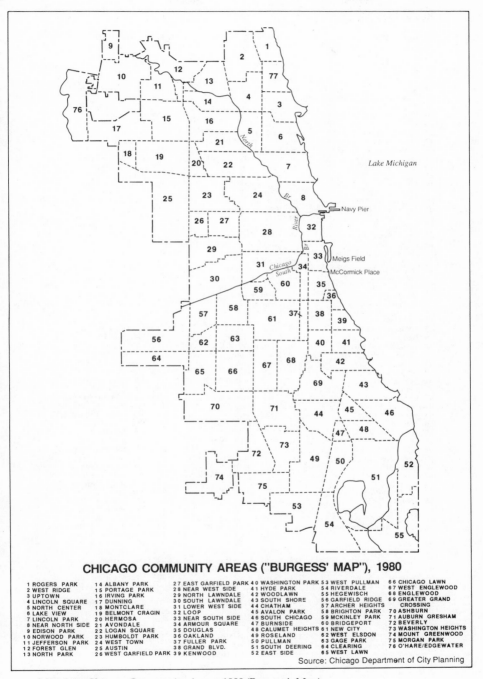

CHICAGO COMMUNITY AREAS ("BURGESS' MAP"), 1980

1 ROGERS PARK
2 WEST RIDGE
3 UPTOWN
4 LINCOLN SQUARE
5 NORTH CENTER
6 LAKE VIEW
7 LINCOLN PARK
8 NEAR NORTH SIDE
9 EDISON PARK
10 NORWOOD PARK
11 JEFFERSON PARK
12 FOREST GLEN
13 NORTH PARK

14 ALBANY PARK
15 PORTAGE PARK
16 IRVING PARK
17 DUNNING
18 MONTCLARE
19 BELMONT CRAGIN
20 HERMOSA
21 AVONDALE
22 LOGAN SQUARE
23 HUMBOLDT PARK
24 WEST TOWN
25 AUSTIN
26 WEST GARFIELD PARK

27 EAST GARFIELD PARK
28 NEAR WEST SIDE
29 NORTH LAWNDALE
30 SOUTH LAWNDALE
31 LOWER WEST SIDE
32 LOOP
33 NEAR SOUTH SIDE
34 ARMOUR SQUARE
35 DOUGLAS
36 OAKLAND
37 FULLER PARK
38 GRAND BLVD.
39 KENWOOD

40 WASHINGTON PARK
41 HYDE PARK
42 WOODLAWN
43 SOUTH SHORE
44 CHATHAM
45 AVALON PARK
46 SOUTH CHICAGO
47 BURNSIDE
48 CALUMET HEIGHTS
49 ROSELAND
50 PULLMAN
51 SOUTH DEERING
52 EAST SIDE

53 WEST PULLMAN
54 RIVERDALE
55 HEGEWISCH
56 GARFIELD RIDGE
57 ARCHER HEIGHTS
58 BRIGHTON PARK
59 MCKINLEY PARK
60 BRIDGEPORT
61 NEW CITY
62 WEST ELSDON
63 GAGE PARK
64 CLEARING
65 WEST LAWN

66 CHICAGO LAWN
67 WEST ENGLEWOOD
68 ENGLEWOOD
69 GREATER GRAND
   CROSSING
70 ASHBURN
71 AUBURN GRESHAM
72 BEVERLY
73 WASHINGTON HEIGHTS
74 MOUNT GREENWOOD
75 MORGAN PARK
76 O'HARE/EDGEWATER

Source: Chicago Department of City Planning

Map 3.1. Chicago Community Areas, 1980 (Burgess's Map)

Key to Map 3.2

1. Rogers Park
2. West Rogers Park
3. North Town
4. Edgewater
5. Andersonville
6. Uptown
7. Ravenswood
8. Ravenswood Manor
9. Lincoln Square
10. Bowmanville
11. Budlong Woods
12. Arcadia Terrace
13. Peterson Woods
14. North Park
15. Hollywood Park
16. Peterson Park
17. Albany Park
18. Mayfair
19. Crazy "K"
20. Sauganash
21. Jefferson Park
22. Wilson Park
23. Forest Glen
24. Gladstone Park
25. Edgebrook
26. South Edgebrook
27. Old Edgebrook
28. North Edgebrook
29. Wildwood
30. Edison Park
31. Oriole Park
32. Norwood Park
33. Old Norwood
34. Big Oaks
35. Irving Wood
36. Belmont Terrace
37. Belmont Heights
38. Schorsch Village
39. Montclare
40. Galewood
41. Portage Park
42. Belmont
43. Cragin
44. Hanson Park
45. Belmont-Central
46. Hermosa
47. Kelvyn Park
48. Belmont Gardens
49. Kilbourn Park
50. Park View
51. Avondale
52. Logan Square
53. Lakeview
54. Belmont Harbor
55. Lincoln Park
56. Park West
57. Wrightwood
58. Sheffield Neighbors
59. Old Town
60. Near North Side
61. Cabrini Homes
62. Gold Coast
63. The Loop
64. Near West Side
65. Wicker Park
66. Buck Town
67. Garfield Park
68. Humboldt Park
69. Austin
70. Lawndale
71. "K" Town
72. Little Village, or South Lawndale

73. Pilsen
74. Chinatown
75. Hicks Homes
76. Dearborn Homes
77. South Commons
78. Prairie Shores
79. Lake Meadows
80. Groveland Park
81. Woodland Park
82. Ida B. Wells Homes
83. Oakland
84. Kenwood-Oakland
85. Hyde Park-Kenwood
86. Hyde Park
87. East Hyde Park
88. South Side
89. Robert Taylor Homes
90. Bridgeport
91. Wentworth Gardens
92. McKinley Park
93. Brighton Park
94. Back of the Yards
95. Canaryville
96. Fuller Park
97. West Kenwood Homes
98. Gage Park
99. West Elsdon
100. Archer Heights
101. Sleepy Hollow
102. LeClaire Courts
103. Garfield Ridge
104. Clearing
105. Lawler Park, or The Village
106. West Lawn
107. Chicago Lawn
108. Marquette Park
109. Lithuanian Plaza
110. South Lynn
111. Englewood
112. Hamilton Park
113. Park Manor
114. Woodlawn
115. South Shore
116. Parkside
117. Jackson Park Highlands
118. O'Keefe Neighborhood
119. Bryn Mawr West
120. Bryn Mawr East
121. South End West
122. South End East
123. Windsor Park
124. Chelten, or Cheltenham
125. Rainbow Beach, or South Shore Drive
126. South Chicago
127. The Bush
128. Millgate
129. South Shore Gardens
130. Veteran's Memorial Park
131. Slag Valley
132. South Deering, or Irondale
133. Jeffery Manor
134. Marionette Manor
135. East Side
136. Fair Elms
137. Pill Hill
138. South Shore Valley
139. Stony Island Park
140. Stony Island Heights

141. Avalon Park
142. Marynook
143. Grand Crossing
144. Burnside
145. Chatham
146. West Chesterfield
147. West Chatham
148. Lillydale
149. Princeton Park
150. Greenview
151. Brainerd
152. Gresham
153. Foster Park
154. Highburn
155. Beverly Terrace
156. Wrightwood
157. Ashburn
158. Scottsdale
159. Ashburn Estates
160. Crestline
161. Beverly
162. North Beverly
163. Beverly Ridge
164. Vanderpoel
165. East Beverly
166. Southwest Beverly
167. Ridge Homes
168. Beverly Manor
169. Ridge Manor
170. Morgan Park Manor
171. Mount Greenwood
172. Morgan Park
173. West Morgan Park
174. Kennedy Park
175. Beverly Woods
176. Ada Park
177. Maple Park
178. Victory Heights
179. Longwood Manor
180. Washington Heights
181. Mount Vernon
182. Euclid Park
183. University Highlands
184. Roseland
185. North Roseland
186. Fernwood
187. Rosemore
188. Rosegrove
189. Sheldon Heights
190. Gano
191. Kensington
192. West Pullman
193. Colonial Village
194. Pullman
195. North Pullman
196. South Pullman
197. London Towne
198. Cottage Grove Heights
199. Altgeld-Murray Homes, or Altgeld Gardens
200. Golden Gate
201. Eden Green
202. Riverdale
203. Hegewisch
204. Avalon Trails
205. Arizona
206. Island Home Trailer Court

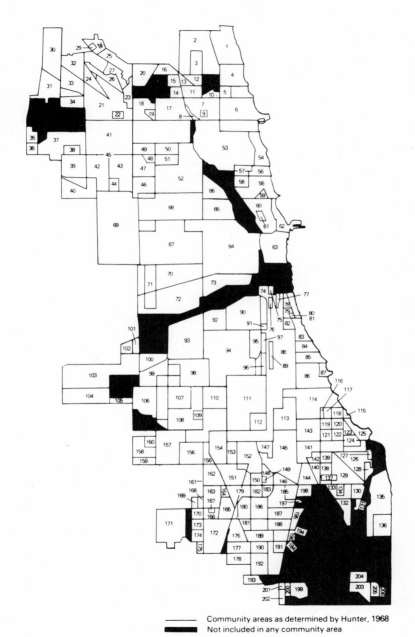

Community areas as determined by Hunter, 1968
Not included in any community area

Map 3.2. Chicago Community Areas as Determined by Hunter, 1968

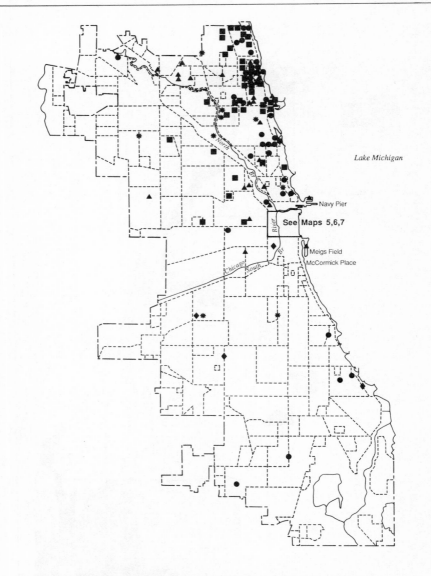

Lake Michigan

Navy Pier

See Maps 5,6,7

Meigs Field
McCormick Place

- ■ Subsidized housing, social service center location, designation as renewal area
- ● Conversion to condos, construction of private housing, landmark designation
- ▲ Conversion to public use, infrastructure improvement, rezoning for new development
- ◆ Industrial/commercial location or relocation, revitalized shopping strips
- ✳ Proposed shopping centers or malls
- ⊡ Neighborhood boundary

Source: Chicago Department of City Planning

Map 3.3. Land-use Changes Under Way or Proposed, 1978–1982

could not be attracted to the area so long as the city's school system remained hopelessly inflexible (Suttles 1972, 1982) and HUD continued to use the area as a way of expanding housing for blacks.

A number of white investors have eyed the possibilities of a growing black middle class, but most of those I talked with thought they would need a black partner and that "all that's out there are preachers and community activists." South Shore is a partial and interesting exception (Taub et al. 1984) which will warrant further discussion.

The other sectors of the city—the extreme southeast, west of the Pacific Railroad and northwest beyond the Kennedy-Edens Expressways—are occupied largely by a white population quite apprehensive about racial succession, although their public statements focus almost exclusively on displacement and gentrification. As one moves toward the edge of the city, much of this area is scarcely distinguishable from the built-up suburbs. As one moves inward, however, many of the neighborhoods are aging, and for the residents there is a heightened awareness of themselves as "white-ethnics," a category that seems to be defined only by what it excludes: blacks and Yuppies (Boylan 1985). A soft housing market, opposition to gentrification, and a sense of being an embattled minority serve to reduce new development, especially where federal funds might carry with them the requirement of affirmative action.

This population is not replacing itself, but it remains the object of a sentimental portrayal as the "real Chicago"—Sandburg's hog-butchers and stackers of wheat. It is also the population most frequently dismissed as simply racist and, indeed, neither federal judges nor civil rights lawyers have had quite the courage to impose subsidized housing upon them. Successive studies (McCourt 1977, Boylan 1985), however, show less a picture of uncomplicated bigotry than a thorough distrust of developers, city officials, and "do gooders." This distrust is not altogether unfounded.

Just west of the Central Area[2] and running north along the lakefront is the battle ground of residential development. Always an extremely diverse area, it includes pockets of practically every population in the city: rich, poor, black, white, ethnic, gay, southern white, middle income, singles, boat people, Cubans, Yuppies, Buppies, POSSLQs (people of the opposite sex sharing living quarters),

2. The eastern portion of the "Addams Area" (Suttles 1968) has been tucked into the Central Area while much of the remainder is undergoing effective gentrification.

Neighborhood Redevelopment from Above

ex-hippies, ex-Yippies, street people, Caribbeans, college pro-
fessors, and ex-mental patients. Often regarded as atypical of the
"city of broad shoulders," it is still a substantial area with a population about that of the central city of Boston.

The extraordinary diversity of the area means that no single
group can extend its presence to a considerable area, so that there
are always some places "ripe for development." This does not mean
that development has advanced without a struggle, for all along the
lakefront groups are entrenched in a many-sided contest over landmark preservation, high-rise construction, subsidized housing,
fast-food outlets, hospital expansion, shopping centers, the conversion of open space, and disused public buildings. In part, this is due
to the area's location; the lakefront is the city's chief amenity. But
probably more important is the fact that private developments
seems to beget development.[3] Starting just north of the Gold Coast,
housing rehabilitation gradually extended through parts of Lincoln
Park in the 1950s and 1960s (Warner 1979). Occasionally it would
leapfrog a few blocks north or west, but usually it hugged close to
the established sliver of high- and middle-income residences along
the lakefront or near some beachhead not far away: wherever, one
might argue, that private investment has not been endangered by
public investment.

Early observers attributed much of this to the presence of "vintage housing" (Berry et al. 1976), but now one can find examples of
gentrification in housing that must be some of the most poorly constructed in the city.[4] The movement is contiguous only right at the
lakefront, and there is considerable leapfrogging at the boundaries
as entrepreneurs seek to anticipate a rise in land values or a lapse in
local resistance. Beyond Lake View, however, there are only tiny
pockets of imperiled pioneers and, in the northernmost community
area of Rogers Park, gentrification scarcely exists despite an unusually good beachfront location and what appears at first sight to
be a better-than-average housing stock.

As this movement advances it also sputters, halts, and circum-
vents some areas in ways that are inexplicable from a purely

3. The south lakefront, between 35th Street and 40th, has not attracted similar development because the siting of substantial public housing has dissuaded private
developers. See Chapter 6 for a discussion of the lakefront area between 12th Street
and 35th Street.
4. Below grade, frame structures with asphalt siding, sometimes referred to as
"Polish revival." The term is not pejorative but ironic, indicating the exceptional ability of the Poles to turn shabby housing into livable housing.

ecological point of view. The fine-grained structure is a kind of crazy quilt of redevelopment, ballooning in at some points, strangled off at others, and going around one island after another. Only at the highest level of aggregation could it be called a single "zone."[5] To speak of urban redevelopment here as a single unified movement, then, is quite misleading. It is as much an unstable balance between contending groups and corporate actors as it is an individual marketplace. For every developer who might further gentrification, there seems to be another who would hasten clearance or conversion to some use that drives out private investment. City decisions that appear to favor redevelopment are often paired with others that might weaken it. Above all, redevelopment here depends upon a highly unstable public-private partnership that defies easy prediction.

This public-private partnership introduces a whole new level of spatial uncertainty where well-publicized professions of high purpose engage an unpredictable range of opposition and participation. This partnership is not limited to the principle investors but extends to community groups, their attorneys, the federal courts, numerous city and state agencies, and especially political leadership. The result is a kind of public theater which often starts as heroic drama but frequently unravels to become irresistible comedy or theater of the unreal. The overriding impression created by this public theater is one of deception and manipulation.

Manipulation and deception are not new to Chicago, but like the City itself they are supposed to "work." Guterbock (1980) called this pattern "defended venality," that is, manipulation and deception that delivers. When defended, venality does not deliver, however, even Chicagoans may become critical and alarmed.

Two City Dramas

The most extravagant of these public dramas occurred in the 1978–1982 debates over scatter-site subsidized public housing. Chicago already had a well-documented (Bowly 1978) record of mismanaging public housing, and it is the subject of frequent parody or pathos depending upon one's sympathies. Throughout the 1950s and early

---

5. Or, if considered a "sector," it is a peculiar one with the higher-income residents located near the CBD and the poorer ones at the city's edge.

Neighborhood Redevelopment from Above

1960s, large-slab high rises were placed in all black neighborhoods, and tenant selection progressively seemed to favor the more destructive. After the heights of the Civil Rights movement, rents were not raised, maintenance lapsed, and city officials made regular pilgrimages to Washington for emergency operating funds.[6] In 1966, the *Gautreaux* decision prohibited further construction in all black areas and mandated new construction, much of it in all white areas.

For the next eleven years, political leaders simply stonewalled the court's decision while at the same time obtaining considerable funding from the Department of Housing and Urban Development (HUD). HUD itself did construct 125 sites for subsidized housing in the interval, but in early 1978 had to announce that over 60 percent of these units had failed under private management. Later that year, federal officials thought they had found strong evidence of fraud in the expenditure of $141 million of community development funds. But nothing came of this and, up to this point, one can say that local elected leaders were occupying the high political ground. Despite the horror stories that regularly emerged from public housing, their response was pleasing to most whites and demoralizing to most advocates of public housing. Privately some took the "hopeful" view that the larger developments would simply self-destruct.

The Irresistible Comedy

In her 1979 mayoral campaign, however, Jane Byrne took a strong stand on providing assistance to low-income households, and no more than one hour into her administration the chief of HUD notified her that the Carter administration was sending her $21 million for public housing rehabilitation.[7] Six weeks later HUD made available another $100 million in community development funds

6. They were astonishingly successful, so that by February 1982 the Chicago Housing Authority was the most heavily subsidized in the nation while HUD reported one month later that it was the worst run housing authority in the nation (*Sun-Times*, 21 March 1982). As late as 1981 tenants paid 25 percent of their income up to a maximum of $250 a month regardless of apartment size. Previous experience (*Tribune*, 19 February 1982) seemed to show that tenants moved out when rental costs exceeded that figure. Some took this to mean that public housing was no longer "affordable" at the higher figure, but it seems more plausible that once the figure rose above $250 residents preferred a private to a public slum landlord.

7. The previous mayor had applied for the funds, but HUD had shown no similar urgency in granting them.

Neighborhood Redevelopment from Above

(CDBG), and the federal district court came to a settlement on the imposition of *Gautreaux*. The new mayor promised speedy and firm action: 2,223 new housing units, half in white areas, half in black areas. Again, general admiration for a gutsy if not altogether popular position. The mayor went further, saying she would involve community groups closely in site selection and design (*Tribune*, 21 May 1979) and that *none of the sites would include more than six units*.

What was promised was much more than additional public housing. There was to be a new partnership with public financing, private developers, the inclusion of not-for-profit management, and "local participation." Some were a little skeptical inasmuch as the preceding court negotiations had been carried out in secrecy, and some ACLU lawyers attributed her resolve more to pressure from the Carter administration than to the "I will" spirit of the new mayor.[8] The residents of Edgewater were even more skeptical as they were opposing a private developer of some 280 units at one site which the new mayor had not planned but quickly endorsed (*Tribune*, 23 May 1979). Still, she occupied the high moral ground if not the most popular political ground, and generally city-wide opponents of subsidized housing were silenced.

It was not until early December that the mayor baffled thousands of public housing residents by presenting them with small, plastic Christmas trees. Overcome by the irony of the situation, the residents of Cabrini-Green roundly jeered her (*Tribune*, 10 December 1979). Then, five days later it was discovered that about 25 percent of the new HUD funds had been spent to pay off snow removal costs from the previous winter. As it turned out, HUD had quietly approved the deal, leaving some doubt about the sunshine policies of the new, open government and its promise of "local participation."

By January of the new year, Senator Proxmire's committee provided a national forum in which Chicago's tenant union leaders could show pictures of the shabby condition of local public housing. Since virtually no progress had been made on new subsidized housing by April, the ACLU attorney asked that the federal court appoint an overseer. The judge waited for five weeks, then actually threatened to appoint one in the next six months if the CHA did not make substantial progress. Less than three weeks later, the FBI began in-

---

8. The city's motto and one characterization of the mayor's inaugural address (*Tribune*, 18 April 1979).

vestigating alleged financial abuses in the CHA, and the Carter administration seemed to be turning on the heat. The next day, Charles Swibel, head of the CHA board for nearly twenty years and often blamed for its deplorable condition, announced a program to provide 8,000 additional units of subsidized housing. The lack of actual accomplishment seemed to require an enlargement of what was promised. "This is not going to be a scare program," Swibel added. Only those who "want [these developments] will get them" (*Tribune*, 11 July 1980). An incredulous Alderman Pucinski still thought there might be a great "hue and cry" about this much-wanted subsidized housing but "this has nothing to do with racism. It's economic" (*Tribune*, 12 July 1980). As it turned out, he was right about the first 326 units. Practically all of them were sited in black and Latino areas. That seemed to quieten things down city wide, if not in the neighborhoods.

Almost, but not quite. In October a Rogers Park group filed suit against the siting of subsidized housing in an area already 30 percent black and in clear violation of the *Gautreaux* interpretation to exclude areas more than 15 percent black. For a while Chicagoans thought they might be able to observe a test of wills between two federal judges. But no, the attorneys for CHA argued that the first judge had *required* them to use the 1970 Census, and the present judge dismissed the suit without offering any reason. For some, this confirmed a growing suspicion that the speed of Swibel's announcement was also dictated by the urgency of avoiding the 1980 Census. With the expansion of the city's black population, the only all-white areas left were in the "white ethnic" regions where it was said that any realtor who even mentioned selling property for subsidized housing was in danger of having his legs broken in three places.

In early 1981, these skeptics had their suspicions confirmed. In yet another "final" agreement on *Gautreaux*, the judge in his wisdom ruled that one-third of the housing would be placed in "limited" (black) areas and that the remainder would be placed in "revitalizing" areas (*Tribune*, 18 January 1981). In this post-*Gautreaux* demography, the revitalizing areas were those along the north lakeshore, not primarily the better-off areas near the Central Business District but those weaker and poorer toward the north. It was enough to reaffirm one's faith in the Chicago School of Ecology. The judge had picked precisely those areas along the lakeshore most likely to undergo transition. Judicial wisdom seemed only to make lawful what was likely to occur (Berry 1979).

Community leaders along the lakeshore were for the most part angered, but by now they were not too surprised. They already had about 20 percent of the city's subsidized housing (much of it for the elderly), and now they were to get several thousand more units. Reactions to this, however, were very complicated, because most north lakeshore community groups had gone on record as favoring subsidized housing, and while some were unwavering advocates others were opposed to its concentration or had voiced support on the assumption that the term "scatter site" was to be taken literally. This brought into relief yet another fracture line for community divisiveness between unwavering and unconditional supporters of public housing and those who still saw the Section 8 program as a way of assuring its location elsewhere, in mixed developments. At the time both sides to the settlement were more concerned that it would unravel if the incoming Reagan administration cut back on support for subsidized housing. They did not look ahead to 1984, when the predominantly liberal lakeside voters, the only largely white population whose leaders had favored subsidized housing, went for Ronald Reagan (*Chicago Reporter*, August 1984).

Well before this expression of public opinion could register itself, another set of events riveted public attention. During the first nine weeks of 1981, ten residents of Cabrini-Green Homes were murdered and another thirty-five wounded.[9] As the body count grew, the now recognizably inconstant Mayor Byrne still managed to astound everyone by saying that she and her husband (an ex-- *Tribune* reporter) would move into Cabrini-Green. It would be her "in-town" home, just a short limousine ride from the one she already had on the Near North Side. The news media went into overdrive. Vernon Jarrett (*Tribune*) solemnly declared that she was after publicity and that she did not deserve it nearly so much as black leaders who had been fighting gangs in public housing for several years. "No," wrote Joan Beck (*Tribune*), Byrne was creating "a new generation in political symbols." Roger Simon (*Sun-Times*) also thought it a publicity stunt but noted she could learn something if

9. Cabrini-Green has about 14,000 residents. The Black Panthers invaded it in the late 1960s. They were well armed, as were the remaining residents soon afterward. Just to the west of the Gold Coast and a short ride from CBS and NBC studios, it is a favorite site of media attention.

Neighborhood Redevelopment from Above

Mayor Byrne Pacifies Public Housing.

she would only listen to the residents. After all, "a lot of reporters, myself included, have gone into the projects for a few days or night to do pieces" (24 March 1981).[10] Suddenly a South Side alderman said he was going to move into Robert Taylor Homes,[11] and one member of the CHA Board urged all the others to join him in moving into public housing. Bob Ciccone (*Tribune*) thought he saw a vast social movement underway and imagined that we might soon see Ronald Reagan packing his bags for Watts over the objections of Nancy.

Even before Byrne moved in, heavy security arrangements were underway, and a strange quiet fell over Cabrini-Green. Bob Weidrich (*Tribune*) likened it to the effects of saturation bombing and suggested that his metaphor be extended to practical action. The cartoonist Stayskal (*Tribune*) depicted the mayor greeting her fellow residents through the barrel of a very large tank. Burk of the *Sun-Times* had her descending into the maws of hell itself, suitcase in

10. Apparently they did not tell them that they disliked having public housing referred to as "projects."
11. Almost as notorious as Cabrini-Green, the Robert Taylor Homes is a series of highly visible slab high rises flanking the Dan Ryan Expressway and the largest single development in the country.

hand. Olimphant (*Sun-Times*) thought she would be delivered in a Brinks armored truck.

Nonetheless, on April first, just after a $150 a plate fund raiser, the mayor moved into her in-town home. For the next three weeks the media gathered at her doorstep. NBC came. CBS came. Georgia Ann Geyer and Gary Wills had already filled feature articles: Geyer (a Chicago native) thinking that it might be at least an improvement over the city's Capone-era image, while Wills (not a Chicagoan) seemed to take it dead serious. Ms. Byrne, apparently with some help from her journalist husband, filed a daily "diary" in the *Sun-Times*. Michael Killian (*Tribune*) responded with an imaginary one of his own which had her alternately stomping cockroaches and wondering if it was appropriate to have chablis with a cold TV dinner (the electricity was off again). The cartoonist McNelly (*Tribune*) had her inviting the neighbors over for an informal Derby Day brunch as soon as they finished removing someone else's TV set. Basil Talbott (*Sun-Times*) gave the whole operation a code name: "Cabrinifest."[12] Although an eleventh resident was rubbed out in the first six days of her residency, the new level of law and order was too much for some Cabrini-Green residents who marched to protest the approaching "police state." Recalling their plastic Christmas trees, they bore signs reading, "Beware of strangers bearing gifts." Mike Royko (*Sun-Times*) responded to say that a police state might be just the thing for Cabrini-Green. Since the news media were in such regular attendance, other groups from elsewhere in the city came in to capture their cameras with fresh causes.

Three weeks later Mayor Byrne moved out saying (with a straight face) that next time she and her husband might want to try some public housing for the elderly. Afterward she did reserve an apartment at Robert Taylor Homes "for surprise visits" but, in the meantime, another drama began to overtake this one. Almost two months before Ms. Byrne's change of residence, a CHA official had announced that the agency might not be able to meet its payroll by

12. A mocking reminder of "Chicagofest," a large downtown festival initiated by Mayor Bilandic and eliminated by Byrne until popular objection led her to restore it. Despite its popularity, the festival had become the object of criticism for several reasons. Some said it was only "bread and circuses," others that it was an inappropriate public expense, and still others that it included too few minority contractors. After his election, Mayor Washington eliminated the dreaded symbol, essentially by renaming it (see below Chap. 8).

Neighborhood Redevelopment from Above

April first, the fateful day on which Ms. Byrne took up residence at her "in-town" home. Others, however, offered assurance, and their case was at least arguable since an outside accounting firm could not make heads or tails of the agency's financial records (*Tribune*, 11 February 1981). And, providentially, five days after the mayor moved into Cabrini-Green, President Reagan's Secretary of HUD recommended a $16 million advance in funding. There were conditions: rents would have to be raised, employees laid off, and the housing authority would have to undergo an audit. The audit was unfavorable, but the loan was advanced anyway. Eleven days later the agency was said to face still another financial crisis, and within a week the mayor acted to scrap the entire scatter-site program so as to release the funds for current maintenance. No! editorialized the *Sun-Times* (19 October 1981). Regrettably yes, editorialized the *Tribune* (31 October 1981). The ACLU lawyers, the federal court, and HUD stood pat, but in November HUD did send more money.

Apparently it was not enough. Throughout the 1981–1982 winter, there were publicly released horror stories about the elevators and heating systems in public housing as the mayor and CHA negotiated for more federal funds. HUD responded by demanding that Charles Swibel be ousted from his chair on the agency's board. A number of state legislators and Jesse Jackson joined this Republican show of resolve only to have the mayor harden in her defense of Swibel, one of her chief fund raisers. It was all a "smoke screen," she said, they want to "blow up public housing" or "sell it" (*Sun-Times*, 2 March 1982). Next day she added that one HUD official was a front for some "fat-cat" real estate operators who wanted to turn public housing into private residences. The mayor took out ads extolling the reforms she had made in public housing, and there were no more news releases about the elevators. Eventually, Swibel did go but only after the state legislature agreed to the face-saving device of making his position a full-time appointment that would have interfered with his business practice. As he stepped down, Swibel congratulated himself on having worked to "isolate" the CHA from political considerations (*Tribune*, 14 July 1982). It brought the house down.

Community Theaters of the Unreal

If the city-wide drama of public housing was played out as irresistible comedy, the scatter-site program in the neighborhoods took on the appearance of a theater of the unreal. Although a majority of the community groups and elected officials along the north lakefront were on record as favoring public housing, the range of positions ran from private and unremitting opposition to some who openly embraced it as a moral crusade. As a result, opening statements often took the form of passionate avowals of good intentions whatever their position. These statements were just as regularly countered by allegations of diabolical intent. Some called public housing "file cabinets for the poor," while at least one advocate called it "heaven itself." Some praised it as "integrated housing," while others praised it as "minority housing," a kind of modern-day white man's burden. "This City has a 'historic commitment' to public housing," it was said. "We are only protecting our neighborhoods which we've lived in all our lives" was one response. "Race had nothing to do with this" was a common opening to which there was a common reply, "Racist!" "Subsidized housing will have no effects here. It's only incremental," some said. "We're just at the tipping point," others replied.

Within the extremes of these assertions a ready-made vocabulary of reduced images found increasing use. People no longer spoke to one another, they "dialogued." High-rise buildings became "Yuppie towers." For some there was only two kinds of housing: "luxury," or "moderate to low income" (i.e., subsidized housing). "White Appalachians," apparently a more sympathetic figure (suggesting coal miners rather than Alabama's George Wallace), almost completely replaced "Southern whites." Community groups clothed themselves in exalted names: "Every Person is Concerned" (EPIC), "Save Uptown Neighborhoods" (SUN), "Voice of the People" (VOP). Real estate developers of subsidized housing did likewise: "American Development Company," "Grass Roots Development Company," "City Centrum Company." Subsidized housing developments acquired elegant names: "Pines of Edgewater," "Peterson Plaza." The latter was also called "Edgewatergate" by its opponents.

There were heartrendering displays on either side. An old, arthritic white woman was trotted out as the typical resident of subsidized housing. One youth opposed to subsidized housing threw himself in front of a bulldozer. There were dozens of demonstrations and legal suits. These morally charged displays and vocabulary of reduced terms did not so much polarize people as they led to a growing sense of unreality in which every generalization was subject to dispute and every term subject to doubt. Community meetings were often carried out in an extremely high state of suspense, as if one were walking on eggshells. People would tremble as they spoke. Their voices broke. Sometimes they cried. Some resigned their memberships. Others seemed to gain such confidence in their moral position that they would send a whole flock of the less certain into retreat.

The federal court had concluded its decision with the novel terms of "limited areas" (e.g., black) and "revitalizing areas" (i.e., areas in transition). HUD officials compounded this novel demography by alternately referring to its irrevocable "mandate" and by dismissing announced guidelines as "only guidelines." Where HUD and the city officials attempted to treat the "guidelines" separately for different phases of the scatter-site program or yet other housing programs, most community leaders tried to aggregate the different programs as a single program. People found themselves talking about "different things," only there did not seem to be any difference. Both the language of public officials and that of community groups were cast through the prism of the mass media from which they returned as stylized, almost archetypical confrontations. Progressively, then, the world of community controversy became a kind of fiction in which representative figures—pathetic Appalachians, an even more pathetic black underclass, yuppies, closet bigots, do-gooders, crusaders, the truly needy—did battle without quite resembling anyone you have met.

The result of all this was not a highly uniform sequence of events that marked the progress and conclusion of each site for subsidized development. Rather, the experience of all the different sites seemed to get aggregated together, providing a sort of cumulative experience which may be said to have a "natural history." The parts of that history presented here come only from the community areas of North Park, Rogers Park, Edgewater, Uptown, the Near West Side, and South Shore. These are the community areas most affected by the scatter-site programs, but they are also the ones I know best.

While community groups generally (60 percent) got wind of the location of new public housing, the way they did so frequently added to their uncertainties. Sometimes it was through the grapevine connecting such groups, sometimes through a stray back-page neighborhood newspaper article, or occasionally from a public hearing on another topic (e.g., zoning). In making notification, HUD and CHA officials often distinguished between "their" scatter-site program (the 223 units or possibly some phase of their construction) and the remainder to be constructed through the larger Section 8 program. Private builders did occasionally notify local community groups but only after quietly obtaining options on land or buildings to the surprise of nearby residents. In eight instances, private developers initially obtained zoning variances (increasing the "envelope") for "luxury" housing only to later announce that they were going to obtain financing for subsidized units. Local aldermen usually received some notification but were rather selective about who they notified. When lists of addresses were published in the daily press, they were described as if construction agreements were already etched in stone.

City and HUD officials often defended these practices, but only to enlarge the uncertainty. In making a sharp distinction between "their" scatter-site program and other Section 8 housing, they undermined occasional "promises" that this "will be the last subsidized units in your community." Two such promises were subsequently said to apply only to Phase II. Or was it Phase I? Was there to be a Phase III? Private developers said that the only way to obtain sites was to do so quietly; to do otherwise would be very expensive. When they shifted from "luxury" housing to subsidized housing it was said that the market for the former was too soft and that construction was possible only with public funding. When buildings scheduled for 20 percent Section 8 were changed to 100 percent Section 8, developers said that they could not rent apartments at market rates in buildings occupied by Section 8 residents. When some community groups objected, the same developers queried, "Just why do *you* judge someone on the size of their pocketbook."

Thus, what people had been led to believe was a court-designed remedy became modified by market considerations. "Our hands are tied" (by the court) was nonetheless a frequent statement made to community groups. On one occasion, however, when Mayor Byrne changed her mind and wanted to increase the amount of public housing to be placed in North Park, she was outraged that the residents had got wind of it and met her with aroused resistance. She had wanted to announce the good news herself. On another occasion the CHA had a better reason for not notifying local residents. They had misassigned a census tract to a community area that al-

Neighborhood Redevelopment from Above

ready had its quota of subsidized housing. After that they left some of the buildings vacant so that they were vandalized.[13]

Frequently (30 percent), the scatter-site program seemed to violate its own guidelines. Apparently minority population changes since 1970 were ignored, or possibly (it is difficult to tell) they were ignored some places and not others. High-rise buildings were sometimes (10 percent) proposed for family housing, although community objection could be effective here if the Chicago Plan Commission had to approve a zoning variance. Previously, however, the Illinois Housing Development Authority had usually authorized funding.[14] The Northeastern Illinois Planning Commission had only advisory authority, and most of the informants I talked to thought it only another way of giving some semblance of systematic decision making. In one instance, HUD approved a high-rise building in an area where its own study five years previously had shown to be heavily congested and polluted. "Things which are true five years ago aren't always true today" said the regional director of HUD (*Sun-Times*, 29 March 1981). Local residents were able to document his statement by showing that the area was now more congested and more polluted than in the previous HUD study. When still another high rise was opposed because of congestion, a HUD official offered the opinion that "congestion around an inner-city is not considered unusual" (*Tribune*, 20 October 1980).

Both Edgewater and Uptown community groups frequently found themselves in the peculiar position of proposing that some particularly dilapidated buildings be rehabbed through the Section 8 program, while the CHA chose alternate sites that resulted in displacement.[15] Altogether, community groups were able to eliminate four sites, modify two others, and not able to do anything about the remaining ones they opposed. Some of these victories seemed to have been pyrrhic; the builder simply moved down the street and

13. One of them was still vacant in 1986.

14. This agency attracted widespread dislike and an effort to require it to notify the public of its pending authorizations.

15. Some of the housing had been converted to tiny apartments. When consolidated into larger units for family housing, some displacement was probably inevitable even if the promise of local preference had been kept. This promise was seldom kept nor could it be kept in view of the *Gautreaux* settlement which required that each site take at least a third of its tenants from existing CHA waiting lists. This very unselective group of tenants was usually enough to dampen anyone else's enthusiasm to live in public housing. The courts disallowed keeping apartments empty when it became difficult to recruit anyone other than blacks into each housing site.

Neighborhood Redevelopment from Above

started over. No census tract was to have more than 15 percent subsidized housing, but that did not preclude site selection that
clustered subsidized housing at the boundary between two or more
tracts.

Once a site was selected community opposition was not always forthcoming, and in many cases there was only weak
opposition or divided reactions. Sometimes there was a compromise on the proportion of units to be subsidized, but the more
frequent case was for the number to be increased once approval was
obtained if it were not already 100 percent. Some groups, particularly in Uptown and South Shore, strongly supported subsidized
housing. In the latter community area, Rescorp[16] carefully cultivated local opinion to favor subsidized housing and rehabbed 446
contiguous units that were quite acceptable to this almost entirely
black community. The same nonprofit firm tried to cultivate a favorable response in mostly white Rogers Park but achieved more mixed
results to be described later. Throughout the "limited" (black) areas,
site selection seemed to have proceeded without any newsworthy
opposition that I could locate. In one largely white area there was
general support for the Section 8 rehabilitation of some particularly
dilapidated housing, but one group strongly opposed it. The local
alderman and members of the machine ward organization simply
joined the organization and reversed its stand. Leaders of other local organizations were left with feelings of awe and apprehension.

Court suits were a frequent recourse (25 percent in this heavily
publicized sample) for community groups who opposed subsidized
housing, and occasionally (10 percent) there were countersuits by
builders. Some builders had an attorney present their plans at the
very outset. One of the most effective of the local community leaders was himself a lawyer, and several community groups retained
attorneys even when they did not file suits. The cumulative pattern,
however, seemed to be one of legal chaos. In one suit a community
group successfully opposed a high-rise building for family occupancy, while another lost a similar suit against an equally high building

16. A division of the South Shore Bank which is sponsored by several religious and
charitable groups. Taub et al. (1984) take this instance to demonstrate the viability of
Section 8 housing throughout Chicago and, indeed, this site does seem to have been
well managed and widely accepted in the local, largely black, community. I could find
no sites on the North Side, however, where Section 8 housing had stimulated further
investment or any widespread belief that it would do so. Advocates and managers of
Section 8 housing, of course, maintained their support of it.

Neighborhood Redevelopment from Above

also for families. In one case the courts sustained community objections to a twenty-four-story building but accepted it when it was reduced to "only" seventeen stories. One "luxury" high rise was opposed unsuccessfully by one community group because it included no subsidized housing. Afterward the builder included subsidized housing in order to obtain cheap financing, and another community group brought suit to prevent that. The builder withdrew because of the long delay before any court decision was made.

Indeed, threats of legal suits or "tying things up in court" were often regarded as a more important strategy than that of obtaining a favorable ruling. One reason community groups did not invariably resort to the courts was that court decisions tended to be final; it was an all-or-none strategy. So threats, delays, and out-of-court settlements—all vague in their principles—were the most frequent device for settlement. Community groups also found themselves on opposite sides in these suits, and in one instance a single site for subsidized housing was divided into two spatial units: one under legal challenge, and the other subject to informal negotiation. All this seemed to be acceptable to the courts and, indeed, I suppose one could argue that it is entirely within the best American legal tradition to provide diverse judgments for a diverse people. Nonetheless, it did contribute to the sense of uncertainty and unreality. "Going to court," said one informant, "is like going to a lottery."

Following site selection and some agreement on the number of units, local attention usually focused on the speed and quality of construction and rehabilitation. A few buildings were allowed to deteriorate further, and builders would sometimes cease maintenance when their project was tied up in court or negotiations. One rather large project was abandoned with the buildings now in worse condition. Although the number of sites where this happened was relatively small, they became real "horror stories" to haunt neighborhood groups. Where new construction or rehabilitation occurred, the quality of work was not a widespread issue.[17]

17. With publicly secured low-interest rates, firms did not skimp on their investments. Rehabilitation of each unit was reported to cost about $35,000 while new construction on the one building for which I have complete data ran to $95,000. Subsequent annual subsidies are said to run to about $6,000 per unit. These high costs were sometimes reported in the press, but they were not a neighborhood issue. In such a morally charged controversy where one's good intentions and some sign of caring for the poor were so important, it seemed wrong "to just quibble about money," as one informant put it.

After 1982, the Reagan administration did publicize the claim that providing subsi-

A subject of much greater concern was tenant selection and management. Although local residents were promised some preference, the results were quite variable. CHA housing tended to be filled from its lists of applicants, which meant black tenants from various parts of the city. The League of Women Voters strongly and sometimes successfully opposed local preference in all white areas but ignored it in black areas. Housing for the elderly tended to fill up mostly with whites in white areas, entirely with blacks in black areas. Ethnic and religious groups, who developed some housing for the elderly, were generally able to selectively recruit tenants of the same background by providing special "services" (e.g., kosher or oriental food services). One housing development for the elderly was widely regarded as occupied by "card carrying" white Democrats. Almost all the "family housing" with several bedrooms was occupied by blacks, although one community group temporarily integrated some family housing with immigrant Russian Jews who were said to show a remarkable willingness to obtain any kind of public assistance. They soon left, and a member of the community group observed, "At the rate they were going, they're probably in Skokie by now."

Latino groups, who had advocated large units to accommodate their families, found that very few Latinos were willing to live in subsidized housing. One Mexican I talked to said there was a good deal of harassment of Mexicans who tried to live in public housing, but others I talked to disclaimed this or any knowledge of it.[18] Ironically, it was only in the more transient parts of Uptown that

---

dized housing for all those eligible would absorb the entire federal budget. The Section 8 vouchers provided by that administration, however, have aroused other concerns. The vouchers seem almost ideally suited to slum landlords who make some modest cosmetic improvements and assure themselves of full occupancy at higher and more reliable rents. Most other landlords refuse to accept the vouchers because they find that once they accept Section 8 tenants they cannot attract market rate tenants in the same building. Proponents of Section 8 housing now use this observation to argue for "100 percent Section 8" conversions at all sites.

18. It is extremely difficult to get any informed observations on the harassment of minorities within public housing by those who constitute the majority. In Chicago, however, public housing is so closely identified with blacks that it is usually regarded as simply "their" piece of the public pie. White "intruders" might easily be regarded as trying to chisel in on someone else's public goods.

I have never lived in public housing, but I have done a total of five years of field work in two developments that accommodated approximately 5,000 families. They housed only three whites. One, an elderly Jewish lady who had lived there for over twenty years, was well accepted. "She was here before us," it was said, and she

community groups were able to integrate some Section 8 sites. Here, two all-white community groups adopted somewhat the same militant rhetoric common among black advocates of public housing and were actually able to insist on a white presence in some sites. A leader of one of these groups told me, "It's really very hard. Once you take the quota forced on you by CHA. And finding local people who will live there."

By 1985, when I last inquired, none of the subsidized units included in this study had gone into default. Two rather large developments were said to be so poorly managed that the better tenants were leaving because of the housekeeping standards of those remaining. One informant wryly remarked, "They need to 'Section 8' it again so that they can throw out the tenants." Most of the rest were regarded as reasonably well managed, and those few managed for and by a single racial, ethnic, or religious group were said to be managed very well. Indeed, the more militant and exclusive the private managers of Section 8 housing, the more likely they were to get high marks as managers. It would appear that such a rhetoric makes it possible for them to be quite selective in who they accept as tenants. As champions of the poor, they are able to use their own discretion and to resist the unselected tenants proposed by CHA. They are, so to speak, a step ahead of the official advocates of public housing.

Almost everyone I talked to regarded housing for the elderly as benign, except for a few merchants who complained of a downturn in business. "All we get are cut-rate drug stores," one of them said. A few others also thought that the concentration of housing for the elderly along some heavily traveled streets was a rather grotesque "final solution" to the problem of aging. The chief concern, however, was with those sites managed by CHA. Two subsequent reports (Marciniak and Jefferson 1985; De Zutter 1986) seem to bear out these fears and recommended the extension of private (usually nonprofit) management of all Section 8 housing. None of the community leaders I talked to, however, thought that private management alone was an institutional guarantee of effective control over

---

scarcely ever went out of her apartment. A white woman married to a black husband was persistently harassed as were her two interracial children. A single white male was totally unscathed. He was a precinct captain and said to have ties to "the outfit."

Recently, when I asked building managers about harassment, they either said that it did not occur or that "it's no worse than what blacks face in a white neighborhood." I would guess that the latter statement is pretty near the truth.

family housing. Rather, they felt that only their own constant vigilance could assure adequate management.

This may be self-serving, but it is worth noting that the two developments said to be poorly managed by private agencies were not subject to this kind of vigilance. One lay outside any organized community and was surrounded by industry and vacant land. The other made up a part of a small black residential island, and the nearby, largely white community groups were "afraid to interfere." A few remembered that Chicago Public Housing had once been reasonably well managed and that "it [a lapse in management] can happen again and when they go, there's no going back."[19] One longtime observer of public housing in the city cautioned, "A private manager can do pretty well when the buildings are new or recently rehabbed. Once there is a good deal of wear and tear, they will have a hard time unless they can get HUD to cough up a lot of money for maintenance." Few of these reservations extended to the private groups managing new Section 8 housing. Assured by two reports on the comparative success of private management, they were more firmly convinced of the moral correctness of their original position.

Shopping Strips and Regional Malls

It is not surprising that subsidized housing is very controversial, that it prompts high levels of uncertainty, and that it may lower confidence in local government. But similar conditions also seem to surround a whole range of land-use changes we sometimes unreflectively think of as in the "private marketplace." Regional malls and shopping strips are a good instance of this.

Chicago has far too much land zoned commercial. Harold

19. Practically everyone, including the older tenants of public housing, seem to report a "golden age" of public housing in Chicago when it was integrated, well run, and only a temporary form of assistance that helped people "get on their own feet." Whites tend to place this golden age in the period when many of them still occupied public housing. Blacks tend to place the golden age at a more proximate time, "When we first moved in," or some dimly reported period "before they let it fall apart."

The myth of a golden age has obvious appeal to whites who want to distinguish their own period of occupancy as something far superior to what is presently the case. Among blacks the myth seems to provide an explanation for why they moved into public housing and how they differ from those currently moving into public housing.

Mayer pointed this out in his famous 1955 address when the city had at least a half million more residents. Routinely every half-mile road was zoned commercial if not industrial as were several angular roads and much of the expanding Central Area. Despite the widespread recognition of the problem, little is done about it because it raises many of the same issues as does gentrification. Great sentimental value is often attributed to these shopping strips, although these sentiments seem to extend to effective patronage only where the strips are "museumized" (Suttles 1984) for an upscale trade. Otherwise, most shoppers seem to prefer one of the newer regional shopping centers that ring the city boundary (Berry et al. 1976, p. 45). These provide ample parking, air-conditioned space, and an experience that is relatively safe and free of clutter once you get past the parking lots.

The intensity of competition along shopping strips is very high, but it seems less to reduce the number of businesses than to lower their quality. Thus, many of the shopping strips would appear to serve just about one social class lower than the one that lives nearby. Some places are vacant, some are boarded up, turnover is high, and a large proportion are so marginal that they would not meet building or licensing requirements if these were strictly enforced. This makes the issue of displacement all the more difficult. The struggling small businessman is a very pathetic figure. This can be especially true if he is a recent immigrant, a "boat" person, or an elderly couple eking out a living in the same spot for the last thirty years. When the confrontation is between a large national chain "bully" and some small struggling merchant, the sentimental favorite is obvious.

The merchants themselves are unusually difficult to organize, not only because they are independent spirited but because they are fearful of a city code that is selectively enforced and of disclosures of illegal conversions or the use of "sweat" (illegal alien) labor. Merchant organizations do exist on most strips, but the discipline they impose is slight. This is especially so in transitional areas where even informal efforts at social control are apt to be seen as efforts at ethnic or racial exclusion. The advantages of the large shopping center are its uniform hours, shared parking and promotion, selection of new entrants, and the control of facades and foot traffic so that the shopper who comes for one product is likely to see all the others. Within the built-up city this kind of control is very difficult to achieve even among very powerful merchant associations. The

State Street Council has been unable to control the duplication and quality of shops selling essentially the same thing along the city's best known shopping strip. Dominant anchors on some shopping strips can be effective only if they threaten to leave, an all-or-none strategy that does not always work. Nor do anchors always follow the strategy of the shopping mall. In the Belmont-Craigen shopping district one owner controlled about 40 percent of the floor space but sought to turn it into a center for selling shoes throughout the North Side rather than into a variety of shops for the local residents.

Although the image of the regional shopping mall as providing a sanitized and manipulated shopping experience may be more nearly an expressed than a revealed preference, there does seem to be a groping desire for "something different." An older pattern of unselective slumming is now quite dangerous, especially to the relatively uniformed from the suburbs. And, if one looks at the more successful of Chicago's inner city variations on the suburban mall (Water Tower Place, Century Mall, and Piper's Alley after it dropped its 1960s funky for 1980s upscale), they all provide a well-controlled commercial experience, although it is also one that is distinctly urban in appearance (no cedar shakes and unpolished stone), one that hides the automobile in enclosed structures, and one that attempts to recall (sometimes with neomodernism) a previous urban period. The much-admired Rouse projects are all of this sort. Chicago's own Rouse project remains on the drawing board. Although there are some interesting efforts to market "old ethnic" shopping strips, these are struggling ventures which have only recently obtained much public support. For fifteen years the alternative strategy has been one that seems almost calculated to arouse public opposition while not offering "something different."

Early city plans (e.g., the 1966 plan) were aimed at reducing and concentrating shopping in large, island-like malls. As that plan unraveled,[20] the practice seems to have become one of opportunism—the encouragement of in-city shopping without any reduction in strip shopping. The first Chicago regional mall (1952)

20. Something like it was accomplished in the Hyde Park–Kenwood Co-op near the University of Chicago. Popular liberal reaction, however, was almost entirely negative, and students still listen to the recording of an old Nichols-May routine satirizing the renewal program of the area. University reading lists still include Jane Jacobs's (1961) criticisms launched from the distance of Greenwich Village, while Brian Berry's study (1968) showing that transition would have resulted in equal displacement goes almost unread.

A recent issue of the student newspaper, welcoming students to the university,

was perched right inside the city in the Evergreen Park area. The second (1965) was located just inside the city boundaries in an area of low density. All but two of the subsequent fifteen regional malls have been located in the suburbs. Harry Chaddick, a good friend of Mayor Daley and once chairman of the board of Zoning Appeals, developed the second of these in-city malls. It so impressed the mayor that he appointed Chaddick chairman of a committee to develop more like it. Chaddick proposed five in-city malls and ten mini-malls. The fate of the five in-city malls is revealing as they show the problematics of public planning when for all practical purposes it is carried out by the developer.

One of the first of Chaddick's malls (Green Acres) was to be constructed on a 160-acre tuberculosis sanitarium site then in disuse. The site, however, was heavily wooded with exotic plants and contained some buildings of remarkable design. Residents, the local alderman, and architectural buffs all opposed it. Although the City owned the land, there would have been additional costs in constructing approaches for this "private" business. There was already a mini-mall four blocks north. The opposition was unified; it pounced on the huge land subsidy given the developer and played heavily upon the destruction of this urban sanctuary. Mayor Daley himself eventually intervened to put an end to Green Acres.[21] A second mall (Humbolt Square) was to be constructed on city-assembled land, but investors quickly withdrew after a nearby Puerto Rican Independence Day riot. Chaddick, now a good friend of Mayor Bilandic, tried again on industrial land facing Lake Calumet (Harbor Mall), but that fell through when another deal for landfill blocked its entrance.[22] Indefatigable, Chaddick then proposed the Stockyards Mall in the Eleventh Ward, home of Mayor Bilandic, Richard M. Daley (Daley's son) and previously Mayor Daley. Mayor Bilandic

included a long article defining for them the tragedies of past displacement. In my own classes at the university I have found it extremely difficult to elicit a more detached analysis of the university's renewal program. Of course, it is understandably difficult to convince someone that Mike Nichols, Elaine May, and Jane Jacobs could be all wrong.

21. However, the errant alderman was not forgiven. When Mayor Bilandic later dedicated a portion of the site as a park, Alderman Gutstein had to sit to one side away from the dignitaries and was the last introduced. Still, he received the only rousing cheer from the assembled residents. He lost the following election to a well-supported machine candidate.

22. Landfill is so scarce that special deals must be made with private scavengers to obtain access to their disposal sites.

first supported him but then withdrew with the statement that news accounts that the residents had objected to potential black shoppers were untrue. Traffic congestion seemed to be the main problem in this lightly used area.[23]

Chaddick did build one of his malls, the Brickyard, which was constructed in a vast hole in the ground that had been excavated to make bricks. No further land assembly was required, and there was at least some fear that it might otherwise be used for landfill. Merchants from the Belmont-Central shopping district strenuously opposed it, but they were unable to defeat it in court where they claimed that Chaddick had a conflict of interest in being both public developer and private manager of the mall. The Brickyard was a great success, so much so that it alarmed not only the Belmont-Central merchants but those from several other shopping strips.[24] Thus, when Chaddick proposed his next mall (Riverview) only a few miles away, merchants from fourteen different shopping districts rose in opposition. This mall would have required rezoning (as did all others), the exercise of condemnation powers, the public construction of traffic approaches, and the displacement of an articulate firm (WGN Studios). After initially supporting Chaddick, Mayor Byrne had to tell this longtime friend of her husband that she was opposed to the mall.

What stands out here, beyond the expectable opposition of competing merchants and nearby residents, is the way that public-private partnerships invite such opposition and change the standards of how the outcome is to be evaluated. Certainly Chaddick did not lack clout in a city where it is supposed to count. He had built several malls in the suburbs with little or no opposition. But as one of his potential mall tenants told me, "Once you put that kind of [public] money in a shopping center, you ought to get something better than Ford City" (Chaddick's first in-city mall). Indeed, Chaddick's presence and his obvious political connections may have disserved the in-city mall committee because they only heightened

23. The last cow was killed in the stockyards in 1971. The International Amphitheater is closed, and much of the land lies empty or is used for warehousing. The area was really congested when the stockyards were in full operation.

24. The Belmont-Central shopping district did experience more vacancies and turnover, but Robert Mier (then at the University of Illinois and now head of the city's Department of Economic Development), who studied the district, thought this might be temporary because there were signs that the Brickyard challenge was forcing some upgrading of the Belmont-Central district. The merchants' organization remains firmly convinced of the harm done them.

fears that "what you'll get is schlock." Chaddick's other malls have attracted good but not top-of-the-line anchors. The Brickyard is regarded as having a pleasing and effective design. Thus, rather than think him a poor developer, I am inclined to say that he met a higher standard, a standard that would have justified considerable public expense. This increase in expectations extended also to a concern over displacement, aesthetic design, the loss of green space, the convincing demonstration of tax returns, and in three instances the legality of Chaddick's proposal.

Public involvement also created multiple occasions at which intervention and opposition were possible: rezoning, land assembly, condemnation, traffic rerouting, investment in infrastructure, and, since Chaddick never controlled his full site, the consideration of alternative land uses. Each of these points of contest invited new opponents: neighborhood groups, competing merchants, architectural buffs, the defenders of parkland, the users of landfill, and other people with clout. Thus, the whole notion of the entrepreneur with wide freedom to dispose of "his" property seems out of place here. The idea that Chaddick's committee was engaged in "public planning" seemed even further from the mark. The ambiguity of the strategy could only invite speculation and enlarge the moral issues involved.

One is inclined to think that neither Mayor Daley nor his successors sensed the growing importance of at least the appearance of a planful process in a population conned once too often and now so fragmented by the unrest of the late 1960s that political leaders had lost their outward signs of invulnerability. To extend Guterbock's term (1980), they now expected "defensible venality."

Fast Foods and Mini-Malls

The growing detachment of blacks from "the Machine" and the conditional nature of the whites' allegiance to it have been accompanied by an increasing capacity for public opposition. Chicago is full of community organizations (Emmons 1986; Harris 1980), and even in very safe wards (such as Mayor Bilandic's Bridgeport) they may take a stand some distance from the local ward organization. This capacity for opposition may draw residents in contrary directions at times, but it also means that even small land-use decisions are now likely to draw some public fire.

Neighborhood Redevelopment from Above

The opposition to mini-malls and fast food drive-ins is interesting because it must seize upon much more modest grounds for intervention. Many of those who oppose them do so for aesthetic reasons, but the more general belief is that they can "downgrade" or tip an area toward transition. They do attract youth from other neighborhoods, appeal to transient motorists, and break up the foot traffic of window shoppers.[25] To be effective, however, community groups must search for some additional arguments.

For example, in Lincoln Park a McDonald's was proposing to demolish an old but sound industrial building to construct one of their restaurants at an El stop. There was opposition for a variety of reasons. Some thought the building worth preserving, others wanted a better class of restaurant, and still others disliked the "suburban" appearance of McDonald's. The older building was being vacated by the owner, and McDonald's needed only a zoning change. Opposition in this affluent community, however, was intense and determined. Dozens of community meetings were held, and local media people were enlisted in the cause. Increasingly, the opposition singled out the fear of attracting gangs. These fears had some basis: Cabrini-Green lies somewhat to the west, although so far away that no one from that community thought to defend the fast food place as among "their rights." Besides, Lincoln Park is a well-organized community and its boundaries stop precisely at Cabrini-Green housing. Private discussions among opponents centered almost entirely on a "low-quality" restaurant in a "high-quality" community. Nevertheless, gangs were showcased—a winning strategy. After the City Council turned down the zoning variance, community groups helped another lessee come in with a high-quality restaurant and assisted him in obtaining a liquor licence.

Almost the reverse took place in Rogers Park where opponents to a Kentucky Fried Chicken drive-in had to abandon the higher moral ground to its supporters. Also located at an El stop, this drive-in could have been seen as attracting "gangs" and transients. In-

25. Opponents also made the argument that they displaced sit-down family restaurants. When I countered with the observation that I saw more families feeding their children at McDonald's than at more expensive sit-down restaurants, I was unconvincing. Although I could not elicit an articulate response, I was left with the impression that the very appearance of fast-food places conveyed a sense of impermanence and transiency. Since I had to do a number of these interviews "cold," I could not usually get beyond publicly voiced reasons for opposition. One barroom commentary, however, was revealing: "They just like a kid's toy. You could dismantle one and put it somewhere else in two days."

Neighborhood Redevelopment from Above

deed, there was some well-justified fear of that because the site lay directly at the boundary between a low-income black population and a white, largely middle-income population. Community organizers, although mostly white, could not meet in isolation to discuss this fear. Instead, they focused primarily on their fears of a "glitter gulch" and their hopes for an alternative twenty-five-acre shopping mall that had achieved very little backing. The developers of the drive-in quickly hit upon the argument that they would provide jobs for the surrounding black youths. Despite eighteen months of debate, they won their zoning variance.

Still a different turn of events took place in Lake View where both sides armed themselves with moral arguments over the development of a mini-mall. A small shopping center had been proposed by a developer who had a favorable relationship with the Lake View Community Council. Indeed, he was offering to donate some of the space to the council. The land was owned by the city and up for public bidding. The ever-present Harry Chaddick came forth with a bid for a discount grocery store. Although Chaddick's bid was the lower of the two, Mayor Byrne quickly stepped forward to support him. "We need it," she said. "I don't think they [Chaddick's opponents] are taking into consideration the poverty on the west side of the community and the need for people to buy cheap food" (*Tribune*, 7 August 1980). Although the primary concern of community groups was the quality of a discount store at a location that "was turning the corner," they focused largely upon the apparent political favoritism and widespread belief that the mayor opposed the first bidder because he had offered space to the community council. Eventually they were able to obtain the support of three state legislators and, with the threat of a court battle, the discount store withdrew.

Conclusion

One could continue with examples of this sort.[26] My aim is not to be exhaustive, however, but to simply show how the planning process

26. For example, in Norwood Park a mini-mall was opposed because it would have destroyed a landmark building. When the landowner "accidentally" destroyed the building, they had an even stronger case. In Lincoln Park, the residents of Sandburg Village fought off a "vertical mall" partly because they were able to stress the builder's "betrayal" of a promise to build town houses. In Lincoln Square, a similar battle over the "desecration" of an unused portion of a cemetery still rages after five years.

in Chicago has progressively fallen into a pattern of theatrical manipulation. The lack of a public body which makes deliberate and reasoned recommendations draws everyone into a dialogue where the results depend upon who can find the higher moral ground or tar the other with ulterior motives. The city does not lack a planning department, but as the reader can tell it was practically invisible during each of these land-use disputes. The city's mayors were neither simply facilitators responding to the independent proposals of private developers nor possessed with the authority to fully shape such proposals. Rather, the mayors became directly implicated in each initiative while, at the same time, seeming only to serve narrowly defined interests: selected developers and the building trade unions in the case of subsidized housing, Chaddick in the case of the regional malls, political favorites or moral bandwagons in the case of mini-malls or fast food places.

The chief advantage of a systematic planning document and a staff that can articulate it is that it moves public discussion toward the general benefits of land usage. Ideally, it should focus on how to maintain or improve a city's standing in the urban hierarchy of which it is a part. Questions of equity, aesthetic appeal, and moral righteousness, then, are entrained within a broader debate over how to form or reform the city's physical plant to meet the competitive challenges in a changing national economy. Very parochial demands or absolutist moral positions are constrained within a larger argument about general benefits and costs. The alternative of a multitude of public hearings and "local participation" only invites additional dissent, the strategic use of moral claims and, in many instances, community division rather than community consensus. As we will see in the following chapter, local community consensus can be achieved under rather special conditions, conditions that are not easily altered and that make community redevelopment from below almost as manipulative as that carried out from above.

FOUR

NEIGHBORHOOD DEVELOPMENT
FROM BELOW

The three maps in the preceding chapter reveal noticeable changes in both our way of looking at Chicago's community areas and the organization of those areas. The first map was prepared by Burgess and Newcomb in the early 1930s. It is a very famous map, one of the most authoritative ever prepared for an American city and the model for many more. The second map was prepared by Albert Hunter (1974), a close observer of Chicago's neighborhoods in the late 1960s. Where Burgess and Newcomb's map consisted of a series of roughly equal-sized areas that touch but do not interpenetrate, Hunter's map shows an uneven hierarchy of nested neighborhoods, contested areas which are claimed by two or more communities and substantial areas which are unclaimed. The third map was prepared by the Chicago Department of Planning, and no effort is made here to show how smaller neighborhoods are nested within larger community areas.

Many of the differences between these maps can be attributed to the methods used by separate researchers. Burgess sought to create roughly equivalent ecological areas which he thought comprised a community because of a complement of characteristics: natural boundaries, a miniature "downtown" for weekly shopping, a population base large enough to support this shopping district, and a collection of institutions—schools, churches, social agencies—sufficient to serve this population. Burgess's map is interesting because he seems to have shared the widespread assumption that a local community would necessarily arise from these constraints and opportunities. If this community did not reveal itself in the expressed statements of local residents, it was because of the perturbations of succession or some change in natural boundaries which had not fully registered themselves on local opinion.[1] Such

---

1. An examination of Burgess's papers shows that many of his interviews were with local businessmen who, like him, thought of these areas as "shopping districts." Thus, many of the names may owe more to local boosterism than to popular practice. None of the more popular but irreverent names were included in Burgess's map.

Neighborhood Development from Below

communities should have a name, and some of them did. If not, Burgess gave them one. Over time, he argued, each of these natural areas should settle down to realize its identity and achieve some organized level of collective responsibility (Barsky 1974). Communities, then, were not simply lines on a piece of paper but reflected a distinct and bounded "social reality," a reality that gave residents a grounded voice in defending or remaking them.

This assumption seems to have been widely accepted, and Burgess's map came into extensive use and has remained almost unaltered for sixty years. The Chicago Department of Planning regularly publishes copies of it. Several social agencies accept its boundaries for their service areas. The newspapers regularly report heinous murders and rapes by their community location. Political leaders and public agencies persist in fragmenting community areas with their district boundaries lest they face a unified community (Hunter and Suttles 1972). Along with a number of colleagues (Erbe et al. 1984), I recently helped produce yet another *Community Fact Book* in the hope that it would obstruct this kind of manipulation.

Among local residents there was always an uneven correspondence between Burgess's map and their customary usage of local names and boundaries. Hunter's map reveals this uneven fit during the late 1960s.[2] To some extent, the differences between the larger areas in Hunter's map (those in boldface) and those drawn by Burgess is due to the tendency of informants to use highly legible transportation arteries (Lynch 1960) rather than Burgess's natural boundaries. But as Hunter points out (pp. 72–88), many of the differences are due to a kind of status game in which areas of higher social rank attempt to disavow adjacent areas of lower rank while the latter seek to extend their community into a "better" residential area. Some of these better neighborhoods go so far as to become small islands of exceptional social rank while some especially notorious ones become equally isolated through exclusion.[3] Hunter calls them symbolic communities, and his study provides us with a

2. I once asked Henry McKay, Burgess's student and colleague, about the differences between these two maps and he responded, "Burgess knew about all those other areas but he wanted to designate real communities."

3. There are other reasons for this, for example, large public or private housing projects seem to be so legible that they are always singled out. I make no effort to exhaustively compare these maps because I want to focus on differences of social rank as the engine that drives the current pattern of community subnucleation along the north lakefront.

Neighborhood Development from Below

snapshot captured at a single time and consisting of shifting boundaries and evolving identities.

Hunter was a careful researcher and allowed a large number of
informants to express a range of their knowledge about community
names and boundaries. The Chicago Department of Planning simply asked people, "What's the name of this neighborhood?" and
"What are its boundaries?" Even so, this map is informative if we
take it to show those areas where there is an increasing visibility of
one's local neighborhood as against the larger community areas.
Clearly, this sort of preoccupation with smaller areas is most concentrated along the north lakefront, along the North Branch of the
Chicago River, and in the area lying just south of the Stevenson Expressway along the lake. The southernmost area, Burgess's Douglas
Park, underwent almost total clearance during the late 1950s and
was redeveloped mostly as a series of megablock compounds where
the residents of four large private developments have little to do
with each other or the residents of five large public housing developments.[4] This part of the Department of Planning's map closely
resembles Hunter's 1974 map because both essentially reveal the
same highly legible megablock compounds constructed by the early
1970s.

The Near North Side and Lincoln Park (again using Burgess)
underwent redevelopment in the 1950s and 1960s, although here
the pattern was more nearly one of house-by-house, block-by-block
recovery than massive clearance.[5] Once again the pattern of sub-
community formation is very similar to that shown by Hunter. Since
Hunter prepared his map, however, redevelopment has advanced
well into Lake View, opened up a few islands in Uptown, and leap-
frogged into Edgewater and the North River areas. Here the
Department of Planning map shows considerably more subcom-
munity formation (or visibility) than was apparent in Hunter's 1974
map. The heightened visibility of subcommunities, then, seems to
follow or anticipate redevelopment. Thus, rather than seeing them
as just symbolic communities, we might want to think of this subnucleation of the urban landscape as a more or less self-conscious

4. I lived in the area doing fieldwork for two years in the early 1970s. The only residents who referred to it as Douglas Park were a small group of people who tried to
organize the area after consulting the *Community Fact Book*. They were unsuccessful
and the large projects dominate local spatial references (Suttles 1972, pp. 83–84).

5. Only one megablock development, Carl Sandburg Village, was constructed.

Neighborhood Development from Below

effort to withdraw into a "defensible space" (Newman 1973) where residents can try to regulate the process of redevelopment.

Just what "regulate" means here, however, differs greatly depending upon who one talks to and the weight one assigns to their statements. For example, some of the smaller areas (the Villa, Ford City Village) are little more than the invention of real estate entrepreneurs hoping to promote an "exceptional" neighborhood which has been (or is to be) rescued from its surroundings. Still others are partially contrived "ethnic neighborhoods" (Ukrainian Village, Lithuanian Plaza) which have been invented or revived through a political process in which some evidence of ethnic presence has been seized upon to promote a commercial district or increase local control.

Andersonville is one of the more "authentic" of these ethnic areas, having been known by that name since it was settled by the Swedes at the turn of the century.[6] Almost all of them have left, but in the last few years the area has been saturated with banners that announce its identity, and there have been several favorable news articles on its ethnic ambience. This helps to promote the area not only for return trade by Scandinavians but to a broader public who may find themselves surprised by the number of Greek, Middle Eastern, and Asian outlets.[7] More important, it extricates Andersonville from Uptown, a neighborhood that has gained an awesome reputation for being populated by drunken hillbillies,[8] bums, street people, and transients. This is not just a symbolic statement; it is an organized effort to escape the clutches of yet another organization

6. About one in every eight Swedes has the last name of "Anderson."

7. A Mexican population in Pilsen does much the same thing by insistently retaining this name despite the criticism of a more nationalist group in the community (Muller 1983). Despite much poverty, the Mexicans are avid entrepreneurs and well aware of the need to attract outside trade.

8. Except when quoting others, I will use the term "hillbilly" rather than "Appalachian white." I avoid the latter term because it is an academic contrivance used to assert the equivalence of primordial groups and to lobby for Appalachian whites as another damaged people.

The extensive, almost universal, reference to all Southerners in Chicago as Appalachian whites is puzzling because at best it could include only about half of those centered in Uptown (Harwood 1966). I can only assume that in the early 1960s, when the term came into general use, it was better to be mistaken as an Appalachian white than someone who resembled Bull Conner with his cattle prod in Selma, Alabama. It would appear that the forgiving features of this region were discovered twice, once in the South by northern missionaries, and again in Chicago by a new set of missionaries (Shapiro 1978).

that would turn this part of the city into a kind of reservation for the poor.

The Ukrainian Village is a much more recent and more obviously contrived neighborhood that seeks to do much the same thing with the development of additional ethnic establishments to supply evidence of occupancy.[9] Even more obvious is the proposal for an "ethnic village," a kind of modern, "old world" shopping center, in Marquette Park where the local white ethnics hope to "stabilize" the area. The city itself has promised to assemble the land and become a coinvestor. Indeed, all across the North Side and Near West Side one finds small residential and commercial areas that seek to obtain special city services (additional police protection, annual street fairs, landmark designation) and public investments (plantings, traffic controls, brick sidewalks) that will designate them as a special kind of area for potential shoppers and residents. The most obvious are the revival of "old" ethnic areas, but there are others trying to find a niche in the market for a distinct housing preference (e.g., "live where you work," "enjoy old world craftsmanship") or some suggested ambience ("Wrigleyville," the "Villa"). The historic designation of some twenty-one residential areas is probably the most advanced stage of this kind of local exceptionalism.[10] However, by now the city government has conceded to numerous local groups who post eye-catching banners along main thoroughfares giving the name of the neighborhood and suggesting something of its aspirations ("Buena Park: A Historic District").

In a way, all of this is quite familiar, for local boosterism has always contributed greatly to neighborhood names and reputations. The high frequency of terms like "estates," "heights," "park," "terrace," "square," "green," "view," "brook," and "manor" make this rather obvious in Chicago. But over the last few years, several

9. The proliferation of ethnic cultural centers has increased the competitive pressure to the point that a much wider range of items must be stocked, especially in restaurants. When I first arrived in Chicago in 1961, there were only two or three Northern Italian restaurants, almost all of them located in the Central Area. Now there are so many that I cannot keep track of them, and a small area on the Southwest Side has come to specialize in this cuisine. Slumming, as it was known in the 1920s, is probably too dangerous for most Chicagoans, but they can still demonstrate an exceptional urbanity by eating in the less "discovered" places.

10. Just about half of these landmark districts lie right along the north lakefront. The others are in the Central Area, in Hyde Park–Kenwood, on the West Side near the Central Area, or on the far Southwest Side where the residents are already preparing for the possibility of succession.

Neighborhood Development from Below

Chicago neighborhoods seem to have gone past the mere claim to comfort and status to where they attempt to establish themselves as a quasi-legal corporation which can lay claim to public investment and protection in much the same way that firms can negotiate with city governments for special services or financial arrangements. Of course, local development corporations do take on a clear legal status, but the more generic pattern in Chicago seems to be an informal one shaped by repeated negotiations with city government, institutions, foundations, and newsmakers rather than a general legal treaty. Businessmen and local political leaders may be involved, but often they are only riding a bandwagon launched by resident organizations.

This also is not without precedent, for many large American cities have informally protected their Chinatowns as part of the tourist industry. These arrangements permitted, indeed required, the agglomeration of Chinese businesses and residents as if they were a single firm. Unlike other efforts at self-segregation, it was publicly acceptable and not legally challenged because it was "voluntary" self-segregation and economically justifiable. Chinatowns made economic sense in the same way that industrial parks make sense. Now that practically all the ethnic groups left in the city are minorities, not even the League of Women Voters can get too exercised over their self-segregation.

To a considerable extent, the Chicago pattern of local community subnucleation can be seen as an extension of this Chinatown practice. No one is overtly excluded, but substantial affirmative steps can be taken to selectively recruit businesses, consumers, and residents. Even the language of minority rights can be adjusted to disarm potential criticism: "We also have a right to our culture," "We are not excluding anyone but they must tolerate us," "We want our next generation to live in this city too," "We have our right to neighborhood pride," "We are part of the rainbow of this city." Blacks and "do-gooders," of course, are the most obvious audience for such disarming statements, but the broader claim is to extend minority rights to practically any residential enclave.[11]

Within these enclaves there is also the advantage of increased

11. With the decline in Chicago's European ethnic groups, they have become numerical minorities. The term "minority," however, has been extended to include so many groups (gays, female-headed households, the elderly, the disabled, etc.) that most Chicagoans see themselves as members of an embattled minority.

Chicago never had a very large WASP population although WASPs often did oc-

Neighborhood Development from Below

homogeneity and the frankness that prevails among people of similar background. Public meetings that draw representatives from a very large area tend to be very cautious to the point that they are almost entirely ceremonial or provide only a stage for moralistic grandstanding.[12] At such meetings nearly everyone is for a diverse, balanced community with a high quality of life. Smaller, more intimate groups can talk about how actually to do this, that is, to retain self-supporting individuals and exclude those who are entrapped in a subsistence pattern than combines welfare payments, the gray market, and scavenging: a pattern of shared poverty where income is no longer separable property. The most obvious objections are to blacks, hillbillies, ex-mental patients, and some recent Caribbean immigrants, but increasingly the term "underclass" has caught on as a more neutral term. As with the extensions of the language of minority rights, class designations seem to assume greater public acceptance in these defended neighborhoods (Suttles 1972), and informants frequently told me, "I think it [self-segregation] is class, not race." Since any ethnic or racial group might conceivably want to avoid this underclass, the term can be used to assert a kind of equivalence among people of any background. "We are only doing what respectable people of any background would do," it might be said.[13] Assertions of this sort seem especially likely to be combined with statements that attribute the origins of "the underclass" to state mismanagement of the welfare system, the displacement of American workers, or the "dumping" of mental patients by state hospitals.

These references to social class are now widespread, and eventually one might suppose that class discrimination could replace the longer-standing practices of racial and ethnic discrimination.[14] Despite the growing use of this terminology, however, one

cupy such prominent positions that they could serve as a generalized "they" to justify one's own self-segregation. Now that the blacks are very nearly a majority, the generalized "they" seems to take on a class definition or, sometimes, an empty abstraction—"the system."

12. These moral entrepreneurs may come from every extreme of the spectrum: a businessman who quotes the "bottom line" as if it were scripture, a Catholic nun who includes everyone in her mission of shared poverty, a black militant who mau-mau's the guilty and sinful, and the lame and the halt who simply open up their wounds for public sympathy. These are embarrassing moments, but there is a sliding scale of tolerance as to how long anyone is allowed to claim the others' time.

13. The standard phrase is, "They don't want those people in their neighborhood either."

14. A growing body of sociological and popular literature attributes to social class a special ontological status, something real rather than reified. The popular acceptance

cannot simply assume its acceptance in broad social contexts. One reason for this is that some of these smaller residential enclaves are organized specifically to defend this underclass. The Heart of Uptown, for example, is an organization represented by a number of professional advocates of the poor. Some of them were seasoned in the social movements of the 1960s, and they continue a running battle with anyone who would openly defend class discrimination on behalf of anyone other than the underclass. There are also a number of other advocacy groups, such as Hull House, the Voice of the People, and Organization of the Northeast, who do not have well-defined turfs but engage themselves in a broad range of confrontations over issues such as displacement, the location of social services, and the construction of "luxury" housing (i.e., anything but subsidized housing). These advocacy groups are quite expansionist in their effort to engage opponents of the underclass, and their moral certitude makes them a formidable adversary. It is partly to avoid this kind of underclass advocacy that other residents have withdrawn into small enclaves where they can speak with a unified voice and characterize any intrusion as "outside interference."

Advocacy groups on the North Side are concentrated primarily in Uptown and, as one can tell from the three community area maps, this district has been whittled away gradually through the secession of several subcommunities and especially by the designation of Edgewater as an official community area in 1978.[15] While this probably indicates some reduction in the range of influence exercised by advocacy groups on the North Side, it should not be overemphasized. Some of these organizations have gained a toehold in other community areas where they have become the managers of subsidized housing or they run social agencies. Unlike almost all other community groups who are nonpartisan in political elections, some of the advocacy groups are quite partisan, and occasionally this may redound to their favor among political hopefuls

---

of class terms owes something to this idea, but the more general attraction of class language seems to be that you are not guilty of discrimination on the basis of language, creed, race, or sex.

15. Marciniak (1981) provides an account of the separation of Edgewater from Uptown but, where he sees it as a "natural" expression of the growing demographic and ecological differences between the two areas, I place greater emphasis on the effort of Edgewater to extricate itself from the advocacy groups in Uptown. While I have relied on Marciniak's study, I have also carried out my own interviews to evaluate differences in our interpretations.

who have no one else to turn to on the North Side.[16] They also have remarkable ability to capture the media and to gain recognition as the "real" representatives of the poor. This allows them to solicit funds from a variety of sources who are either sympathetic to their ideology or believe that their contributions will more directly benefit the poor.[17]

The expansionist tendencies of these advocacy groups are quite overt, but similar tendencies occur in a less obvious way among other local groups, even those who have retracted their boundaries to very narrow and defensible limits. The vast majority of community leaders on the North Side adhere publicly to the objective of a balanced, stable community, but in practice some of them are closet gentrifiers, others hope to retain an undisturbed ethnic community, and still others are torn between their sympathies for the poor and the fear of being themselves displaced by the poor. The pattern of redevelopment itself is quite unclear outside of the Near North Side and Lincoln Park and, in many areas, disinvestment is more apparent than new investment. There is a widespread but not too openly voiced belief that the choice is not between stability and gentrification, but between disinvestment and gentrification. As the threat of disinvestment gains or recedes, there may be a rethinking of local objectives. All this may be complicated by their relationship with outside investors, particularly bankers and developers who are usually outspoken gentrifiers[18] and expect a similar attitude from cooperative neighborhood groups. Machine politicians on the North Side further complicate things because most of them are out of office and find any division within community organizations an irresistible opportunity for cultivating a new constituency. Further generalization, then, is difficult, but there are repeated patterns as one examines separate community areas.

16. For example, Mayor Washington has cultivated the support of the Heart of Uptown despite some embarrassment created by the organization's leader, Slim Coleman, when he tried to physically attack Alderman Vrodolyak. The subsequent disclosure that Coleman is not a "white Appalachian" but from a well-to-do Houston family and a Harvard graduate was the source of some media amusement.

17. The Heart of Uptown regularly conducts fund-raising drives around the University of Chicago and Northwestern University. They arrive with cylinders and little hearts like those of the American Heart Foundation.

18. Except when they are seeking low-interest loans to construct or rehabilitate low-income housing. On these occasions they can become highly moral advocates of the poor.

Neighborhood Development from Below

Edgewater and Lake View: Good Fences Make Good Neighbors

Edgewater and Lake View illustrate a widely accepted model of community formation in Chicago, but they are exceptional in having actually achieved it. Both are formally designated areas on current city planning documents, but while Lake View was designated in Burgess's earliest map, Edgewater achieved separation from Uptown only in 1978 and then after a considerable struggle. For over a decade some Edgewater block clubs and the local council tried to single themselves out from Uptown which was badly divided between advocacy groups, businessmen pressing for gentrification, and city officials who were going to "renew" the area. When Jane Byrne ran on a proneighborhood platform in 1978, Edgewater residents caught her in a vulnerable moment and Edgewater appeared in the city's Community Development Block Grant Program shortly after her election.[19]

As a result, Edgewater's boundaries are exactly those proposed by the local council and made all the more visible by roadside banners which proclaim its presence and antiquity ("We Celebrate the Edgewater Centennial").[20] The entire community is checkerboarded with thirteen block clubs (each includes several city blocks), all of which are members of the local community council, each possessing a distinctive name and a procedure for developing positions on separate issues. Theoretically the local council is a separate organization, and individuals may belong to it as well as other organizations which are not territorially defined. Indeed, anyone can join whether or not they live in Edgewater, but in the main the organization takes its form as a confederation of local neighborhoods with some allowance for a small staff who may extend considerably its initiatives beyond those of the local block clubs. Most of the community now lies within a single ward, the result of a redistricting in 1972, and one of the reasons that the community was able to sever itself from Uptown. The alderwoman is an ex-president of the Community Council.

19. At the time a member of the Department of Planning told me that he feared that "the entire city will be balkanized" by small neighborhood groups hoping to negotiate separately with the city rather than share power in the larger community areas previously designated. Edgewater's designation is the only one of this kind to ever appear on city planning documents, although Nortown is now arguing for similar recognition.

20. The current residents may be nearer the truth than was Burgess. I combed through his papers and could find no reference to Uptown other than his own. However, I did find an old *Chicago Tribune* map (n.d.) that clearly delineated Edgewater.

Neighborhood Development from Below

The outer boundaries of Lake View are only slightly less clear. The northwest tip, two census tracts Burgess placed in Lake View, are conceded to Uptown by Lake View residents, although the residents themselves prefer to say that they are in North Center. South of Diversey there is a river-edge area where the Concerned Allied Neighbors sometimes side with the Lake View Citizens Council, sometimes with the Lincoln Park Conservation Association, depending on who is the more likely to help salvage this largely white ethnic community. Otherwise Lake View closely resembles Edgewater. There are twelve organized subcommunities, a regularized procedure for developing positions on local issues, provisions for individual and group memberships in the council, and a staff who may choose to enlarge upon local ambitions. The local alderman is an ex-activist of the Lake View Citizens' Council.

Both Lake View and Edgewater have attracted considerable investment over the last two decades. In Lake View this investment first occurred right along the lakefront which is now almost saturated with high-rise apartments and mostly upscale retail establishments. In the last ten years, however, Lake View has developed "hot spots" throughout the eastern half and, in some places, there is almost continuous redevelopment to Halsted Street, which lies about one-third of the way inland. North of Lake View lies Uptown, and over the same period many of the local groups there opposed new high rises beyond the tiny strip that had previously existed. They were so effective that most investors moved further north to Edgewater where another canyon of high rises were constructed along Sheridan Road.

As these high-rise strips filled in, both communities tended to develop an inner corridor where property owners often neglected their buildings in anticipation of lucrative land sales to still more high rises. This happened first in Lake View, and some high rises actually took root in the corridor before opposition led to a more mixed form of redevelopment which has gradually erased much of this low-income corridor and formed a bridge to several areas to the west where much of the redevelopment is house by house, block by block. In Edgewater, opposition to further high rises occurred at about the same time, partly because several community groups, including those in Edgewater and Lake View, supported a lakefront ordinance which limits rezoning for additional high rises. While very few of the residents or organizations in either of these communities would want to abandon the lakefront ordinance, it has left

Neighborhood Development from Below

Edgewater with a long corridor which has undergone years of disinvestment and a substantial population who are poor and often black. Bridging the relatively high-income area along the lakefront and the remainder of Edgewater, then, has proved difficult despite continuous efforts to impose housing codes and spotty instances of revival (Marciniak 1981). Certainly there are affluent bargain hunters in Edgewater and isolated signs of thoroughgoing restoration, but it does not have the consolidated "hot spots" or upscale shopping strips only too obvious in Lake View. Nonetheless, rumor has it that Edgewater is the "next place" after the bargain hunters get priced out of Lake View.

Despite some recent improvement in the Edgewater corridor,[21] it continues to confront the residents with a set of issues that are both unifying and divisive. Certainly they are opposed to more high rises, at least where zoning does not already permit them. The concentration of subsidized housing in the corridor is a more divisive issue but by no means insurmountable. The more troubling issue is what now to do with the corridor since further "improvement" might displace a number of blacks and, what still others fear, create such a hot real estate market that the entire character of the community would change in the direction of Lake View.[22]

In Lake View, something like this corridor once existed, but it has been so obscured by redevelopment that it does not present an obvious moral obstacle or constitute a consolidated turf from which low-income black residents (i.e., their advocates) can lay claim to a separate voice in the local council. Thus, while Lake View and Edgewater closely resemble each other, Lake View's poor are more scattered around. In most other respects, however, the two communities would look remarkably similar to a demographer. In the 1980 Census, Lake View was 6.9 percent black, 13 percent lived below the poverty line, and 20.4 percent lived in owner-occupied housing. The corresponding figures for Edgewater are 11.1 percent black, 15

21. Marciniak who knows the area as both a resident and sociologist has argued (1981) that the problems of the corridor have been effectively resolved. His views, however, are not that fully shared by some investors I talked to, and there is still some concern that the concentration of Section 8 housing is a barrier, especially if it were to "self-destruct" the way that public housing has.

22. Anyone who visits the area might think these fears unfounded, but some media attention has already alerted people to the possibility. For example, Don DeBat (*Sun-Times*, 20 October 1980) once characterized a part of Edgewater as a "jewel in a green velvet setting." Such excesses are common in the real estate sections of the local press, but they may be taken seriously.

percent below the poverty line, and 23.2 percent in owner-occupied housing.

As one moves west in both community areas the density falls off, sharply just past the lakefront, more gradually thereafter, with some peaks along major commercial strips which often have mid-rise apartments above retail establishments. A third of the way into Lake View and just past the corridor in Edgewater, neighborhoods are said to take on a more "ethnic" character, and a little over two-thirds of the population in both areas reported some European ancestry in the 1980 Census. However, reports of multiple ancestry outnumber single ones by a ratio of two to one, and no ethnic group constitutes more than 7 percent of the population in either community area.

What is meant by this ethnic character, then, is not the overwhelming presence of any one ethnic group but modest concentrations which are sometimes made more visible by commercial establishments (restaurants, bakeries, delis) that antedate considerable population change. Actually, the most typical pattern seems to be an agglomeration of "white ethnics" who see themselves as "nationalities" as distinct from color or racial groups. Since some Koreans, Japanese, Chinese, and Middle Easterners are moving into each community, the term "nationality" has the advantage of extending to include them while implicitly excluding blacks, hillbillies, and unpedigreed "Yuppies." The distinction is important to many of the residents, for as some of the older European groups fail to replace themselves, Orientals, some Hispanics, and people of very mixed European ancestry are seen as favorable replacements. The more inclusive term, "nationality," then, still provides some claim to a common descent. Blacks are obviously excluded, but so are Yuppies, a population that has also come to signal displacement or, more indirectly, a style of life that is antithetical to another that emphasizes home, family, and church.

The term "Yuppie" most obviously applies to young singles who are heavily preoccupied with their night life, exploring the new reaches of consumerism, and staying abreast of the trends. However, the term also has the advantage that it can discriminate without overtly facing the issue of sexual preference. Some of the Yuppies are gay, and they are widely regarded as the most adventuresome in locating or creating the next residential hot spot or in developing new businesses—restaurants, bars, craft industries, retail outlets—which appeal to an affluent, cosmopolitan taste. What, then, is feared is not so much displacement as the appearance of a way of life that seems downright unnatural to people whose existence is organized around their family, the church, and the traditional holidays and celebrations of nationality and kinship.

In the eastern portion of Lake View, gay entrepreneurs and customers are well out of the closet while in Edgewater they are said to be far fewer in number and still less overt.[23] The time when one could openly discriminate against gays is long past, and both of Chicago's recent mayors have made a point of marching with the annual gay pride parade. The city has no ordinance to protect them from discrimination, but there are almost annual efforts to pass one. The Windy City Gay Chorus has achieved national fame, and gay protective associations are as active as other antidefamation societies in the city. Yuppies you can openly discredit, and in Chicago that term has achieved exceptionally wide usage.[24]

This kind of resistance to Yuppies or gays was quite apparent in one of the shopping districts in the westernmost part of Lake View which was proposed for redevelopment as an "old" ethnic area for cosmopolitan trade. Some of the restaurants, delis, and bakeries were already there, and all that was needed was to restore their facades so that they would be "genuine," bring in a few upscale shops, add parking, and spend some money on promotion. A great deal of planning and expense went into several proposals, and potential investors were lined up. As proposal after proposal met with unenthusiasm, it became apparent that what was wanted was a strip redevelopment that "wouldn't bring in those Yuppies east of here." Although this effort to redevelop the area failed, some of these "Yuppies" began to make their way into the area after 1985 as residents and, without much planning at all, the strip is beginning to show the expected changes, even to include some places that are detectably gay (e.g., you can pick up a free copy of *Gay Life*) but not

23. It would be hard, almost impossible, to fully document this, but the number of well-known gay bars (say those listed in *Chicago Gay Life*) would certainly support it. Both the straights and gays I talked to were convinced of the exceptional business talent among gays. Indeed, some straights attributed to them much the same clannishness attributed to Jews or the Chinese. One gay informant also complained of this, saying, "In Lake View you can live and work entirely among the gays. It's like a total institution. It's not a normal life."

24. Although Bob Greene of the *Tribune* is credited with being the chief popularizer of the term, the media does not seem to use the term to single out gays. However, the antifamilialism and unconventionality conveyed by the media nicely fits its usage as an occasional code word to single out gays.

overtly so. Some tension continues to exist in the neighborhood, but one older community leader told me, "We've got along all right. They're not too open about it. Still I don't see many people wanting to raise their families here."

Similar tensions exist in Edgewater although at a much reduced level. There is only one gay bar which has been there for years, and a recent TV strip joint failed after a brief period. Still, there is a sprinkling of gays, and some have become active in community affairs. They are widely admired for their business skills, and one informant pointed out to me that, with so many women in the labor force, gays are a possible replacement for community group volunteers. The result, however, is not always a comfortable relationship, and relations were especially strained when some gays sided with the remnants of the local political machine in a community election. As one observer put it, "They are strange bedfellows, I know, but the machine is always looking for some way to cause trouble."

In both Lake View and Edgewater one also runs into the occasional claim that the community councils are "too close" to their "independent" aldermen. To some extent this is a problem for each community council because both aldermen began their career within these councils and are very responsive to them. It is important that community councils remain nonpartisan, not only because they can recruit widely that way but because open partisanship undermines their claim to represent the "whole" community. Lacking direct power, they must retain the image of consensus as their principal asset.

Despite all these rifts and periods of contention, the confederation of neighborhoods and community councils in Edgewater and Lake View seem to provide an effective representational structure for most negotiations. First, they are accepted as "unit actors" who, once a position is established, allow leaders to more or less ignore a vast array of individual opinion that may lie behind their position. Second, one can often abide by the rule that the neighborhood most affected by some land-use change should have the first and strongest voice in opposing or supporting it. In Lake View, for example, one neighborhood was divided on some proposed Section 8 housing. Almost all other neighborhoods were opposed to similar site selection in their area. This was no problem, however, because everyone could go on record as being neutral on the first site and opposed to the others. Similarly, when the Edgewater residents op-

Neighborhood Development from Below

posed "luxury" housing in one instance, it did not keep them from turning a blind eye toward it in another instance.

This kind of "unprincipled" representative structure can work, but it works best where site changes and their effects are narrowly confined to one neighborhood. For example, a center for battered women in the Edgewater corridor had some appeal to nearby residents who were from single parent households, but it was widely objected to elsewhere because of the "traffic" it would create through all the surrounding neighborhoods. It was defeated. Shopping strips and widely used public spaces also present a problem on which there can be division. Shopping strips often lie at the boundaries between neighborhoods and, in any case, they may be claimed as the separate turf of businessmen's associations. The development of gay bars, fast food "hangouts," second-hand stores, porno outlets, wig shops, massage parlors, and package liquor stores may be the source of some contention between local merchants who simply want to fill the storefronts and residents who are fearful of "who they might bring in."

The selective use of public space also becomes problematic when the level of investment and type of facility would seem to invite wide usage. Throughout Chicago, school grounds, play lots, vest-pocket parks, even empty lots are seen as being reserved for local use whereas larger recreational facilities that include some exceptional amenity—swimming pools, meeting rooms, auditoriums, etc.—are taken to be open to a wide population and, if not the whole city, then certainly more than one neighborhood. Thus, when the Edgewater Community Council, after a long struggle, managed to get the Park District to purchase the last open spot along the lakefront in their community, there was considerable interest among the older high-rise residents that it be a "passive park," that is, one that would not attract teenagers, especially black teenagers who are only a stone's throw away in the corridor. But the expense of the park ran to several million dollars, and one or possibly two old mansions were to be converted to high-cost space. The high-rise residents soon found themselves to be regarded as Yuppies and their passive park a lost cause.

All this may leave the impression that the main achievements of community councils are that they manage to stay in existence, that they fight off some new investments and attract very little in the way of new enterprise. Many potential investors would certainly subscribe to this generalization. But it is misleading. In both Lake View and Edgewater, their chief accomplishment has been to conserve a housing stock from public or slum lord management and to face off further megablock encroachment. They are still credible communities for the sort of house-to-house, block-to-block capital development that appears to appeal to small investors and the new urban bargain hunters who find the city an alternative to the suburbs. It is probably true that some of the redevelopment in Lake View would have taken place without the presence of the Lake View Council (e.g., high rises along the lake), but the choice that developers face is not the absence of a community council or a very pliable one but between the presence of a community council that will negotiate with investors and the kind of ingrained suspicion and divisiveness that exist in Uptown. No community in Chicago is simply unorganized. The important question is how it is organized.

Actually, the Edgewater and Lake View community councils have done a number of things which go beyond housing conservation and gatekeeper. In Lake View there are several small developers who work with the council, and while their investments are relatively small—a storefront here, a three-flat there—their accomplishments are exactly what draws in larger investors: the new supermarkets, the better chain retailers, and off-Loop office conversions. New home construction is a far more difficult objective for almost all large builders are fixed upon the slab high rise. These structures can be quite profitable especially where the Illinois Housing Development Authority provides below-market loan capital. Some Lake View informants were aware of the possible benefits (higher income customers and, possibly, some street level shopping space) of even this kind of home construction if it could be scattered and oriented away from the lakefront. They were among the first to add, however, that most large builders are too cautious to leave the lakefront and that it is almost impossible to convince residents that one high rise would not be followed by several others. Precedent would warrant this conviction.

In Edgewater there is far less new commercial development than in Lake View, and the main sign of change is a growing number of Oriental businessmen, many of them selling much the same thing, dry goods and food. The local council, however, has had some success in attracting public investment, most notable the conversion of an old armory into a community center and the development of the new lakeside park. Both efforts are interesting because they required a sustained piece of showmanship that reached over several years.

To renovate the armory the council first had to mount a campaign that would mobilize their state and congressional leaders. This involved not only widespread canvassing among residents but the development of a site plan with cost estimates—in other words, the same kind of marketing study and "conceptual" site plan as is frequently presented by architectural firms.[25] A crucial point came in the identification of a Department of the Interior program with funds to finance the conversion. Eventually, ten congressmen were ferried to Chicago for a site visit. Undoubtedly, the site plans and marketing approach helped get them there, but what happened thereafter was almost pure theater. Each congressman was met by an Edgewater family who drove them into town and quietly lobbied along the way. There was a daylong presentation, but most agreed that the high point of it was the "bubble gum parade," a series of young children of "almost every nationality" imagining aloud what they would do if the old armory were turned into a community center. It stole the show, and Edgewater was a winner. Just ten years after the campaign started, the community center opened.

There is also a story behind the lakeside park. I will not relate it except to say that after having finally prevailed over a reluctant Park District, the proposal to name the park after a prominent Chicago family, one of whose members just happened to be commissioner of planning, led the council to enlist that family in their effort to enlarge the park by converting a second old mansion to park usage. Anyone who can manipulate the Chicago Park District—a bastion of acknowledged political patronage—is a force to be reckoned with.

Rogers Park and Uptown: Advocates and Adversaries

At first sight, Rogers Park and Uptown would appear to be very dissimilar local communities. Lying right at the northern edge of the city, Rogers Park is often thought of as an exceptionally visible community, heavily Jewish, and resembling a small town (Welter 1982).

25. With the additional resemblance that the original site plan does not look too much like the finalized community center.

Neighborhood Development from Below

A well-known stop on the North Side El, it is the site of Loyola University and the only community along the lakeshore not walled off by a row of high rises or the eight-lane Lake Shore Drive. The community area just to the west is officially designated "West Ridge," but most of the residents there referred to it as "West Rogers Park" until recently.

But these items of appearance are deceptive. Rogers Park is one of the most densely settled areas in the city ranking just behind Uptown. Single-family homes are quite rare (4.7 percent),[26] and only 13 percent of all dwelling units, 2 percent more than in Uptown, are owner occupied. Uptown is certainly poorer (28 percent below the poverty line as against 15 percent in Rogers Park), but income levels are declining more rapidly in Rogers Park. Between 1970 and 1980, the income rank of Rogers Park declined more than that of any other community area in the city. Over the same period, the residents of West Rogers Park reexamined their identity and asserted their distinctiveness as West Ridge.[27]

Where Uptown and Rogers Park most nearly resemble each other, however, is in their internal organization. Both have many local organizations; frequently they are at odds with one another, and most aim at capturing constituencies rather than territorial communities. Things have not always been this way in either community. In Uptown one can still find previously recognized neighborhoods (Ravenswood, Glenwood) which persist essentially as home improvement associations and two relatively new neighborhoods (Buena Park and Sheridan Park) which are attempting to single themselves out as historic districts. But at present, these turf-bound organizations are only contenders in a larger contest with other organizations claiming to have constituencies throughout Uptown and in other communities as well.

This situation first developed in Uptown in the 1960s when most white protest organizers found themselves frozen out of black neighborhoods and hit upon Uptown—heavily transient and quite diverse—as the most likely place to cultivate a class-based social movement (Harwood 1966; Gitlin and Hollander 1970).[28] The Up-

---

26. Unless indicated otherwise, all figures are from the 1980 *Local Community Fact Book* (Erbe et al. 1984) which uses Burgess's community designations.

27. Initially, some residents sought a still more distinctive identity in the term "Nortown," but "West Ridge" won out in a local referendum.

28. Uptown was not the poorest community area at the time, but it was among the least able to resist the incursion of "outsiders." It is the city's chief dumping ground

town Chicago Commission, dominated by local bankers, went precisely in the opposite direction, supporting slum clearance, new high-rise construction and, later on, condoization. A substantial portion of the community was designed as a renewal area and, while this made it eligible for federal funds, Chicagoans usually regard such designations as only a prelude to the withdrawal of private loan capital.[29] There was widespread (unsuccessful) resistance to this designation, to further high-rise construction (successful), and substantial clearance (unsuccessful). For a short period turf-bounded and constituency groups seemed to have been united against the commission, but this level of unity was short-lived. They quickly came into conflict over condoization, subsidized housing, and the growing number of welfare service centers. These divisions center on the differences between homeowners in the southern and western sections, the businessmen in the commission, and a number of constituency groups run by professional advocates. They are compounded by organizational competition and fragmentation. The home improvement associations do not combine their efforts. The constituency organizations compete for the same members. The commission is regarded with ambivalence or hostility. One might think these divisions entirely expectable given the community's composition and settlement pattern. Such divisions are expectable all along the lakefront. It is just that in Uptown and Rogers Park such divisions actually occur. In both cases it is hard to avoid the importance of organizational choices taken as much as two decades ago.

One reason for the present ambivalence or hostility toward the Uptown Commission is that the local banks started three large-scale rehab programs (200–400 units) during the late 1970s and early 1980s when interest rates increased to the point that new sales could not finance further rehabilitation. The result was a lot of boarded-up buildings, partially occupied buildings, and sublet condos. The more militant organizations have taken this as definite evidence that

---

for ex-mental patients, has the largest concentration of dormitories for street people, and is a center for day labor recruiters. The state and the city seem to have been the chief corporate actors creating its special vulnerability.

29. This did not occur in the renewal area of Hyde Park (Rossi and Dentler 1961) or Lincoln Park (Warner 1979) where there were strong institutions (Northwestern University, DePaul University, and several hospitals) and prominent individuals who could exercise some control over the banks and draw on their own considerable resources. Elsewhere, designation of a "blighted area" usually did mean the withdrawal of private loans.

Uptown cannot attract the new urban bargain hunters and that the community must remain a kind of housing reserve for the minority poor. A recent study (Sander et al. 1985) by the Organization of the North East makes a very forceful argument in support of this position while also attempting to reassert Uptown's "stability" and continuation with Edgewater. The report is interesting because it shows how one can take demographic data to support exactly the reverse argument made by the defenders of Edgewater's separation (Marciniak 1981). Each group finds its demographic "signs of homogeneity" by looking for them selectively, and at times diversity itself can become a claim for drawing boundaries (Sanders et al. 1985, pp. 27–29). As with similar reports, there is both a tendency to insist on the inexorable drift of past demographic characteristics and the organizational capacity to overcome them either by "stabilization" in the first instance or by servicing the poor in the second.

The latter possibility is unconvincing to the homeowner associations who see more service centers, more subsidized housing, and more public demonstrations as only an endorsement of the revolving door pattern which has characterized Uptown in the past. As one homeowner put it, "If only we could keep the population we have for a while!" Businessmen's associations are even more opposed, sometimes blaming the advocacy approach for the earlier collapse of the condominium market. Contrary efforts have been made to improve Uptown's image, and Warren's 1979 report is a rather forthright effort to correct its "conventional stereotype" (p. vii). But the message one takes from this may be that Uptown is not all bad and should attract selective investment or that it is only a revolving door and ought to be cast more effectively in this role.

As a result, investment in the area is very limited and for the most part occurs at the edges of the area where home-owner associations are strongest. The city has invested in some trees and sidewalks along shopping strips, but there was no obvious correspondence with business revival as of 1985. The one Local Development Corporation strip in the area is indistinguishable from the other shopping strips, and a scattering of fairly recent Oriental and Hispanic businesses seems to bear no relationship to either public or private initiatives. Ironically the only business strip that shows a concerted effort at revival is along Argyle where a group of Oriental merchants have located at their own initiative. Initially this strip was promoted by some Chinese businessmen as a "new Chinatown," but many of these places failed as the Chinese resi-

Neighborhood Development from Below

dents themselves moved out of the area. They have been replaced by a number of merchants from Korea, Vietnam, and Cambodia despite earlier resistance from the Chinese.[30] A few city planners and business organizations take some credit for this development, but it apparently owes much more to ethnic solidarity and unconventional sources of financing.[31]

In the southeast of Uptown, adjacent to Lake View, one does see some signs of private housing rehabilitation in the Buena Park historic district and, to the northwest, the Sheridan Park neighborhood has made a bid to become a second historic district. The organization of the North East has opposed this designation because the area has no exceptional unity of design but fearing, at the same time, that it might succeed in raising home values. These fears may be justified for one can detect in the area an effort to create a unity of design to justify the designation.

Uptown's most affluent population is located right along the lakefront in a sliver of high rises. Often referred to as "Yuppies," fully a quarter of this population is over sixty-five: old people looking for a safe high rise with a doorman. The remainder are relatively young, mostly singles and couples living in apartments before they can afford home ownership. Although there are some block clubs along sections of the lakefront, they are often said to be unreachable by the ordinary practice of door-to-door community organizing. High-rise residents seem increasingly to use the available option of not responding to inquiries through their intercoms.

One major investment that the city and state did make in the area was the construction of Truman Community College almost squarely in the middle of Uptown. Yet some advocacy groups opposed it because it replaced about 200 dwelling units. The "Heart of Uptown" has since put in place a mural which stares down at the college to declare, "The eyes of the Community are upon you." Yet local groups do not make much use of the college and, when asked to develop joint programs, community groups have failed to respond. The college has experienced some declines in enrollment, and earlier minority programs have been cut back. The student population is increasingly nonwhite, but Truman remains the second

30. Some of those remaining, however, are ethnic Chinese from Indochina.

31. It appears that some Southeast Asians receive direct loans from their home countries, either from relatives hoping to shelter savings in the United States or by banks hoping to establish a reverse flow of dollars in repayment and remittances.

most diverse of the city's community colleges and whites still feel comfortable enrolling there. There is a small program of meetings and seminars for people interested in economic development, but most of Chicago's LDCs oppose cooperation with the city colleges. They see them as competitors for the same "soft money" and leadership in their respective communities. Recently Truman College has cooperated with a residential group's campaign to vote dry an adjacent precinct where day-labor contractors rotate single men from flophouse to day-labor jobs and to the local taverns in a pattern that resembles debt servitude. The Heart of Uptown opposes them because of the presence of one remaining "responsible" barkeeper. Unlike private colleges (e.g., University of Chicago, Northwestern, DePaul, Loyola, and North Park) which have been active in community renewal (three have threatened to leave the city), public colleges must be cautious lest they experience political retaliation. So far Truman College has been sufficiently cautious.

Local political representation also splits the Uptown area which belongs to three different wards. The alderman who presides over the largest portion draws most of his support from the lakefront, and he has supported renewal in the area, at first cautiously and later more aggressively.[32] The northern tier of Uptown has an independent alderman in Marion Volini and, although she is very popular in Edgewater, some of the advocacy groups in Uptown remember her as a woman who helped separate Edgewater from Uptown and called for a moratorium on subsidized housing. A strip along the western part of the area falls into the ward of a machine alderman who usually sides with the local homeowners but would seem to prefer that they approach him with sufficient humility. Ed Kelly, the Democratic committeeman in this ward, is the well-known head of the Chicago Park District which has been heavily criticized for entrenched patronage and very high expenditures (*Tribune*, 1985). At an earlier time, Chicago aldermen and committeemen could turn these signs of venality and manipulation into evidence of their attachment to the underdog (Guterbock 1980). But claims of this sort seem to be a lost cause among the newcomers in Uptown. Increasingly, the elderly, the Orientals, the single parents, and the urban pioneers in Uptown seem to find their flawed heroes outside the Chicago machine. Some of them look to the independent reformer while others look to the remnants of Harold

32. In 1987 he lost his office to an activist from the Heart of Uptown.

Neighborhood Development from Below

Washington's administration which has carved out its own definition of the underdog.[33]

One thing that practically everyone agrees on is that Uptown is
extraordinarily diverse. But this is true of all the areas north of Lincoln Park. A third of Uptown's families are headed by females, but at
least a quarter of all families in Lake View, Edgewater, and Rogers
Park are also headed by females. Forty-one percent of Uptown's
households are nonfamily, but the same is true of 43 percent of Lake
View's households, 37 percent of Edgewater's households, and 28
percent of Rogers Park's household.[34] These differences make a difference only if you pick and choose among them and ignore other
areas of the city.

Yet only Rogers Park shares the "organizational diversity" of
Uptown. During the early 1970s Rogers Park had the reputation of
being one of the best organized communities in the city (Welter
1982). The Rogers Park Community Council included at least seven-
ty-two member organizations and many individual and business
members as well. It was especially active in monitoring the housing
stock, in providing services for the elderly, and in publicizing the
community as a good place to live. But very few of the council's
member organizations were turf-bound groups. There was a Tenant's Council, a citizen's action program, an arts center, a Council of
Jewish Elderly, and a very long list of religious and charitable
groups. A few block clubs came into episodic existence, but little
effort was made to systematically cover the community with similar
organizations.

Just why this occurred is difficult to unearth. People present
and active at the time simply say, "It wasn't done. It didn't seem
necessary." One point that reoccurs in these accounts, however, is
the pride that local leadership took in the area's ethnic hetero-
geneity. Rogers Park was, as the local council often put it, a place of
"neighbors of many faces" (Welter 1982, p. 36). Yet, if one looks

33. The new "underdog," of course, is primarily black. Harold Washington did
make substantial headway in assuring Puerto Ricans and Orientals that his administration will "err" in their favor. Some criticism by the media may have only given
credence to this new direction of defended venality. Washington, however, had difficulty in convincing whites that his favor would extend to them, and Jesse Jackson's
"rainbow" does not include the color white. Uptown and Rogers Park were important
to the Washington administration because they included white political aspirants
who sought to extend this conception of the underdog to some white groups.

34. One might try to make something of these differences, but they have fluctuated
over the last two decades without any corresponding variation in community organization which has temporal priority over demographic changes.

closely, the area was not that diverse or no more so than many others. Welter's estimate for 1970 puts the Jewish population at 37 percent and the "Irish," although frequently of mixed ancestry, may have made up near a quarter.[35] Actually Rogers Park was probably best described in 1960–1970 as a community of second settlement where the residents were a bit more proud of not living in "the ghetto" than of their ethnic background. By emphasizing census reports on "nationality" rather than religion, the community could be made to look like one of the more integrated in the city.

Underneath this imagery, however, the Jewish and Irish leaders seem to have worked out a rather special division of labor. For most of the postwar years the Irish dominated local politics, sometimes receiving the benefit of machine support but always voting independently enough to gain the confidence of the remaining population. The Jews were the community's social leaders, organizing its council, its charities, its watchdog groups, and much of its recreational life. Until the 1970s this was apparently a very durable way of doing things, and it worked best when ethnic differences were obscured. Turf-bound groups could only have brought into relief these ethnic differences, for the Jews were very concentrated north of Pratt, and the Irish were equally concentrated below that street.[36]

In the late 1960s and throughout the 1970s many of the Jews and Irish left Rogers Park, and it became a genuine community of many faces. Initially, many of the newcomers were East Indians, Japanese, Chinese, Filipinos, and Koreans who, in general, have remained outside the community's civic life despite some overtures to include them.[37] At one time the area probably had as many as 2,000 Russian Jewish émigrés who were represented by existing Jewish organizations, but many of these people have left the community. By 1980, there were somewhat more than 4,000 Mexicans in the area, and they have remained almost invisible in the community's civic life. The largest and most visible growth was in the communi-

35. These are very high concentrations for white and non-Hispanic areas in Chicago by 1970. Even at an earlier date, entire community areas seldom reached the 50 percent figure before succession began.

36. All the synagogues were on Pratt or further north. There is an old adage that "the blacks follow the Jews," meaning that the Jews "soften" the legal defenses of a community to the point that the blacks can get in after them. This does not seem to have happened in Rogers Park. However, there may be a more general tendency for Jews to establish constituency groups which lead to the same thing.

37. The pattern here seems very similar to that occurring among strip shopping associations.

Neighborhood Development from Below

ty's black population which reached 5,000 by 1980 and is very concentrated in the northeastern edge of the community. With the location of subsidized housing in this section, they are becoming still more concentrated in the "North of Howard area." Always somewhat distinct,[38] the North of Howard area became especially so after it was organized by advocacy groups into what is now Rogers Park's most clearly defined turf-bound group (HACC, the Howard Area Community Conference).

All these population changes placed a great deal of strain on local political and community organizations. Some constituency-bound groups continued their mission of defending and serving the underdog. Others felt that it was time to retrench, to oppose subsidized housing, to being an investment program along the shopping strips, to more fully enforce the housing code, and to encourage home ownership through condoization. Issues first came to a head in the 1977 aldermanic election when an incumbent ran a weak campaign against a newcomer who was not part of either the old Irish political wing or the Jewish social circles. His support seems to have come primarily from activists, from constituency-bound groups; once in office, he quickly mounted a campaign to establish rent controls and to place a moratorium on condoization. Neither campaign was successful, but they did alarm his opponents and solidify his supporters. As member organizations in the council began to take sides, it became progressively difficult to maintain its image of political neutrality or to find any compromise which might be presented as the "community interest."

Finally, the local council experienced an open rupture over the placement of subsidized housing in the North of Howard Area. At an unusually stormy[39] public meeting, the council called for a vote on the exclusion of further subsidized housing in the area. The vote carried but at the expense of several member organizations which withdrew from the council. The independent alderman, who had supported the location of subsidized housing, is now remembered

38. Until 1893, it was part of Evanston. Once incorporated into Chicago, Howard Street became a favored place for the residents of Evanston (which was not only dry but the headquarters for the Women's Christian Temperance Union) to pick up liquor. This gave the street an unsavory reputation, and its economy plumeted when Evanston finally got legal liquor in the 1970s.

39. Although the discussion was very heated, one observer noted, "Not once did they mention race or ethnicity. Only income categories were used." I did not attend this meeting but have observed several other local meetings at which the same practice prevailed.

Neighborhood Development from Below

by some as "the man who brought public housing to Rogers Park" and "the one who put a chill on condoization."[40] This evaluation, of course, is reversed among his supporters, but as of now neither political nor civic leadership can present itself as a nonpartisan voice.

Signs of decline, however, were quite visible in Rogers Park well before either the 1977 aldermanic election or the confrontation over subsidized housing. The leading edge of this decline was probably the inability of the area's shopping strips to reform themselves during the postwar period of rising incomes. As in most other parts of Chicago, these strips are pathways for the incursion of residents outside the reach of proximate social control. The level of upkeep is often so tolerant as to invite abuse and even more often so permissive as to demoralize the "home proud." The residents above street level are not responsible; the shop people below are seldom owners, and the owners are less frequently residents. The shopping districts in Rogers Park are not far off the low standard maintained throughout the city, but they do make an unusually stark contrast to the residential streets which underwent steady improvement through the earlier of the last three decades.

The southernmost shopping intersection at Devon and Sheridan is heavily concentrated in the hands of one owner. There is no formal merchant's association, and the shopkeepers complain that while initial rents are low they rise rapidly "once you make it." Vacancies are frequent and the level of maintenance uneven. Several vintage facades have been disfigured with suburban shakes, ersatz modern, and fast-food cute. A vast theater has fallen into disuse and presents its decaying facade as the first visual impression to those entering from the south. There have been several proposals to revive the theater either as a shopping center or as a performing arts center. All these plans have fallen through as investors and owners wait for the other to take the first step.

Rogers Park's northernmost shopping strip is the southern boundary of the North of Howard neighborhood, and its fate is viewed as heavily dependent on the stability of the area to the south. Two owners control a substantial proportion of the store-

40. It is difficult to assess this latter allegation. However, one fairly large building that was being turned into condominiums had to be auctioned off at the time of the location of subsidized housing in the North of Howard area, and some of the rehabbers previously active in the area point to the alderman as the reason they have withdrawn. But Rogers Park consistently had the lowest level of condoization of any of the north lakefront communities.

The southern entrance to Rogers Park.

Neighborhood Development from Below

fronts, but there are many other owners and lessees. Plans for the strip have ranged from a very ambitious suburban-like mall, to a short-lived Local Development Corporation, and most recently to an incremental effort that is to begin with the renewal of another disused movie theater. Each proposal seems to have different supporters who have drawn a stalemate.

The last shopping strip is Clark Street with a "T" that extends along Morse. Much earlier, in 1959 (Welter 1982, p. 33), there was also an ambitious plan to construct a shopping mall along Clark that would compete with those in the suburbs. Although supported by local bankers, the problems of land assembly were insurmountable and the plan abandoned. Now, some see the Clark Street strip as doing better than the other two. Lacking any grand design, it has filled in here and there with fast-food outlets, a car dealership, a major grocery chain, and a regional discount store. All this is pretty much what the market delivers along a major traffic artery, and progressively Clark Street itself seems to be oriented toward the passing traffic and away from the local community.[41]

Loyola University is the community's chief private institution and, despite earlier proposals to move the campus (Welter 1982, pp. 31–32), its recommitment to the area, the continued presence of its students, and a scattering of faculty now help to anchor the adjacent area. In the last few years, the university has established a small faculty home loan program and a community relations office. The university's primary advantage, however, seems to be the perception of it as a neutral ground where contending community groups can at least meet and talk to one another. The university manages this by its own cautious approach and acts primarily as a host rather than a partisan. Recently, a member of the Chicago Department of Planning has seized upon this neutral ground to draw together a series of local groups for the discussion of "Rogers Park's future." The university appears to be the only feasible location for such discussions. These meetings, however, proceed with so much caution that one wonders if their rhetoric of tolerance will not become only a high-minded statement of resignation.

Although this approach lacks the corporate sponsorship and political allies that have been so important to communities like Lake

41. Yet Clark Street remains one of the best publicized shopping strips belonging to old, immigrant Chicago. I can only assume that the total absence of control of outdoor advertising leads newsmen to think that they are observing authenticated natives rather than hurried motorists.

View and Edgewater, it does occur at a time when some Chicago
communities might actually achieve the socioeconomic balance and
racial integration so often recommended in broad public statements
of high purpose. The black population of Chicago is growing very
slowly and may actually top out within the next decade (Bogue
n.d.). Much of the white population that found its chief attachment
to the city in the exclusive, parish-like urban village (Suttles 1968;
Gans 1962) has either left for the suburbs or remains in peripheral
locations. Those who remain are a select population more reconciled to limited "integration." All along the northern lakefront and
considerably inland, then, one finds white populations more willing to experiment with some kind of interracial balance. Since
Harold Washington's mayoral victory, blacks have begun to shop
much more widely for housing, moving beyond the ghetto inter-
face. In selected areas this has already interrupted the block-by-
block advance documented by the Duncans (1957).[42] The constraints on black real estate firms described by Berry (1979) also may
have relaxed somewhat.

Seizing upon these trends to produce a "balanced" community, however, demands more than good intentions. Essentially, it
requires a corporate actor and political allies who can "ration" housing to low-income or minority populations without engagement in
the rhetoric of absolute voluntarism and social justice. The territorial
confederation of neighborhoods can adopt this pragmatic course,
but its formation seems to depend upon a historic moment, a moment that may have passed in Rogers Park. Just how this formation
occurs is best illustrated in the North River Area.

The North River Area: From Generalists to Specialists

The North River Area consists of a series of relatively small
neighborhoods whose residents never relied much on Burgess's
community designations. The northernmost of these neighborhoods (Hollywood Park, Ravenswood Manor, and North
Mayfair) possessed what were essentially homeowner's associa-

42. The best evidence for this is the much wider spatial distribution of interracial
incidents following the movement of black householders into previously all white
areas (*Chicago Reporter*, January 1985). The accounts included in the *Reporter* portray a
much more confident home seeker among blacks than the ones described by Berry
(1979) no more than ten years earlier.

Neighborhood Development from Below

tions which had been enlarged and aroused by the first of Chaddick's proposals for a regional mall in the 1960s. In 1962 the North River Commission was founded in a very self-conscious effort to promote business and housing development when areas to the south began to show signs of population transition and growing secondary usage along the Lawrence, Montrose, and Irving Park shopping strips. The commission was largely the idea of a single faculty member at North Park College, a private institution. The college, along with an affiliated hospital and a local bank, provided the initial financial base and relied heavily upon the existing home improvement associations for its early membership.

At first sight, the North River Commission closely resembles the Uptown Commission, but where the former differs is in systematically developing additional home improvement associations to blanket the area as it expanded southward toward the commercial and residential sections in which it has become most active. The North River Commission, then, essentially established its own allies as it proceeded. This has obvious advantages, but it had the additional one of establishing a rather clear division of labor. The commission could focus itself almost entirely upon economic development while the "civic associations" (as they are termed in the NRC) were much more concerned with the management of social or public services. "We do not provide social services," its director emphasized to me. "We'll help the civics obtain their own services. Show them how to do it themselves or get them from agencies. But we are into economic development!" This specialized aim seems largely to have circumvented a host of other demands that frequently mire community organizations into the imponderable debate over social redistribution and justice. The civic associations must take upon themselves responsibilities for how public and social services are allocated. The commission staff focuses on investment in commercial space and new housing construction. This positive assignment of responsibilities excludes an enormous range of dispute which can be found in other areas (e.g., Rogers Park and Uptown) of Chicago.

Nonetheless, the North River Commission does occasionally find itself in a stormy relationship with some of its member organizations, primarily over this division of responsibilities.[43] One local

43. The argument that private firms shoulder redistributional objectives is a persistent issue even when the firms have only a marginal chance at best. At a conference

Neighborhood Development from Below

improvement association recently pulled out of the organization, and two others have threatened to do so. So far, however, the commission has stood fast, and an approximate division of labor prevails. The improvement associations help to identify trouble spots (e.g., abandonment) and occasional investment opportunities, and they provide some generalized support for the flow of funds into the area. In turn, the Commission is heavily engaged in assembling loan pools, promoting specific investment opportunities, and helping to manage the city's oldest and most effective Local Development Corporation. The Lawrence Avenue Development Corporation was also the first in the nation, and to a considerable extent it has been able to rescue most of that strip from secondary usage. The facades are beginning to show some signs of coordinated treatment, and there are scattered instances of similar logos. The merchants association has been strengthened to the point that on one strip they are willing to begin a form of self-taxation, although there is still some nonparticipation.

The commission was able to develop nonprofit management for most of the area's subsidized housing, thus avoiding management by the Chicago Housing Authority. It also runs one of the city's best-known energy conservation programs which is an effort to make existing rents cover maintenance rather than a charitable enterprise. They have helped to promote the Old Irving Park Area as a place for housing restoration or gentrification.

There is also a long list of things the NRC has opposed, usually with community support: Chaddick's Riverside Mall, the commercial development of Rosehill Cemetery, the location of high density housing without adequate parking, and so on. All this has its limits. None of the North River neighborhoods show the kind of trendy shops, nightclubs, or craft industries that one can find in Lake View. And, with the exception of the Old Irving Park Area, it is mainly an area in which new immigrant entrepreneurs are trying to find a foothold rather than a place that can attract the more highly skilled and trained "urban pioneer." The Orientals have insisted on separate merchants organizations, but so far the commission has managed to include them as federated units.

The commission loan packaging and strip redevelopment pro-

on "incubator industries" I attended, many black community organizers were quite critical of this approach to expand a niche for high-risk entrepreneurs without targeting specific minority individuals for employment.

jects have reached some level of routinization, but it continues to face an uncertain future. Some of the community organizations and merchants associations are said to feel that they give more to the commission than they get. In turn, the commission has argued that the local residential organizations must achieve a level of self-sufficiency that will allow them to insist on uniform public services without caving in to the kind of subservient exchange the Regular Democratic Ward offices often require.

This has not always satisfied local leaders, and it is even less popular among local political officeholders. All three of the local aldermen are machine sponsored and see in the commission a competitor or troublemaker. The commission, in turn, deals with the local aldermen at arms length or, at times, simply as adversaries or agencies to use. This relationship, however, is not quite so acerbic as this suggests. There is an implicit agreement not to embarrass local aldermen during election periods and to avoid any appearance of partisanship. At an earlier date when an independent candidate and an active member of the commission won a single term as alderman, he was asked to resign from the commission. Actually, what seems to occur most frequently is for the commission to present its plans or projects first to national or state political officeholders and, having gained their support, to confront local political leaders with little alternative than to go along. With the recent change in the mayor's office, this sort of direct contact is being extended to some of Washington's appointees as agency heads. Overjoyed at the prospect, the commission's director told me, "I hope we never have another mayor for more than one term." However, there are all sorts of cracks showing in the Cook County Democratic machine, and even a two-term mayor probably could not avoid this kind of manipulation of one level of the organization against the other.

What would seem critical for the North River Commission is to maintain its momentum, to continue to capture loan programs, foundation grants, and organizational allies before they can become hostage either to patronage organizations or to welfare-oriented groups who "tax" similar programs with the burdens of redistribution. The North River Commission's task here might be considered easier than that of Rogers Park or Edgewater because most of its neighborhoods lie to the west of the older housing and commercial strips along the lakefront. The northernmost of its neighborhoods are dominated by middle-income residents, although a number of them are recent Russian immigrants. South of Foster, however, the

Neighborhood Development from Below

area begins to take on much the same appearance as areas to the east, and there is a steady in-movement of Hispanics, blacks, and new immigrants. Lying away from the lakefront is also a drawback because the lakefront is the city's chief amenity and attracts at least those investors interested in high density or upscale development. The North River area invites such development only where there are large tracts that can be cleared or converted to other uses. The residents are usually opposed to both. Thus, the North River Commission must seize upon a very large number of small projects, give them high visibility, and avoid overloading them with social causes. As the commission's director said in a mocking reference to Burnham, "Make lots of little plans."

Local Communities and the Public Interest

Local community organizations along Chicago's North Side achieve their importance not only by their unyielding presence but as one of the main instruments for defining the public interest. They do this primarily by demarcating territorial boundaries which aggregate to form a "full" representation for the community that can claim to articulate the public interest. Where they fail to do this and organize on the basis of dispersed or unbounded constituencies they are drawn into confrontations, and the issues of land-use change open up an unlimited set of moral and social dilemmas. Of course, neither kind of organization actually enlists the participation of a large number of the residents. But where the territorial form can claim to provide equal access to participation, there is always the appearance of serving partial or exclusive interests on the part of constituency-based organizations.

These organizational forms do not come into existence without outside assistance. The organization of Edgewater seems to have owed a great deal to Charles Livermore with the Department of Planning and Ed Marciniak with Loyola University. The organization of Lake View is probably a continuation of a pattern initiated in Lincoln Park and sponsored by a number of people from DePaul University and the local hospitals. The organization of the North River area is sufficiently recent that the role of North Park College and its affiliated hospital can be reconstructed with fair accuracy.[44]

44. Stories of a similar kind, however, can be unearthed from a variety of studies carried out in Chicago. Alinsky (1966) was well aware of the need for outside spon-

Neighborhood Development from Below

In their recent book on community redevelopment in some other areas of Chicago, Taub et al. conclude (1984, pp. 183–84) by emphasizing the importance of corporate actors and the assistance they give to community organizations. I would underscore their observations and extend them. The kinds of corporate actors that can help to initiate and sustain a territorial definition of the public interest are of a special kind, primarily universities and hospitals. These organizations have both the capacity to understand local communities—frequently they mount studies of them—and sometimes include key actors who are active in the community. To some extent, their position as nonprofit employers may staunch the general tendency to look for ulterior motives. More important, they seem to share in a fund of accumulated experience from which similar institutions (University of Chicago, DePaul, Loyola, Illinois Institute of Technology, Michael Reese Hospital, North Park College, Swedish Covenant Hospital, etc.) have "learned their lesson." At an earlier date Michael Reese Hospital and the Illinois Institute of Technology had not learned this lesson and followed essentially a massive clearance program. Those in the know can point to the failures of that strategy in defense of the present one.

Local private firms, even large banks, do not seem to have access to this accumulated experience and may only contribute to fears of displacement. Social movement groups may be familiar enough with the record of previous efforts at community redevelopment, but their aspirations go well beyond the local community to a reform of the wider society or to rectify past injustices. The most immediate result of their efforts is a divided community and the further concentration of a casualty population. Nevertheless, the nobility of their aspirations often earns them the moral endorsement of outside observers. But, like the universities and hospitals, they are corporate actors.

Whether a community takes on and adversarial or territorial form seems to depend upon a historic moment when several conditions come together: a corporate actor who plays to locality groups or to constituencies, the availability of agreeable political allies, and a local leadership with one foot in the local community and the other in some more cosmopolitan place. Up to a point, each type of com-

---

sorship, but he aspired to the complete autonomy of community organizations. Harris (1980) documents the continuing reliance of Alinsky organizations on outside sponsors.

munity is self-perpetuating because it can exclude the other. The territorial neighborhood gravitates toward the defended neighborhood. Its principal weakness is that it can become so exclusive as to be unable to find residential replacements in the city's changing population mix. The community organized around constituencies suffers chronic secession and disinvestment. Eventually, then, each type of community may face another historic moment, a moment when some new corporate actor discovers their vulnerabilities.

FIVE

THE BIG PROJECT AND THE
POLITICS OF URGENCY

Chicago is a city where plans mean action. A record of striking
success and accomplints since 1973 attest to this long standing ax-
iom. Chicago's civic leaders have developed a heritage of
involvement that has carefully shaped the face of the city and continues to do so today!

. . . within the business community of Chicago, there are differing
civic agendas that sometimes lead to misunderstanding, distrust
and conflict among the various business interests. There is little
understanding of or even respect for often conflicting agendas. Executives from big and small business do not know or trust each
other. Companies headquartered in Chicago but who do very little
business there tend to participate in the civic life of the city according to the nature and interest of their chief executive officers. Many
of these companies share the perception that local government has
the least sensitivity to their needs because they are merely headquartered here.[1]

Part of the myth of "the city that works" is the belief that it possesses a unified elite, that the public and private sectors are almost
indistinguishable, and that plans are made almost as an after-
thought to existing agreements. In the last fifteen years, that belief
has become a bit threadbare as an increasing number of downtown
projects have stalled or come to an unanticipated end. In the following pages I want to look at three of these downtown projects which
demonstrate the extremes of this impotence. These case histories
are not meant to be representative. I am sure some will consider
them unfair. But if they are not representative, they are diagnostic of
a number of obstacles and flawed strategies which can be found in a
more inclusive list of similar projects to follow.

1. The first of these quotations is taken from the 1980 Annual Report of the Chicago
Central Area Committee and appears in an article by Cafferty and McCready (1982).
The second is from Cafferty's 1986 *Report on Civic Life in Chicago*.

The North Loop: The Foremost Downtown
Development in the Nation

In early 1978, it was rumored that the state governor had finally decided to locate a new State of Illinois building in the Chicago Loop and that the Hilton hotel chain was eyeing a site one block away for a major convention hotel. Suddenly the long-dormant North Loop project emerged from five years of sleep. A huge project, covering almost seven blocks zoned for high-density development, it lay at the northern boundary of the Loop, just west of State Street. First proposed during Daley's administration, it had gotten nowhere and practically disappeared from public attention. In March of 1978, however, Mayor Bilandic announced that it would be his top priority, and Arthur Rubloff stepped forward to offer himself as sole developer.

A flamboyant figure, often in tuxedo and cape and surrounded by lavish furnishings, Rubloff had been in the wings all five years since, as he claimed, Mayor Daley had picked him to head the project from the start (*Sun-times*, 19 July 1980). Only "the grinding wheels of government bureaucracy" had delayed him (*Sun-Times*, 2 August 1978). Rubloff later also credited himself with the site selection of the State of Illinois building "for free, as a contribution to the state" (*Sun-Times*, 2 August 1978). There were those who disagreed with him and noted that the site selection also rescued the teamsters from a bad debt on a vacant hotel (*Sun-Times*, 2 August 1978). Rubloff brushed aside such criticism, saying that it would be a $900 million project, "the foremost development undertaken in any city in the nation" (*Tribune*, 3 August 1978). There were "billions" of dollars behind him (*Sun-Times*, 2 August 1978), and $250 million of his own money would go into the project. The name of Allen and Co. was dropped, then confirmed. There were repeated leaks about large amounts of "Canadian money."[2] Nothing was too big for Rubloff.

> what's too big for some people is not too big for me. Sand-
> burg Village was something they said I couldn't do, but
> there it is. I've got a track record and I think I've done more

2. Meant to suggest Cadillac Fairview Co., a major developer of the Los Angeles Bunker Hill development. Bunker Hill continued to haunt both the supporters and opponents of Rubloff, with the former hinting at a similar scale of development and the latter emphasizing the open bids and tough guidelines set down in the Los Angeles project (Shapiro 1981).

The Big Project and the Politics of Urgency

for this city than the rest of the profession combined.[3] (*Sun-Times*, 2 August 1978).

Although the city was flooded with rumors of money, a relatively small $25 million Urban Development Action Grant was said to be critical to the project. The city had already been turned down once for the grant, and it was turned down again in July because of inadequate public participation in the plan (*Sun-Times*, 2 August 1978). The city then scaled down its request to $7.9 million, arguing that it was critical only for the Hilton start-up. HUD, however, deferred this grant until it could be assured that the fund would not be used simply to "change the location of a hotel" (*Tribune*, 3 August 1978).

But the local reaction to Rubloff's project turned out to be downright hostile. Community groups, especially the Metropolitan Area Housing Alliance (MAHA), loudly protested the use of UDAG funds for downtown rather than neighborhood development. Hilton's unionized employees were said to be talking directly to HUD about their fears of losing their jobs. Some groups opposed the project because it would drive out most of the low-income blacks who were now the main customers in the area. Others were concerned about the displacement of the over 1,000 existing firms with 23,000 employees if there was no definite assurance that new firms and jobs would more than replace them (*Sun-Times*, 23 August 1978). By far the most sustained issue, however, was the preservation of several landmark buildings. The area contained four buildings on the National Register, and two more were being proposed for that status. Ultimately, fourteen out of the total of fifty-two buildings were to find their defenders. Rubloff met such sentimentalism with scorn. "Look at that dog," he said, pointing to the Unity Building[4] during an interview with Brian Kelly of the *Sun-Times* (2 August 1978). "They want to make that a monument. It's crap." If it were left up to him, he would tear them all down and, when asked again, he added that "[all the buildings are] nothing but junk" (*Tribune*, 3 August 1978).

3. Rubloff's claims were not all hype. He had developed Sandburg Village, although with considerable public assistance and continuing doubt over its strategic importance in the renewal of Lincoln Park. He also developed the region's first enclosed mall, Evergreen Plaza. He may have been the first to call North Michigan Avenue "The Magnificent Mile," but his substantive contributions to its development are in doubt (Krasnow 1981).

4. The Unity Building had housed the offices of Clarence Darrow and had been built by Illinois Governor John Peter Altgeld.

The Big Project and the Politics of Urgency

For a plan that had been five years in the making, Rubloff's did seem a bit primitive. Essentially a floor plan, it simply designated different plots of land, sometimes whole blocks, for a shopping mall, office building, public library, State of Illinois building, hotel, and two landmark buildings. Only five of the intended structures had any backers, and two of them already existed while the other three seemed likely to be built whether or not Rubloff carried out the remainder of the plan. Still, Rubloff had his supporters, primarily the mayor, the building trades unions, and the C. F. Murphy Company who came forward as Rubloff's architects. What the backers emphasized was the massive infusion of capital, new job creation, and an entertainment zone that would be active in the evening hours. These arguments, however, could be easily countered by a concern for the loss of existing firms and the uncertainty over what would actually happen to the plots that had only hatch marks on them. Journalistic opinion turned heavily against the proposal.

Mike Royko (*Sun-Times*, 6 August 1978) held the entire project up for ridicule as a land grab. Jeff Lyon (*Tribune*, 17 August 1978) invited readers to send in letters opposing Rubloff. Bette Cerf Hill, of the Landmarks Preservation Council, noted that while the state was spending a half-million dollars to preserve a theater in downtown Joliet, the city would be spending about that much to tear down a similar one in Chicago (*Sun-Times*, 19 September 1978). Paul Gapp (*Tribune*, 13 September 1978) doubted that the project design could rise above banality. On top of this, the Metropolitan Housing and Planning Council, a private group with prominent business interests well represented, began to pick apart the plans and the lack of any guidelines which would require committed new construction before clearance. Some people even had the bad taste to bring up the Place Du Sable, a massive clearance carried out under Mayor Daley and still vacant.

Rubloff remained on the offensive. He would tolerate no competition, and he insisted on property tax relief for ten to fifteen years. Also, he wanted a commitment to construct the public library on a plot he had already selected. By November, however, a newly appointed planning commissioner was clearly backing away from Rubloff as sole developer. Part of what was at stake was HUD's unwillingness to grant the $7.9 million if the landmark buildings were destroyed. But it was also an election year, and mayoral candidate Jane Byrne was contending that the money could be better spent in the neighborhoods.

The Big Project and the Politics of Urgency

Although opposition to Rubloff's plan had been widespread, there was a strong argument for some kind of plan for the area. New York, Los Angeles, and Las Vegas were all making very strong bids for the convention and the trade show business which is a substantial part of Chicago's downtown economy. Despite all their misgivings about landmark buildings and the use of UDAGs, the North Loop's importance to Chicago's tourism was quite well recognized among many of those least satisfied with Rubloff's plan. To them, the real problem was that his plan did not address the city's need for a major convention center and a series of theaters which could serve the relatively small audiences attending contemporary productions. Some of the older theaters (Harris, Selwyn, and Woods) were almost ideal for this kind of entertainment while the Chicago Theater was an excellent facility for rare large productions.[5] A "theater row" connecting the two theater sites through the convention center was clearly possible but nowhere in Rubloff's plans. Strangely, the competitive position of the city was never fully articulated to the general public, although Lewis Manilow of the Civic Coalition Task Force on the North Loop made a valiant effort to state the feasibility of a theater row.

With the election in full swing in early 1979, city officials progressively moved away from Rubloff and tried to get the UDAG by affirming Hilton's intention to maintain its existing hotel. Two more buildings were added to the list for preservation (*Sun-Times*, 9 March 1979). By March the City Council was asked to approve the project guidelines, and the HUD grant now seemed almost certain. But all this occurred in the waning days of the Bilandic administration—for Jane Byrne had won the election!

When Byrne entered office in April, she was faced not only with her prior opposition to the project but a rather divided public response. Journalistic opinion of Rubloff's plan had been largely negative. However, both the Metropolitan Housing and Planning Council and some members of the Landmarks Preservation Council felt that there was great potential in a project with adequate guidelines. The building trade unions were for almost any project. Downtown merchants were hoping for some kind of plan—if not Rubloff's and the Hilton, people had already expressed a strong desire to talk to Mayor Byrne. Before Byrne could return from a brief

5. Two other large theaters in the downtown area did not oppose the idea of a new theater row because it seemed the only hope of restoring night life throughout the Loop.

postelection vacation, however, the Department of Planning disavowed any further role for Rubloff, and the Chicago Plan Commission approved Bilandic's guidelines for the project.

The new mayor did not even mention the North Loop at her inauguration. By late April, however, Hilton had appointed a new project director who had once been the city's public buildings commissioner. Never one to let past promises stand in the way of future ones, Byrne was on the North Loop bandwagon within two months. Her first announcement was that Continental Bank would help the city assemble $50 million in low-interest loans, thus avoiding having to obtain additional federal funds and the issuance of more expensive general issue bonds. Very quickly, however, others recognized that this would also eliminate the requirement to keep the landmark buildings or, possibly, to keep open the existing Hilton Hotel. The Metropolitan Housing and Planning Council sent Byrne a letter strongly restating the need for explicit and binding guidelines for the North Loop. Martin Oberman led five other independents in the City Council to denounce the "sweetheart deal" with the Hilton chain (*Sun-Times*, 25 September 1979). Byrne recaptured the headlines by backing Edward Kennedy in his primary campaign against Jimmy Carter. A month later HUD officials refused to release even the $7.9 million promised Bilandic unless the Hilton chain again assured them it would not scrap the existing hotel. Hilton refused to make the commitment and within weeks added that it could not construct the hotel without a property tax break as well.

A period of quiet negotiation began, and Byrne appointed an architectural advisory committee to study the project.[6] In May, Hilton agreed to keep its older hotel open for four years, or about the construction period for the new one. Nonetheless, HUD now appeared willing to release the grant. By this time the Hilton project had added half a block for an adjoining apartment tower; the total project cost was said to be $200 million. Hilton gave Byrne a check for $2.7 million. Two months later she came forth with a new coordinator, Charles Shaw and Co., for the entire North Loop project.

Shaw was a respected builder[7] and so painfully shy that he

---

6. However, she ignored its recommendations.

7. He had built Lake Point Towers in Chicago and the new tower for the Metropolitan Museum of Modern Art in New York. Rubloff was bitter, saying that Harry Chaddick and Charles Swibel had voted him out of the Loop (*Sun-Times*, 20 July 1980).

was thoroughly disarming after the theatrics of Rubloff. Then HUD again refused to release the grant, charging that the city had segmented the project in such a way as to allow developers to destroy national landmarks. This revelation was followed by news that Hilton's contract practically gave it full control of the project.[8] Hilton was not pressing for an approval of its tax abatement, but in the meantime Byrne had managed to get herself on the wrong side of the county tax assessor, Thomas Hynes.[9] The request for the tax break passed between City Hall and the assessor's office three times before fairly obvious technical omissions were cleared up and the assessor gave "tentative" approval (*Sun-Times*, 28 October 1980). For the next two weeks the North Loop was alive. Byrne announced that there would be three more hotels in the project (*Sun-Times*, 31 October 1980). The State of Illinois Building broke ground. And Charles Shaw put on his show.

Compared to Rubloff's floor plan it was an impressive unveiling for Skidmore, Owings and Merrill had been retained to do some really glitzy scale models. Six of the landmark buildings would be retained. There would be several new theaters, a residential "project in the sky," and the whole assemblage would be tied together with skyways and underground passages. Shaw, himself, would develop a large office tower and collect 2 percent on all additional developments. But Shaw's office building was sited directly on the plot occupied by the Harris and Selwyn theaters which were to be the western terminus of the theater row. Even more disturbing was Byrne's continual reminder that "nothing in the plan is written in stone" (*Tribune*, 14 November 1980). Richard Christiansen, probably the city's most respected art critic, raised fundamental doubts about Shaw's understanding of Chicago's special mix of cultural institutions (*Tribune*, 14 November 1980). Basil Talbott quickly dismissed this effort to "Manhattanize" Chicago (*Sun-Times*, 16 November 1980). The *Tribune* (23 November 1980) began to wonder just what was written in stone: Shaw's contract? The tax break? The buildings to be saved? Lewis Manilow released his study for the Landmarks

8. Among other things, it required that the city demolish five buildings outside the hotel site and provide a route between McCormick Place and the new hotel. Actually, one could have made a good argument for the new traffic artery, but it was simply slipped into the contract rather than argued for in any explicit way.

9. She was supporting a losing candidate against Richard M. Daley for state's attorney, and Hynes was supporting Daley. Hynes also had his own ambitions to run for mayor.

The Big Project and the Politics of Urgency

Preservation Council[10] which argued for the retention not only of the Harris and Selwyn theaters but the Woods Theater as well. By February of the next year a powerful civic coalition[11] was encouraging the assessor not to grant any tax breaks for the project, and within two weeks Shaw was out as coordinator. Byrne then moved Miles Berger from the Plan Commission to become head of the project, saying that the city itself would coordinate the development.

For the next two years the struggle over the North Loop defies a blow-by-blow description. Byrne first went on the attack, accusing her opponents of representing "special interests" (*Sun-Times*, 28 February 1981). Basil Talbott of the *Sun-Times* was sitting "in the back of the room" making arrangements for the civic coalition (*Tribune*, 26 February 1981). Assessor Hynes continued to string out his requests for clarification on the tax abatement for the Hilton Hotel. Then, in what seemed a complete turnaround, Byrne adopted almost exactly the guidelines proposed by the Civic Federation and said that she would appoint a citizen's oversight committee. There was a brief respite, and Moody's even gave its top rating to the city's proposed bond sale. But now it was learned that the new guidelines would be advisory rather than binding, and Byrne malingered in appointing the oversight committee. Mid America Appraisal came forward with a study stating that Hilton could not operate the new hotel without a tax break.[12] Somewhat later, a coalition of Loop businessmen presented the assessor with another study claiming to show that the city would be essentially paying for the hotel through its tax break. The dean of the Loyola Law School presented yet another study unfavorable to the tax break. The figures in these studies were so far apart that none of them achieved credibility. Thus, by November the editors of the *Sun-Times* threw up their hands and accepted the tax break for Hilton (20 November 1981) while the *Tribune* editors favored the lowered land costs but not the tax break (7 November 1981).

10. The study had been supported by both the National Endowment for the Arts and the Chicago Community Trust. The latter includes many of the city's major philanthropists.

11. Including the Metropolitan Housing and Planning Council, the Civic Federation, League of Women Voters, Better Government Association, Urban League, and Landmarks Preservation Council.

12. Mid America was a firm that Berger had withdrawn from when taking his position on the Plan Commission. This Berger, by the way, is the same Berger who was enlisted by the Edgewater Community Council to secure the use of their lakefront park.

The Big Project and the Politics of Urgency

Already there was wide speculation that Richard M. Daley would oppose Byrne in the Democratic primary almost a year off. Hynes, one of Daley's supporters, tried a compromise by tying the size of the tax break to the levels of hotel occupancy. He had not stopped the project, and he had not given into Byrne. One day later Hilton pulled out of the project. The next day a rumor developed that Hynes would be willing to talk to representatives of the city and Hilton, and the following day Hynes both denied the rumor and added that "we can sit down and talk" if it could be demonstrated that he was wrong (*Tribune*, 12 December 1981). Three days later Hynes and Hilton representatives began talks behind closed doors (*Tribune*, 16 December 1981). Over at City Hall, it was rumored, they were considering bids from other hotels, maybe three of them (*Sun-Times*, 29 January 1982). And, as the talks with Hynes proceeded into the new year, Byrne announced that she was preparing for bids from other hotels if the talks fell through (*Sun-Times*, 29 January 1982). Within a week Hilton and Hynes had come to an agreement, "in principle," tied to hotel profits, although the exact terms were unstated (*Sun-Times*, 24 February 1982). Whatever the exact terms, they did not satisfy Hilton's backers who pulled out (*Tribune*, 4 March 1982). A brief effort to consider using the pension funds of the building trades unions was unable to revive interest in the hotel (*Sun-Times*, 10 March 1982).

Now the city was back to round one, and in June ads were placed inviting competitive bids for all the North Loop parcels. It was the city's first effort at this novel device. Suddenly twelve developers came forth with sixteen different proposals (*Tribune*, 8 August 1982). For a week, optimism soared. Chicago could still attract big investors even at a time of very high interest rates. But, then, it was noted that not one of the proposals conformed to the guidelines. After all, the ads had only urged developers to do so (*Tribune*, 25 September 1982). At an important meeting with the Civic Federation attended by prominent civic and business leaders, there was general disapproval of the proposals, and Mayor Byrne and her planners withdrew to set new guidelines. Within three weeks the new guidelines were out, and all the old bidders and new ones as well were invited to come in with their proposals (*Tribune*, 13 October 1982). The new guidelines were not that reassuring. They did not save the Harris and Selwyn theaters, made no clear provision for a theater row or convention center, and they required that only 2 percent of the construction cost of office space be contributed to the city. The city was now running short of money to obtain any additional land because practically nothing had been sold to establish a cash flow.[13] Even more pressing was Byrne's engagement in a three-way primary race with Harold Washington and Richard M. Daley. Byrne tried to quiet critics of the new guidelines by promising landmark status for the Harris and Selwyn theaters. That prompted Elizabeth Taylor, who owned the theaters, to send her attorneys to oppose the designation (*Sun-Times*, 9 November 1982). Then the owners of the Chicago Theater asked for a demolition permit.

By the end of the year, the North Loop was down to two bids: a relatively small Libra-Americana hotel for the Hilton site and, just to the south, an enclosed shopping mall which actually seemed to funnel people toward the proposed theater row.[14] Before decisions could be made on either bid, Byrne was out and Washington was mayor.

Like Byrne, Washington had run on a platform favoring neighborhood investment over downtown projects like the North Loop. Unlike her he stayed with it for almost two years. At first, investors simply hung back, waiting to see if it was safe to do business in Chicago. Those in the civic coalition, however, were encouraged when he appointed Elizabeth Hollander, former director of the Metropolitan Housing and Planning Council, as his planning commissioner. Certainly she was thoroughly acquainted with all the different plans for the project, and she had good connections in various civic associations and much of the business community. The City Council even approved her appointment despite a run-in with Edward Burke, one of Washington's chief opponents in the rapidly developing "Council Wars." Still, there was little she could do initially because most of the money allocated to the project had been spent, and court decisions had raised some land values to $500 a square foot. Libra-Americana was having problems finding financing and, until they could pay $10 million for the site, there were no funds to clear the other site for the shopping mall. Moreover, even if these funds became available, they might have to be used to pur-

13. The city had sold one parcel for a transportation center, essentially a large parking lot sandwiched between some airline offices at street level and some offices above the garage. It commanded a heavy $7.6 million subsidy and probably would have been widely opposed if people had not been so occupied with the general project (see Lewis Manilow's evaluation in the *Sun-Times*, 9 March 1983).

14. A second bid for the same site was contingent on financial backing and a major occupant.

The Big Project and the Politics of Urgency

chase the Chicago Theater, whose owners were now in litigation asking for the full appraised price of the theater as well as damages. Some were hoping for a land swap, but the one proposed struck almost everyone as a very bad deal for the city (*Tribune*, 8 May 1984).

In the meantime, Washington and the remnants of the Chicago Machine were off to the Council Wars. The issues they chose to divide over were numerous, but the most important for the North Loop was Washington's decision to funnel all federal funds to the neighborhoods for services and new construction. Actually, this was entirely suitable to most aldermen who have no ambitions to be mayor and get elected primarily by bringing projects into their wards. It seemed to take Washington well over a year to realize that he was not just another alderman from the South Side. Nonetheless, he and his opponents found much to disagree about since Washington favored services for the black community while the "Vrdolyak 29" wanted a lot of street paving.

In August the shopping mall was approved, but at about the same time the hotel investors asked for yet another extension to round up financing. They received that extension and another one in December. In the new year, Libra-Americana added a new partner, Urban Investment and Development Co., and asked for another six-month delay. By this time the department was looking to tax increment financing for the purchase of the Chicago Theater and the land for the shopping mall. At least this time people seemed to agree that it would cost the city about $226 million in foregone taxes (*Tribune*, 23 April 1984), or about the price of the Hilton Hotel. In June, however, things were looking up, and the council approved the land sale to Libra-Americana, now Urban-Americana. Three months later they asked for another extension.

By November, however, not all would seem to be lost. A new group of investors had put together a deal for the Chicago Theater that would include live performances[15] (*Tribune*, 3 November 1984). The new State of Illinois Building was taking form, and Helmut Jahn's design was attracting attention despite large (100 percent)

15. The result was a bitter dispute with some members of the City Club who had put forward a competing plan to use the theater as a movie house and the adjacent Page Building as a movie museum. Most of the people I talked with did not think that City Club's proposal could be carried out for the estimated costs or that it was as desirable as live theater. But the Chicago Theater aroused strong sentiments and clouded visions as between those who wanted to recapture there their youth and those who wanted a theater row to compete with New York and Los Angeles.

The Big Project and the Politics of Urgency

cost overruns. By January the Stouffer Corporation had replaced Urban and that pumped fresh hope into the site for a hotel.

That hope did not last long for in April the developers asked for another extension, and the planning commissioner put the block up for new bids (*Tribune*, 2 April 1985). In all these negotiations Washington had kept a low profile; the Council Wars were providing plenty of publicity. When the application for the federal money for the Chicago Theater was finalized, however, he came forth with the governor and with Representative Rostenkowski to become an advocate for the North Loop.[16] "Chicago is on a roll," he said (*Tribune*, 21 April 1985), and for a while it looked like he might be right as two new bidders had shown up for the two-block hotel site. Altogether they offered a 600-room hotel, two office towers, an apartment building, and quite a bit of street level shopping and dining. There was no convention center, really no theater row, but Washington urged their acceptance before the Commercial District (*Tribune*, 7 August 1985). Three months later property owners in the area proposed a glass enclosed galleria which would connect the two blocks, and the money seemed almost in reach (*Sun-Times*, 13 November 1985). Elizabeth Taylor was being uncooperative and had signed a lease to show movies at the Harris and Selwyn theaters, but Hollander released a barrage of studies showing that the theaters would be better used for live shows (*Tribune*, 29 November 1985).

The year 1986 did not start out well for the North Loop. At its beginning Washington and his opponents were facing a $78 million deficit. In a bit of brinkmanship, Washington refused to cut payrolls, and his opponents refused to raise property taxes. The result was that his opponents put forth on the council floor a lease tax (6 percent for anyone doing more than $12,000 worth of business) hoping to force Washington to veto it—it was sure to be unpopular—and then have to cut payrolls. But Washington did not veto it! Shortly afterward one of the bidders on the hotel site pulled out, and the other partners said they would do so as well (*Tribune*, 12 January

16. Washington was out front on a few large public works projects (e.g., O'Hare expansion), but I think this was the first time he showed much enthusiasm for downtown. Like his predecessors, he showed most interest in those projects where the contracts were still to be negotiated and he could exercise some control over jobs through the affirmative action program. For example, the linked development tax included a subsidy to downtown firms giving preference to job seekers nominated by the mayor's office (*Tribune*, 25 August 1985). Later he did press for a 4.2 million square feet office complex that defies any accepted standards of density but includes an affirmative action program which has its political advantages.

The Big Project and the Politics of Urgency

1986). News releases continued to assert that something can still be worked out. But by this time the Washington administration was deeply mired in a bribery scandal, and Byrne was already threatening to reunify the city as its next mayor.

The Chicago Central Public Library: Books in the Attic

Chicago essentially has no central public library. In 1974, the old public library was closed for renovation as a cultural center, and much of the city's collection was stored in a warehouse on the little-known Pioneer Plaza. Mrs. Daley herself had openly opposed the move, but her husband persisted. "She has a right to express her opinion," he allowed, and developed instead a fine reference library at City Hall. One could actually obtain books at the warehouse on Pioneer Plaza, but it was a grim facility with a misleading address on Michigan Avenue and few services. Library use had fallen to less than half its previous level, and in 1978 three ranking library officials, including the commissioner, resigned because of the library's condition. The president of the Library Board was said to be a well-connected book appraiser, but he was better known for the $10,000 fine he had to pay for backdating former President Nixon's papers. He had been president of the board for over ten years.

Shortly after the new Cultural Center opened, Daniel Boorstein, Librarian of Congress and former professor of history at the University of Chicago, addressed a meeting of the American Library Association in Chicago declaring the city's library a "public disgrace" located in "what amounts to an attic" (*Tribune*, 5 July 1978). This criticism was widely repeated in the daily press, and the Bilandics, who had a good reputation for supporting the arts,[17] were moved to action. Two months after Boorstein's remarks, Mayor Bilandic appointed a new library commissioner, Donald Sagar, a man who had achieved high marks for his development of the Columbus, Ohio, library system. Ralph Newman, president of the Library Board, was to ease over into the position of archivist, and a number of new nominees were named to the board; Hanna Gray, president of the University of Chicago; Eliza Gleason, executive director of the Black United Fund and a former professor of library science; and Mrs. Richard J. Daley herself.

17. Heather Morgan Bilandic had been executive director of the Chicago Council of Fine Arts.

The Big Project and the Politics of Urgency

A new library was clearly in the works and, in November, the mayor presented a rough site plan for a 400,000-square-foot library with commercial space at the street level. Arthur Rubloff, who it was thought wanted the library in his North Loop plans, said that he was surprised but delighted (*Sun-Times*, 19 November 1978). The merchants who would be displaced expressed their apprehensions but were assured that they would get first preference relocating in the new building. A few people (mostly architects) expressed some doubts about the inclusion of street level commercial space, but they were clearly outnumbered by others who thought that the cultural center would serve as a sufficiently impressive entrance to the library while the commercial space would draw additional people to dilute the congregation of derelicts who were already there. The commercial space was seen as essential to reducing the costs of the library which was then said to be from 60 to 70 million dollars. Three days after Bilandic's announcement, the City Council approved his plan, and in January of the following year the city's Plan Commission approved the site. Shortly thereafter, Camille Hatzenbuehler, Harry Chaddick's daughter and a vice-president of his firm, was elected president of the Library Board.

Then Michael Bilandic lost the Democratic primary to Jane Byrne. For the next year Bilandic's library simply fell out of public sight. It resurfaced momentarily in late 1979, when it was announced that there would be a reduction in library hours and a 22 percent loss of personnel. In February of the next year it resurfaced again when Patrick Greene, a deputy commissioner in the library and a cousin of Richard M. Daley, filed a legal complaint when Byrne's chief of staff tried to fire him (*Tribune*, 13 February 1980). Eliza Gleason then resigned from the board in a dispute over the computer system to be installed in the library. Shortly after Byrne lost the fight to fire Mr. Greene, she made major changes in the board. She appointed Sally Berger, wife of a well-known developer and subsequently Byrne's head of the Chicago Plan Commission; Melanie Kluerynski, an unsuccessful candidate who Byrne had backed; Evangeline Gouletas of American Invesco; and Cannutte Russell, a black dentist. Also asked to serve because she was "impressed with his business acumen" (*Tribune*, 15 April 1980) was Charles Swibel (see Chap. 3). Earlier Byrne had suggested downsizing Bilandic's library, but now she opted for an entirely new site on South State Street, well away from the Cultural Center. The initial argument for this site was that the city controlled much of the land which had been purchased originally for a downtown college that had been built elsewhere. The new library was expected to cost only $50 million, but it was hoped that the price would be even less if a private developer would come in with a mixed-use facility.

By June it was clear that Byrne was hoping for still more through state legislation which would provide $4 million for construction. This legislation first languished in the legislature; then, when it passed there, it was vetoed by the governor. Still Swibel recommended delay until the next legislative session and, at that point, it became clear that what was expected was not just $4 million in seed money but an annual fund over twenty years to retire the entire indebtedness. Swibel assured the *Tribune* that it could be done (15 September 1980).

Despite growing doubts, the Library Board approved the new site, and a few weeks later Byrne announced that an anonymous Chicago industrialist would give $10 million toward the construction of the library. This mysterious benefactor never reappeared in Byrne's plans for the library. Three weeks later Patrick Greene, Daley's cousin, instituted a second lawsuit (he had already won the first) contending that he was the only one of thirty-two deputy commissioners of the library who had been denied an across-the-board raise. It was then disclosed that Commissioner Sagar had received only a 1.5 percent raise despite the recommendation of a consulting firm that he receive much more. Byrne said it was "blackmail"; her husband said that the judge was protecting "incompetents" and "political hacks" (*Tribune*, 19 December 1980). Judge Bua invited—almost urged—Commissioner Sagar to join his case to that of Greene's. Sager declined, but by January the administration seemed content to sign a consent decree which was accompanied by an apology from the mayors' husband.

Journalistic news of these events was still not sufficient to displace attention from Byrne's ordinance to strip the Library Board of its control over the Cultural Center.[18] Some members complained that they had not even been forewarned. "An outrageous lie," said Swibel (*Tribune*, 17 December 1980), and the ordinance went through. Nonetheless, by April the board was agreeable to an RFP (request for proposal) for firms to bid on the new library design.

18. The Cultural Center was by now a great success, drawing more patrons than the better-known Art Institute and circulating more books than the warehouse library.

Only two local firms submitted bids, the lower of which was quickly approved by the Commercial District. The nine-story library, at a cost of $33.8 million, was to be connected to an apartment tower and extensive office and retail space with a total price tag of $168 million. However, by December it was clear that the plans did not subscribe to the RFP, that the private portion of the development would provide no funds other than property taxes, and that the foundation work for the private development would be provided by the library funds! (*Tribune*, 16 December 1981). By that time the cost of the library had been increased to $51.2 million; it was to climb to $64.2 million later when land costs were factored in.

Before all of these news items were widely publicized, Commissioner Sagar chose to resign rather than be fired (*Tribune*, 12 September 1981). Judge Bua actually blocked his resignation until Sagar appeared in court and declined to speculate on why he was being forced out. Swibel was more forthcoming, saying that political sponsors get people jobs in Chicago and "nothing has changed" (*Tribune*, 13 September 1981). Sagar had just been made president-elect of the American Library Association.

With public confidence in the administration's library plans sinking to a new low, Byrne fought back by sending portraits of herself to all the branch libraries (*Tribune*, 27 October 1981). Then, seemingly out of nowhere, the architectural firm of Holabird and Root released a study showing that the new library might be housed in the vacant Goldblatt building one block north. There was much to be said for the site. A distinguished building,[19] it provided ample space for both the library above street level and retail space at street level. A small building to one side could be removed (if Cook County Sheriff Elrod who owned it could be induced to sell it) to provide an appropriate entrance to the library. The plan was especially appealing to State Street merchants who were faced with a "dead" stretch on a portion of the street which was in shaky condition. Holabird and Root estimated it would cost only $41.4 million. Eleven days later Mayor Byrne jumped on the bandwagon and announced that the city would acquire the site (*Sun-Times*, 10 January 1982). Swibel was even more enthusiastic, saying that the city might save as much as $25 million. Holabird and Root were singled out to do the renovation, but they would have to share the honor with Lester P. Knight and Associates, one of the firms whose bid had

19. It was originally designed by Holabird and Roche.

been approved on the previous site,[20] which later had been converted to a parking lot.

Only Stanley Balzekas on the library board opposed the new site,[21] and once again Byrne seemed to have weathered the storm to find broad support for the new location. Swibel's estimate of savings had slid downward to $10–15 million, but hopes were up and they were extended to the professionalism of Amanda Rudd, the new library commissioner (*Sun-Times*, 23 January 1982). Commissioner Rudd soon cooled that enthusiasm, first when she fired an employee who had worked for a candidate opposing Byrne, and second when she denounced a City Club report calling for the resignation of Swibel. Mayor Byrne also denounced the report and began to use library funds to publish her own *City Edition* newspaper (*Sun-Times*, 14 January 1982). Even the City Council backed off from an additional $145,000 to be allocated in this manner.

Still, the acquisition of the building proceeded, and some renovation plans actually began. In November, Mr. Greene struck again, this time providing information that led to the arrest of the library's chief of security. Commissioner Rudd suspended Greene for this act of excessive zeal (*Tribune*, 29 November 1983), but the court ordered his reinstatement. Vendors complained of being pressured into contributing to a cocktail party for Ms. Rudd (*Tribune*, 14 December 1983), and her $93,000 in expenses drew journalistic attention. But despite these antics, it began to look as if the city would get a new central library.

Then Jane Byrne lost the Democratic primary to Harold Washington. By February 1984 Swibel was out, and Washington began to nominate his own Library Board: Lerone Bennett, Jr., of Johnson Publishing Co.; Dorothy McConner of Johnson Products; Carmelo Rodriquez of ASPIRA (a Puerto Rican community organization); and Marian Pritzker who was from a very wealthy Chicago family. He also reappointed Cannutte Russell, who happened to be his dentist. A month later James Lowry, a black businessman, but a Byrne appointee, was elected president of the board. As it turned out, however, this board had very little enthusiasm for the Goldblatt site. Moreover, the new cost estimate was now said to be $75 million. For a while it looked as if there might be a complete repetition of site

20. Knight and Thomas V. O'Neill, the firm's chairman, had contributed $9,000 to Byrne's campaign fund, and Byrne had named O'Neill to the Joint Commission overseeing the Chicago Transit Authority (*Sun-Times*, 21 October 1981).

21. He was replaced on the board as soon as his term expired six months later.

selection with fresh bids and new developers. Washington had trouble getting all of his nominees through the council. There was continuing criticism of Commissioner Rudd. Finally, in the last month of 1984, the new board approved the Goldblatt site and began the search for a new commissioner. The search proved to be very divisive, with black board members siding with black candidates and white board members with white candidates. For a while Lowry had to take over the library as acting commissioner. It was also Lowry who finally cast the deciding vote in favor of John Duff as library commissioner. A white man, Duff is a former college chancellor with an excellent reputation as an administrator.

In mid-1985 Holabird and Root were actually able to present some of their plans for the new library, and the rumor was that it would open in 1988.[22] That of course was only rumor. At this date the new library is still far off. Washington had not closely identified himself with the new library, but paradoxically it was named in his honor after his death.

The State Street Maul

Like so many other downtown Chicago projects that remain unfinished, the State Street Mall was part of the *Chicago 21* plan unveiled by Mayor Richard J. Daley in 1973. Rubloff was one of its boosters and, typically, it was billed as "the largest mall of its kind in the country." A nine-block strip that included six major department stores, it was already one of the busiest streets in the nation and included altogether 6.5 million square feet of retail space. For Chicagoans the street was probably the most readily available image of the city. Just to see it was to recall Potter Palmer, George Jessel, Big Bill Thompson, Franklin Roosevelt, St. Patrick's Day, Richard J. Daley, Louis Sullivan, Santa Clause, and Frank Sinatra. Nevertheless, sales had been lagging on the street since the early 1960s, and the street's future became especially problematic after the onset of the Civil Rights movement when an emboldened black population made its presence felt and whites largely vacated the street during the evenings and on weekends. Few of the stores stayed open on weekends or past 6 P.M. The presence of blacks was especially no-

22. By 1988 the idea of using the Goldblatt building as a library was abandoned and still another site was being considered. The price now: close to $200 million.

ticeable along the southern end of the street where a series of "bottom of the line" retailers and porno shops lay across the street from Goldblatts and Sears.

The grand plan for State Street was to double the width of the sidewalks, narrow the street to two lanes for buses, and deck the entire street with attractions that would be irresistible to suburbanites; trees, flowers, cafés, fountains, sculptures, transit shelters, seating, live entertainment, and elegant newsstands. All these things would be cast against a background of polished granite. The major impetus for the mall came from City Hall and the six major "anchor" department stores who dominated the State Street Council. But, again like so many other downtown projects, much of the money, 80 percent it was said, would come from the federal government, or the Urban Mass Transportation Authority and the Federal Highway Administration. That is why it was called the "State Street *Transit* Mall."

At this time, however, the two federal agencies were in no rush to reduce the number of roads available to automobiles and, in any case, the city's application was so flawed (*Tribune*, 10 June 1975; *Sun-Times*, 26 October 1976) that the UMTA and FHA found it easy to turn down. So for the next three years the city and the federal agencies exchanged pieces of paper without much progress. Then, in late 1976, as Gerald Ford faced a stiff fight for the Illinois vote, the secretary of transportation announced that an early approval of the $9.9 million grant was forthcoming along with another $120 million for the O'Hare surface line.[23] Ford lost the election, seven weeks later Mayor Daley died, and for a while it looked like the council would be unable to pick a successor (Weisman and Whitehead 1977). Finally, under pressure from the downtown bankers, they hit upon Michael Bilandic as a sign of continuity because he had been such a loyal follower of Daley and had practically no profile of his own. Also, he was white, unlike Wilson Frost who had a stronger legal claim to the position.

Bilandic, who had never run in a city-wide election,[24] was almost immediately faced with the necessity of winning a big one. By March he was on the campaign trail, and his election speech was a

23. Secretary Coleman's announcement came five days before the presidential election and five days after a poll showing Ford and Carter virtually tied for Illinois' twenty-six electoral votes (*Tribune*, 24 October 1976; 29 October 1976).

24. He was alderman in Daley's Eleventh Ward, a position better described as appointive than as elective.

The Big Project and the Politics of Urgency

slide show of Daley era brick and mortar projects. It looked like Skidmore, Owings and Merrill had taken it right out of the *Chicago 21* plan, complete with the obligatory quotes from Burnham. Having been picked to succeed Daley, Bilandic acted as if he should simply duplicate his proposals to win the party and the voters to his side. But Roman Pucinski had already bolted party ranks to oppose him in the primary, and Harold Washington was to do so later on as blacks remained outraged over the treatment of Wilson Frost. Still, Bilandic squeaked through the primary with 51 percent of the vote and advanced easily through the mayoral election which, in Chicago, has long been a needless embarrassment to the Republican party.

Bilandic had featured the State Street Mall prominently in his election slide show, and he quickly moved to have the council approve a special assessment to provide $3 million to finance it (*Tribune*, 8 July 1977). Optimism reigned for the moment, but then negotiations with the UMTA and FHA bogged down, partly because of problems with the application but also because of jurisdictional and design disputes among a host of city and state agencies; the Illinois Department of Transportation, the city Departments of Public Works and Streets and Sanitation, and the Chicago Transit Authority. These disputes were to plague the mall throughout its development and they continually lay behind many of the delays and cost overruns (*Sun-Times*, 12 March 1978). Without Daley to apply the patronage screws unmercifully, the various city departments became baronies, run as much by their unions as by their jurisdictionally conscious administrators. It was not just that power and jobs were involved but that most of these departments have only a few people with the competence to assist in an application to the federal government. Any change of routine is alarming for they work in an atmosphere surrounded by legal threats, racial sensitivities, and a labor force that has its own recourse to political influence.[25]

In March of 1978, the city had still not received final approval of its application, but Bilandic was able to reconstitute much of the special oversight commission to guide the project and overcome some of the infighting among state and local agencies. There were

25. For example, the administrators of the CTA resisted the new rounded canopies to be placed at the bus stops because they had trained their workers to clean rectangular ones. At first I thought it must be a pretext for some other reason, and in a way I suppose it was; they were afraid of labor troubles over the same issue!

new assurances that construction would begin in June and that "this is just the normal way of doing business," as the commissioner of public works phrased it (*Tribune*, 13 March 1978). The cost had gone up, first to $16 million (*Sun-Times*, 4 April 1978), then to $17 million (*Sun-Times*, 11 April 1978). The city would have to bear its "share,"[26] and the federal government was now being asked for $12.8 million (*Sun-Times*, 4 April 1978). Construction actually did begin only two weeks late in June, and a fourteen-month period was announced for the mall's completion. Two months later, however, the mall was already behind schedule, one person had been killed in the unusual bus traffic that snaked through the construction site, and the bus drivers' union had made its first allegation of racism when the buses serving white neighborhoods were placed at the most forward loading stops (*Sun-Times*, 19 July 1978; *Tribune*, 10 November 1978). Ultimately, there were to be at least thirty lawsuits over injuries at the construction site, and despite double crews during Bilandic's campaign against Jane Byrne the mall was still behind schedule.

The State Street Mall remained behind schedule right into Jane Byrne's first year in office although the council decided to have a ceremony anyway. Thus, in October of 1979, Mayor Byrne patted some concrete around a figurative "last curbstone." About half the sidewalks appeared to be completed (*Sun-Times*, 29 October 1979). The bus drivers were still complaining about racism and, when the stops for whites were placed to the rear, they called it "reverse racism" (*Tribune*, 3 November 1979). Nonetheless, the Christmas parade was held in December. And to the outrage of the State Street Council, the crowd trampled the fir bushes, piled on top of the kiosks, and left the new planters in a shambles (*Tribune*, 12 December 1979).

Then, just as people were getting into the Christmas spirit, the council asked Byrne to revoke the permits of the old news vendors who were still plying their trade out of wobbly, rusty sheds (*Tribune*, 12 December 1979). It could not have happened at a better time for Byrne who rushed to the street, embraced one of the eldest of the news vendors, and promised them that they could stay put: "You are a State Street tradition" (*Tribune*, 14 December 1979). She was a momentary Christmas heroine, and the *Tribune* applauded this defense of the press's liberty and chided the Scrooges on State Street who would deny the mall "some of the variety and unexpectedness

---

26. Previously no "share" for the city had been announced.

The Big Project and the Politics of Urgency

of the crowds who visit it" (24 December 1979). The council grudgingly conceded to build more kiosks for the existing vendors.

However, already some of the *Tribune's* variety and unexpectedness had begun to occur. A brief bus strike the week before Christmas had imperiled the holiday trade, sometimes as much as 20 percent of the total. The asphalt tiles, which had replaced the more expensive granite, had been laid so unevenly that they tripped up pedestrians and gathered inch-deep pools of water. And, during the St. Patrick's Day parade, a drunken horde left the mall in shambles, doing some $500,000 in damage (*Tribune*, 10 April 1980). The State Street Council, then, asked that parades be kept off the mall. When the city put a freeze on further parades, even the *Tribune* applauded this restraint of the unexpected (13 April 1980).

The first preacher with a bullhorn arrived at the State Street Mall in April because "this is the place that God sent me" (*Tribune*, 4 April 1980). He was soon followed by several others with less divine guidance. Within weeks one could hear an elevating oration on the threat of international communism, the sins of abortion, the dangers of nuclear war, and a variety of other improving topics. The bullhorns were absolutely essential to these messengers because they were the only way that human speech could possibly overcome the drone of a 700-horsepower diesel engine in a Grumman articulated bus. The bus stops, of course, were the favorite platform for these sidewalk orators; you could escape moral enlightenment only at the risk of missing your place in line. The State Street Council asked for a noise ordinance, and the city's corporate council warned that such an ordinance would also preclude the amplification of Christmas carols or any other music that stores often broadcast themselves. Even the Salvation Army would not be able to use their electric guitars and bells.

The leaders of the council complained that they were being excluded from any control over the street and, indeed, they were having their problems. In October, a Department of Transportation study concluded that the mall was "totally ineffective" (*Tribune*, 5 October 1980): there were very few places to sit, the kiosks were oriented away from the pedestrians, and there was just not much to do on the mall. The head of the council dismissed that as just the view of a bunch of people from New York and Washington (*Tribune*, 6 October 1980), but it was harder to deny the differences within the council itself. The merchants themselves were divided over the presence of competing outdoor cafes, and only Goldblatts, now in serious trouble, had located a cafe outside its store (*Tribune*, 13 August 1980). The council was also divided over the purpose of the mall. Was it to bring in suburban shoppers looking for a chainsaw, or was it supposed to market clothing and high-style items to those already working in the Loop? Sears and Ward's carried a line of goods for the former while Marshall Fields and Carsons were beginning to show increasing attention to the latter type of customer. When Byrne urged the council to accept pushcarts, they first resisted and then unenthusiastically conceded with the provision that there be no hotdogs (*Sun-Times*, 9 December 1980).

By January sales were up only 3.4 percent lagging inflation and the national trend. By mid-year, however, the council had allowed six outdoor cafes in, and later in that year cabs were permitted back on the street during the evening hours. Marshall Field's began to experiment by staying open one Sunday each month, but none of the other stores followed their lead until there was a major shake-up in the management of several stores in 1983. By November, Goldblatt's announced that it was closing after the Christmas season, and in the new year there were rumors that both Sears and Wards would also close. Wards at first denied the rumor but then confirmed it. Sears soon followed with a statement that they would close when a reuse for their building could be found. The Sears building, designed by William Le Baron Jenny and now on the National Register, was eligible for a 25 percent tax credit. It would be far more profitable to restore it for office space above the street level than to lose money for the eighth consecutive year. Wards, also designed by Jenny, had been so defaced by modernization that few cared that it would be torn down and replaced by an office tower. There was some initial hope that the street side of the new building would conform roughly with the existing cornice line and include some retailing business. Subsequently, a seventy-two-story office building rose to face both east and west.

By the spring of 1983, the *Wall Street Journal* seemed to provide a final judgment on the State Street Mall. For three years its sales had lagged inflation and the national retailing trend (9 May 1983), and the southern end of the street was weaker than ever. As Harry Weese, a prominent Chicago architect said, "State Street has been mauled." But the story does not quite end there. That same year Marshall Field's and Wieboldt's followed Carson's lead in a management shake-up, drawing in new blood from those familiar with the notion of shopping as "festival." With the renovation of the Chicago

Theater actually getting underway in 1986, and Lawrence Levy (a North Michigan Avenue restauranteur) and Jerrold Wexler (North Michigan hotels) beginning to show their presence on the street, a new leadership was forming. Even the bullhorns were gone although, under the Washington administration, they were replaced with musicians who provided quite a musical experience when overcoming a Grumman articulated bus. The planned renovation of Sears and Goldblatts and the ongoing construction of the Ward's site would require removal of much of the asphalt tile, and new developers are already making new plans for the mall. Nothing has been announced yet, but maybe this time they will get it right.

Lying Down in a Partnership

What is one to make of these three stories? One could just say, "That's Chicago," and in a way there is something to this. Chicagoans are exceptionally inured to manipulation and chicanery and, without some indication of plunder, they might loose confidence in the seriousness of anyone's intentions to carry through a project involving any sizable sum of money. The established pattern of "defended venality" (Guterbock 1980, pp. 33–68) is not simply remembered; it is often romanticized as part of a golden age of brick and mortal instrumentality. But even Chicagoans grow impatient of failed venality, and after a decade of newsworthy disappoints one must look beyond their pragmatic tolerance to find some additional reason for such clumsy urban planning.

One thing common to all these three case histories is the effort to forge some kind of partnership between investors, sometimes two or more public investors, sometimes public and private investors, and sometimes all three. The North Loop projects, for example, were exceedingly complex for they involved federal, city, and private investors. In its various forms, the library went from being largely a local project to a public-private partnership, and then again to a project financed entirely by the city. The State Street Mall, the only one of the projects declared finished, lingered for five years while the city waited for a fortuitous approval during Ford's presidential campaign. Just like local community leaders, then, downtown business leaders and public officials seem to have a hard time "lying down in a partnership."[27]

27. The apt phrase is Harry Weese's.

The Big Project and the Politics of Urgency

One reason for this is that a partnership of almost any kind seems to raise the public standards of performance. It is not just that more is promised of such a partnership but that partnerships tend to open up the number of chinks and cracks through which information is passed, so that deficiencies are noticed and opposition aroused. Once the Hilton Hotel project was to be partially financed by federal money, the unionized employees of the hotel could approach federal authorities directly to insure their jobs. Land write-downs and tax abatement increased the number of government units involved and fueled public criticisms as well as political competition between the assessor and the mayor. Applications for the State Street "transit" Mall were continually turned down by the UMTA, and local groups repeated their ridicule although they did not stop the project. Public hearings multiplied as Byrne added private partners to her south State Street library, and when it came to light that the city would be subsidizing the private developers rather than the reverse, the project floundered.

One way to examine this argument more thoroughly is to look at six additional downtown partnerships, although in far less detail than the previous case histories. During the same period (1970–1982) these were the major additional downtown capital improvement projects that involved some kind of partnership.[28] The Navy Pier project was a proposal to use the lakeside structure for a mix of recreation, exhibition, hotel, and retail space. The most durable proposal was a Rouse project with some resemblance to Baltimore's Harbor Place. Soldier Field is where the Bears play, and there have been several proposals to enlarge it or to replace it. Expo Park was to be an exceedingly large (10 million square feet) permanent exhibit of capital goods and equipment. At one point it was claimed that it would employ 27,000 persons. McCormick Place is the nation's

28. The Central Area Committee keeps a list of downtown projects that are reprinted in Cafferty and McCready (1982, p. 144). The CAC considers many of them (mixed use in the Loop, River zone, Navy Pier, historic preservation) underway, but they are "underway" in much the same sense that the North Loop has been underway since 1973. Two substantial projects requiring federal funds were completed or are under construction. The O'Hare transit line was completed although marred by scandals when Byrne speeded up construction and costs during the late days of her campaign for reelection. The S-curve on Lake Shore Drive was straightened at a cost of $90 million. Both projects were funded in a "historic" (i.e., long-delayed) agreement between the governor and Mayor Byrne. It is generally conceded that the governor "took her to the cleaners" in an agreement that bargained away half the funds for the crosstown expressway in a desperate attempt to get something started during her administration.

The Big Project and the Politics of Urgency

largest exhibition hall for trade shows, and an annex half as large is being constructed nearby. The Franklin Street Connector is a down-sized version of a larger subway which was to cost about a billion dollars. The Franklin Street Connector was to cost only half a billion. Loop College is the downtown campus of the city's community college system. It was actually constructed by 1986 although after thirteen years of "planning."

Three of these projects (Franklin Street Connector, Loop College, and the stadium) reach back to Richard J. Daley years and he had no better luck with them than his successors. As early as 1971, Daley appointed a committee to select a site for a new stadium. Conservationists quickly rose to protest the lakefront sites selected, and Daley appointed another committee which quietly buried the issue. The Chicago 21 plan did not openly mention the stadium, but some of its color plates showed grass in place of the stadium and many assumed it was to be replaced. Thus, when Daley proposed rebuilding Soldier Field in 1975, he was opposed because it went against his own plan. By that date, however, the Bears were threatening to move to the suburbs. Daley first proposed a modest face-lift for the Bicentennial and, six months later, a much more ambitious expansion and reconstruction of the stadium.[29] The face-lift, at city expense, actually took place, but widespread opposition to the issuance of tax exempt bonds stalled the expansion project. Daley died shortly afterward.

Daley had no better luck with the Franklin Street Connector and Loop College. Funding of both projects depended upon an agreement between the mayor and the governor, and the subway required the agreement of federal authorities as well. Governor Walker had objections to both plans and that eventually opened up the way for more extensive objections from other groups. The media raised questions about the wisdom of putting so much money into a subway that would serve only the Central Area, and the Business and Professional People for the Public Interest opposed it because it would serve mostly whites. Repeated federal requests to clarify the plans and cost estimates whittled away at public confi-

29. Daley also became furious with the Bears, saying that he would deny them the use of the city's name if they moved to the suburbs. There was always some doubt as to the seriousness of the suburban negotiations, but they failed also because of opposition to the use of tax exempt bonds. An earlier proposal by Daley to expand the Chicago Stadium for the Black Hawks failed for the same reason.

dence. By the time of Daley's death, local civic groups like the MHPC had begun separate studies of the project.[30]

The first site selected for Loop College was adjacent to the existing building in the North Loop, and some of the land was purchased as early as 1969. With the encouragement of the State Street Council, however, Daley endorsed an alternative site on south State Street in the hope of bringing some consumer-minded students into the area. There was no pedagogic reason for the shift of sites, and none was given. Thus, it was not long before a number of individuals and groups, most notable the American Institute of Architects, began to propose alternative plans which would have eliminated the "porno row" to the south. The Illinois Capital Development Board, controlled by Governor Walker, opened up the site selection process again, and doubts grew over the advisability of displacing the John Marshall Law School and a number of other businesses and institutions. The college system itself underwent progressively critical examination.[31] By the time of Daley's death, portions of the land site had been purchased, but that commitment was to prove indefensible as a new governor vetoed the funds for expansion.

Several subsequent partnerships under Bilandic, Byrne, and Washington experienced the same difficulties as their proposals inadvertently opened up the evaluation process to a wider public. Under Bilandic, Loop College, Navy Pier, the Franklin Street Connector, and the stadium were under continuous and uninvited review as individuals prompted court challenges (on the pier, connector, and mall) or landmark designations or carried out their own evaluative studies. The most persistent criticism came from the MHPC which pointed out the unconditional financial liability of the city at Navy Pier, gave its own separate recommendations on stadium sites, and provided a revised plan for the subway. In asking for more effective applications and plans for the subway and mall, the

30. There was never a massive protest against the Monroe-Franklin Street subway because it never seemed to get anywhere. Bilandic downsized it to the scale suggested by the MHPC, and Byrne bargained it away in her transportation agreement with Governor Thompson.

31. There were faculty strikes in 1973, 1975, and 1978. At one point the faculty voted no confidence in the college president who had presided over the system since it was founded. The system experienced declining enrollment over much of the period after 1973. Despite an annual budget of $159 million in 1980, employers do not take its graduates seriously. In 1981, only 8 percent of those enrolled in the high school equivalency program could pass the final examination (*Tribune*, 3 October 1981).

The Big Project and the Politics of Urgency

federal government raised questions which prolonged the decision-making process and encouraged doubt and criticism from other groups, such as conservationists and landmark preservationists.[32] The state legislature and the governor found in these delays additional arguments for their own resistance or political ambitions. Similarly, both the stadium and Navy Pier became bones of contention between the patronage-minded Park District and the mayor's private developers. The coordination of city and state departments, especially the Department of Streets and Sanitation, the Department of Public Works, and the Chicago Transit Authority created persistent difficulties. Daley may have been able to overcome at least this kind of opposition, but his successors were more dependent upon popular support.

In almost every instance, especially in the post-Daley years, the mayors and governors found in these projects some claim for their own reelection or for the weakness of their adversaries. Governor Walker held up the funds for the college to embarrass Daley. Bilandic hastily embraced all of Daley's projects without any indication of priority or before they could be revised to assemble broader support. Byrne seemed almost breathless as she raced from one project to another, promising more than she could deliver at Navy Pier, the North Loop, and the library.

Probably the most premature of Byrne's announcements was the public release on Expo Park which, she said, was to break ground just as her reelection bid began. The developers had only an option on a portion of the land site and no agreement with financial backers. There were many people who thought that a permanent industrial exhibit was a grand opportunity, and they were willing to work hard to build support for it. Some people, however, had objections to the extent of the lakefront site (e.g., MHPC), and still others (South Side Planning Board and South Loop developers) had alternative plans for much of the site. The developers of Expo Park had a history of difficulty in finding financial backing (*Tribune*, 24 June 1984), and without a firm land site and a general agreement on how it would link up with other projects (especially the 1992 World's Fair) there seemed little chance of financial backing.

When Washington first came into office he backed off from

---

32. Part of the plan for the Franklin Street Connector included the removal of the downtown El which preservationists had gotten placed on the National Register.

many of Byrne's projects just as she had backed off from Bilandic's projects. He did give formal support to the new Central Area plan and Navy Pier. The latter, however, slipped through his fingers and into the Council Wars before he could recognize that the Rouse company had an outstanding affirmative action program. Washington, however, was at his best in the negotiations over the Chicago Theater in the North Loop where he stepped aside and let his planning commissioner negotiate a firm deal before running to the media. When he declared that "Chicago was on a roll," he only set himself up for a fall when his lease tax bombed and threatened the remaining projects in the North Loop.

None of this should be taken to imply that any of the downtown projects aroused massive opposition throughout the city. Instead, the usual pattern was one of prolonged delay in negotiations, an increase in critical media attention, and the gradual emergence of organized opposition, sometimes from established civic groups, sometimes from another unit of government. All of this resulted in a decline in public confidence and, frequently, a political candidate ready to take the opposing view. The thread that runs most obviously through all these projects, then, is the rather desperate use of them as an electoral platform to run on or to oppose. The result was a planning process that depended almost entirely on showmanship.

Of course, even when the confidence game becomes transparent, it does not always exactly fail, and three of the nine projects mentioned above did survive to some sort of completion. So long as you count your successes that way, however, the costs go unrecognized. One additional project so well illustrates these costs that its description can conclude this chapter.

McCormick Place and the Illinois Theater State

As early as 1979, it was recognized that McCormick Place, the world's largest exposition center, would have to be expanded to meet the competition from other cities and to accommodate the growing scale of trade shows. By that time the exhibit hall's board had adopted the slogan, "Two Million [square feet] by 2000," but it was not before 1982 that studies for expansion got underway. Late that year, just as Byrne was facing Washington in the Democratic

The Big Project and the Politics of Urgency

primary, plans were released. Hastily assembled,[33] the plan called for a bargain basement building of undistinguished design crouched directly on the Outer Drive. At all the meetings I attended, including the unveiling, there was disappointment in its appearance and location, but resignation to its necessity. According to its designers, Lester B. Knight and Skimore, Owings and Merrill, it was supposed to come in at about $150 million.

Byrne, however, lost the election, and Washington was reluctant to take his first step by supporting a 1.5 percent tax on the city's "hospitality industry" (*Sun-Times*, 3 November 1983). The state legislature was no more eager to impose the tax without Washington's support so they just deferred action on the matter. It was over six months before the restaurant and hotel tax was abandoned and the legislature approved the use of tax exempt state bonds. Already the figure was up to $252 million.

There was a momentary pause when it was discovered that the annex and its parking lot would wall off almost a mile and a half of lakefront. An old 1919 ordinance requiring public access was exhumed by the planning commissioner. The exhibit hall board took the position that an ordinance frequently violated in the past could be flagrantly violated in the present. Desperate for time, however, the board gave in and added almost $2 million to its budget for walkways, and the Chicago Plan Commission approved the project.

The construction director was a thirty-three-year-old architect who had never managed such a large site, but what he lacked in experience was made up for in assurances that the building would come in on time and under budget (*Tribune*, 4 May 1985; 21 July 1985). The first cost overruns were publicized in February of 1985, but that was not too bad; they only cut into much of the reserve fund. However, as cost overruns continued, what was to be a budget building became an austerity building as amenities and comforts quickly disappeared (*Tribune*, 21 July 1985). By May there was a minor scandal when it was learned that the exterior panels of the building might not be fireproof and had been approved by a committee including a consultant from the firm manufacturing the panels (*Tribune*, 7 May 1985). The panels were replaced before they could be tested, but there was still a delay in construction. By mid-June, it was no longer possible to ignore the cost overruns, and the

---

33. The investigative committees were to reveal that the general practice was a "design as you go" construction schedule (*Tribune*, 21 July 1985).

board began to lobby the state legislature during the waning days of their session for an additional $55 million (*Tribune*, 16 June 1985; 21 June 1985). Angered by having practically no time to consider the request or to manage some concealment for their impotence, the legislature adjourned without any decision on the additional allocation.

At that point the curtain was raised on the Illinois theater state. It was somewhat like Rashomon would be if staged by David Mamet. The suburban-based Republican house minority leader started the action with a declamation on the purificatory powers of a state takeover of the exhibit hall (*Sun-Times*, 20 June 1985). The Democratic Speaker of the House then spoke of "smokescreens" (*Sun-Times*, 29 June 1985) and, indeed, it was revealed that the firm with the highest proportional overrun was the major contributor to the minority leader's political fund (*Tribune*, 7 July 1985). The governor, "Big" Jim Thompson, already chafing by some unnecessary[34] criticism for the 100 percent cost overruns on his State of Illinois building, said that the House Speaker was in a jocular mood (*Sun-Times*, 29 June 1985), toying with the press.

Now the board arrived to dialogue with two legislative committees. It could not be their fault; they had only forgotten to have the contracts signed (*Sun-Times*, 24 July 1985) and bent the rules to accommodate minority contractors and please the mayor (*Sun-Times*, 30 June 1985; *Tribune*, 21 July 1985). "Not me," said the politically well-connected contractors.[35] They had informed the project director they would need much more money shortly after they had won the contracts at very reasonable bids (*Tribune*, 2 July 1985). An

34. Unnecessary because there was not much anyone could do about it. The state building was not a partnership, and it went into the ground before anyone could do anything about the large overruns. Actually, there was not much criticism—only cynicism.

35. The largest contract went to Schal and McHugh, the latter being run by a partner and brother to a member of the Park District Board. McHugh hired AIC Security in which it had a part ownership along with Alderman Vrdolyak's brother. Larry Bullock, a state representative and leading advocate of the $252 million bond issue, was given a 40 percent share in one of the firms contracting for the project. John Simon, a close friend of Governor Thompson, handled much of the legal work on the bond issue. Eugene Heytow, part owner of the adjacent McCormick Hotel, had previously served as chairman of the exhibit hall board during its early plans for expansion, and as chairman of a local bank had made substantial loans to both the managing director of McCormick Place and Governor Thompson. The plans for the annex included an underground walkway directly to the unprofitable hotel Heytow had taken off the hands of the teamsters union.

The Big Project and the Politics of Urgency

executive of Lester B. Knight added to this chorus that he had warned the project director that the bid rules were being consciously subverted to assist a firm headed by Alderman Vrdolyak's brother (*Sun-Times*, 24 August 1985) and a state legislator who had led the drive to fund the annex (*Sun-Times*, 1 July 1985).

Since practically everyone seemed blameless, all eyes turned upon the general manager of the exhibit hall who had received rather extraordinary loans from the banker-owner of the McCormick hotel which is adjacent to the annex (*Sun-Times*, 11 September 1985). One member of the board, an ex-U.S. special attorney whose very name strikes terror in the hearts of corrupt judges, solemnly observed that appearances are realities and that the general manager must go (*Sun-Times*, 18 September 1985). Exit general manager, ex-Chicago school superintendent.

Despite this courageous act of self-purification, a trio of gubernatorial candidates unsettled the apparent resolution with an unflattering exchange on each other's character. Stepping aside from this exchange between "quitters," "henpecked husbands," "imperial potentates," and "dismal failures" (*Tribune*, 1 September 1985; 23 October 1985), "Big" Jim brought forward an almost holy man, a man who came from the Daley years.[36] He had just one tragic flaw. He had opposed Washington in his contest with Byrne, and it was said that he might run later as the Republican mayoral candidate. Now the mayor and the governor were locked in combat over who would be the white knight to rescue the annex. Finally, the governor stepped aside and in a soliloquy asked for "reason and patience" (*Sun-Times*, 2 October 1985). What happened, however, was that the construction firms began to pull out of the project and there was the threat that they would file for the $70 million in anticipated profits (*Tribune*, 3 November 1985). This *deus ex machina* brought a sudden quiet to all on stage, and like all good comedies this one had a happy ending. In a "bargain worthy of Solomon" (*Tribune*, 12 November 1985), the governor got his holy man as a trustee on an interim board, and the mayor got to name its chairman. There was also a final act of purification. The $60 million for the annex would be funded with a sin tax on cigarettes.

I use Geertz's image of the theater state here, not only because it seems an apt description of such a show of power but because

36. Ex-Governor Richard Ogilvie who, although a Republican, had set a high watermark for cooperation with Daley.

The Big Project and the Politics of Urgency

Geertz suggests that the more elaborated the display of power, the weaker its substance (1980, pp. 121–133). The confidence game had become too transparent to sustain public conviction. True, the annex got its financing, but it cast a long shadow over the city's 1992 World's Fair. Chicago's plans for the 1992 fair were put to rest by the state legislature about nine days after officials from McCormick Place began to lobby them for an additional $55 million.

SIX

FROM THE CITY BEAUTIFUL TO THE COMMUNITY UNDER GLASS

Many observers will notice that so far I have omitted any reference to Chicago's most successful and impressive example of recent land-use planning: the South Loop or, as it is now termed, Burnham Park. Unquestionably Burnham Park is a well-executed instance of a new community. Lying just south of the Loop, the area had become a collection of underused industrial buildings, warehouses, converted storefronts, downscale taverns, and single-room occupancy hotels. It is now the site of expensive loft apartments, two new large-scale residential developments, several smaller ones, and a number of retail outlets that can attract a growing night-time trade from Loop visitors. It has over 10,000 residents, land values have soared, property taxes have increased, and investment is spreading to adjacent areas.

The planning for Burnham Park reaches back into the Daley years, and many of those responsible for it attribute its success to the exceptional alliance he fostered between investors and city administrators. There is some truth to this, but it seems to me that Burnham Park also owes much of its success to a learning experience that stretches back eighty years and includes a series of more flawed developments that provide the variation from which a more effective planned community could be designed. The planning for Burnham Park is informed by the most persistent problem of American cities, the absolute need for assurances of social control. From this overriding consideration, one can more fully appreciate the importance of its site (adjacent to downtown), building design (passive and active security systems), housing mix (distinguished buildings, rental and for-sale property) and, above all, its dominance by middle-income residents.

Since this learning experience is articulated only in the scattered recollections of individuals and fugitive pieces of literature, let me begin by recounting some of the more flawed efforts that preceded Burnham Park. They begin with a rather utopian vision and follow an irregular course toward the essential recognition of social control as the defining parameter of residential planning.

The City Beautiful

The City Beautiful movement had one of its better moments in Chicago with the 1893 Columbian Exposition. Burnham's Fair was both a demonstration of the promise of city planning and a display of a controlled environment which managed a great congress of people within what was essentially a model of urbane civility.

> Specially organized police and fire forces, new water and electrical systems, novel transport devices all supported the visitor surges. There was an obsession with demonstrating the orderly management the expositions enforced on the perils of social congestion. These affairs were to be safe, clean, peaceful and easy to move through.

> ...Artists delighted in showing the [Chicago] Fair with well dressed, refined, obviously cultivated ladies and gentlemen strolling through its avenues, sitting in gardens, admiring its monuments. Americans could wander with a permissiveness national police made possible in Old World Cities, but not in the New.

> ...The Fair was a city that worked. While it retained the appeal of urban contrasts, it attempted to freeze them into peaceful coexistence, seeking to control their energies as well as their picturesqueness. This was, if you will, both the great problem of the American city, and the Chicago Fair's accomplishment. (Neil Harris 1984, pp. 8–9)

Sullivan (1956), of course, complained of the exposition's backward search for architectural leadership, and others (Scott 1969, pp. 100–109) have cited the fair's impotence in imposing its vision on our cities. But the fair was a great popular success, and one can hardly start a conversation on urban planning without some mention of it. The Columbian Exposition was one of those contested but exemplary events. It heightened aspirations for a controlled environment and at the same time raised doubts about its democracy.

Despite this nagging doubt, the aspiration to reshape the conduct of the lowest social class has stamped many other Chicago efforts at urban planning. At the time of the Columbian Exposition, this aspiration captured the imagination not only of architects and reformers but that of the captains industry as well. George Pullman was probably the most ambitious of these entrepreneurs, creating an entire community of 12,000, complete with model institutions and nearby employment. At first regarded as one of the marvels of the industrial age, the town of Pullman progressively came under criticism as being responsible for the manipulation of one class by another (Buder 1967, pp. 92–104). Then, in the 1894 strike against the Pullman works, the effort at paternalism simply came undone when Pullman the employer lowered their wages and Pullman the landlord raised their rents. By 1907, the community was sold to private bidders. By 1930 it was a "run-down, lower working-class neighborhood pock marked with blight" and commanding rents "well below the surrounding area" (Buder 1967, p. 226).

The story of Pullman, however, does not end there. George Pullman had built on such a scale and with sufficient architectural quality that middle-income investors have filtered in over the last two decades and thoroughly gentrified the place! It is now an island which commands rents *well above* the surrounding area. Highly legible (Lynch 1960) with clear boundaries and a self-contained set of private and public facilities, it is *defensible space* (Newman 1973). If it could not reform the poor, it could capture a new middle-income resident increasingly attracted to the comparative rarity of "period" housing.

Although the initial fate of Pullman must have been discouraging, Marshall Field opened his much smaller (628 units) Garden Apartments in a "run-down Italian slum" (Marciniak 1986, p. 23) in 1928. Hoping to set a higher standard of home maintenance for the neighborhood, the Garden Apartments were never able to draw rents that would cover operating costs and, within a decade, had come to resemble the level of home maintenance in the neighborhood. Philanthropy had failed again for the Garden Apartments were not large or self-sufficient enough to create the defensible space that appeals to post-World War II gentrifiers. After several changes in ownership, it is now sometimes referred to as "Cabrini North" (Marciniak 1986, p. 154).

Julius Rosenwald, a contemporary of Field, made a similar effort with his Michigan Boulevard Apartments which were built on about the same scale on Chicago's South Side. These apartments, also recognized for their exemplary design, enjoyed a few years of superior tenancy but then succumbed to the deterioration around them. Attempts to renovate them under nonprofit management failed twice because of tenant opposition. They are now under the

From the City Beautiful to the Community Under Glass

management of the Chicago Housing Authority which thoroughly removes them from any "danger" of gentrification. This danger, of course, was never very great. Two small to dominate their site, they also lacked self-sufficient or nearby commercial and public facilities. They were buildings, not a defensible community.

By the time of the Great Depression, Chicago philanthropists could point to three clear failures at community building and no successes. The burden of providing exemplary housing for the poor became the responsibility of federal and local government. I will not repeat the dreary history of that effort, but only say that the Chicago Housing Authority repeated most of the errors of the philanthropists and added some of their own. They did not build defensible space with its own self-contained services. They were buildings, not communities. Certainly they were highly legible and built on a scale sufficient to dominate their site, but they are so lacking in architectural merit that it is hard to believe that they can ever attract anything but a dependent population. In a way they repeated Pullman's error in management. Public authorities became both landlord and chief provider of income with the twist that this landlord could not sell off the properties, insist on self-sustaining rents, or engage in mass evictions. The only limit to costs was the frequency with which the plight of the residents could be dramatized so as to embarrass successive presidential administrations to provide more money.

The first planned departures from the extension of public housing in Chicago were Lake Meadows (1956–1960; 2,000 units), Carl Sandburg Village (1956–1960; 2,000 units), and Prairie Shores (1958–1962; 1,700 units). The first of these consisted of a series of high rise buildings, widely separated from one another by large parking lots and open space. The development, however, did include a retail shopping center and one building that was billed as a community center but functional mainly as a restaurant.

Prairie Shores flanked the west side of Michael Reese Hospital a few blocks to the north of Lake Meadows, and the buildings were placed close enough together that the intervening space did not seem a no-man's land as it did in Lake Meadows.[1] Both developments were assisted by land write-downs, but they were able to ask

---

1. Galen Cranz made systematic observations on the use of open space in both areas. More people used the tiny open spaces around Prairie Shores than the much larger ones around Lake Meadows.

for market rents. Despite the proximity of over 5,000 units of public housing, both became occupied by middle-income renters and, initially, they were able to attract both black and white residents. In 1968, Lake Meadows had a 70 : 30 ratio of blacks to whites, and Prairie shores was just about the opposite. These ratios were possible because of an affirmative action policy that favored whites, for before 1968 this was tolerated in private housing.

After the racial unrest of the late 1960s, however, it was progressively difficult to attract whites to Lake Meadows which became almost entirely black. By the 1980s HUD began a much more aggressive policy of affirmative action for blacks, and Prairie Shores also became largely black although still middle income. During the same period the shopping center in Lake Meadows failed. Nonetheless, both developments were constructed on a scale sufficient to create relatively defensible space, and each has maintained a middle-income residential population. Many people are critical of the design of both developments, but they are still functioning and self-supporting pieces of the landscape. Their most notable failure is their inability to prompt any additional investment into the area. I will more fully explore some of the reasons for that in the next section.

Carl Sandburg Village is a much more controversial development because it was built in an area (the Near North Side) which was already undergoing gentrification. It was also financed with the promise that it would include some subsidized housing which was later eliminated from the plan. In some ways, however, the village was a "great success." It quickly filled up with self-supporting people, redevelopment in the adjacent area accelerated, and it has subsequently been sold off to a homeowner population. People still complain about the lack of subsidized housing and the profits made from its sale, but it too is a functioning piece of the landscape.

By 1970, one could stand back from all these "natural" experiments and begin to draw some lessons. House-by-house recovery was occurring only on the north lakefront while there were vast areas of Chicago elsewhere underused or practically vacant. Pioneering these areas would have to occur on a large scale, and public housing was not the way to do it. One would have to create defensible space, that is, buildings close enough to provide informal surveillance. Local self-sufficiency or daily consumer needs would be essential, and a local school would especially enhance the community if it was to be integrated. It would have to be dominated by middle-income people. One might attract families to such a development—maybe people from the suburbs!

The Suburb in the City: South Commons

It was exactly this sort of deliberation that went into the planning and construction of South Commons. The developers were McHugh-Levin who had been encouraged by Mayor Daley to build a model community. He would do his best in insuring financing and city cooperation. Gordon and Levin, prize-winning architects, were to be the designers. Morris Janowitz consulted extensively with the developers and brought to their discussions an informed understanding of communities from a career spent largely in studying them. I entered these deliberations relatively late, well after most of the design decisions had been made, but when the first building opened I became a charter resident with the objective of evaluating its "success." All I had to do was to understand it and to publicize it. Or so I thought.

The financing for South Commons included 220 and 221 (d)(3) funds which meant that it would have an income mix of residents. The site lay only two blocks to the west of Prairie Shores, so we were confident of a similar racial mix and could anticipate that the two developments would add to the street life and commercial possibilities of the area. The design and placement of the buildings was innovative because they consisted of a mix of high rise, mid rise, and town houses grouped around four common areas that included shared space (swimming pools, play lots) to overcome the impersonality usually experienced in other high-density developments. Although each group of buildings was placed in a park-like setting, all the open areas were readily accessible to visual inspection and within earshot of the residential buildings. The town houses added for-sale housing to what was otherwise a rental community of 1,500 units. Visually there was no way of telling the subsidized from the unsubsidized buildings. There was an ingenious provision to have the income from the shopping center provide support for a community center. The community center was built on top of the parking lot where it could obscure automobiles and house a school that would integrate the racial and income mix in South Commons and a small portion of the student population from Prairie Courts (public housing and not to be confused with Prairie Shores) who were all black and low income. The district police station was adjacent to what was to be the shopping center. There was direct bus service to the Loop, and the South Side El was only two blocks away. Much of the surrounding area was vacant, but here and there you could see the spire of a Baptist, Lutheran, Catholic, and Episcopal church that had escaped "renewal."

The construction and rental of the first group of buildings (which included no subsidized housing) left us all optimistic. The racial ratio was 70 : 30 in favor of whites, about the same as that in Prairie Shores. We were surprised at the small number of children, even among blacks. Still, there was a scattering of school-age children and enough to start a KG-3 school which would include a number of children from the nearby school in Prairie Courts. Children from a small residential compound adjacent to the Illinois Institute of Technology were included to enlarge the number of white children.[2]

The effort to establish the school was an enlightening experience. Perhaps the most notable difficulty was that practically any decision (hiring of teachers, curriculum, selection of students from Prairie Courts, testing of students, etc.) required a time-consuming trip downtown to negotiate with top school administrators. To some extent this was overcome by having an assistant superintendent sit on an advisory board that already included the district superintendent, principal, one of the developers, two local ministers, representatives from Prairie Courts, parents from South Commons, a consultant from the University of Chicago Department of Education, an occasional parent from IIT, and myself. (There was only about sixty students in the school and about twenty-five members on the board.) While this could slightly speed up our negotiations with the school administration, it soon became obvious that the administration was very shy of the experiment. They were alarmed by the use of racial quotas, the exceptional enrichment of the program (e.g., foreign language training), the hiring of three teachers outside their order of seniority, the insurance coverage for moving children between school buildings, a privately sponsored annual pre- and post–testing program, the private usage of schoolrooms during the

2. IIT included a small fenced-in residential compound. The fencing of the compound was among those "stories" that Prairie Court residents recounted as a parable of past betrayals. The inclusion of the children from IIT heightened thee apprehensions of future betrayal. At first, however, few of us understood these parables of betrayal.

From the City Beautiful to the Community Under Glass

evening hours; indeed, almost anything that differed from standard practice in Chicago schools.[3] As one school administrator told me later, "It all looked so unfair."

Indeed, it was "unfair" if one's aspiration was to replicate the shoddy performance of other Chicago public schools. We aspired to create a superior school which might first influence the "sister" school in Prairie Courts and then prove a model for wider efforts at ad hoc experiments in the racial and economic integration of public schools.[4] The school administrators, however, were just emerging from a brutal confrontation between Martin Luther King's massive marches to get rid of the previous school superintendent and Daley's intransigence in doing so.[5] The previous superintendent had been replaced, and a large number of black teachers from marginal institutions had been hired. Heavily dependent upon union protection for their jobs, they were strong supporters of the union and at the time were said to be the best paid teachers in the country.[6] School administrators, then, were extremely anxious not to give the teachers or the parents any cause for complaint lest they inflame a situation that had only partially subsided. Raising the standards in any one school might lead to charges of favoritism.

These charges were not long in coming. The board representatives from Prairie Courts were not primarily the parents of children but older people who had some time on their hands and some depth

3. Many of the things we were requesting are done by a few innovative principals who either do not inform the administrators of what they are doing or get around them in ingenious ways, for example, able teachers are told to apply for a position well in advance of a last-minute announcement of an opening.

4. Previous experience had dissuaded us from attempting any system-wide changes through the administration either because they would prompt resistance by the union and administrators or suffer what David Street (1969, pp. 1–15) has called "death through incorporation." That is, an announcement is sent out saying that a particular practice is now required in the school system without any training or oversight to see if it actually occurs.

5. Superintendent Benjamin Willis had been the main target of King's civil rights marches in Chicago. He was known as "Ben the builder" because of the number of new schools constructed to house black students rather than sending them to underused white schools.

6. Local blacks from Prairie Courts made a sharp distinction between "dedicated" teachers, most of them hired before Willis's tenure, and teachers who "left at 2:30." During the time I lived in the area, there was a teacher's strike, and my discussions with the teachers revealed a similar division between those who saw the strike's aim as "better working conditions" (i.e., local selection of teachers, control over curriculum, and classroom composition, etc.) and those who said its aim was higher wages. Although this division of opinion reached the press, it would not have been obvious to the casual reader as to what was meant by "better working conditions."

of experience as community leaders. In no sense were they "militants"; they came from an earlier period in which self-help and status equality had been the main themes of black community organization. They were particularly likely to disagree with others, like myself, who had read the Coleman report to mean that black students would benefit educationally from direct contact with white students if neither group numerically dominated the other. Their view was that white schools were better because they got better books, smaller classroom sizes, newer buildings, or more resources in general. They were opposed to keeping class sizes small to preserve a numerical balance between income and racial levels, they were suspicious of the choice of books for the South Commons school which were different from those used in "our school" (the school in Prairie Courts), they were concerned over the amount of time the principal spent at South Commons, and they lobbied very hard to have an equal number of students transferred to "our school" (South Commons never became "our school") as was being transferred in the opposite direction.

What was being asked for was fundamental and exact reciprocity, almost the same kind of standardization that school administrators preferred. Eventually, the extension school board did adopt a language that evaded as nearly as possible all references to race, income, ability, and residence. But that did not quite solve the problem. Neither the black nor white parents in South Commons would send their children to the school in Prairie Courts in any number. Black and white parents from South Commons wanted enriched classes while the representatives from Prairie Courts wanted basic education. The representatives from Prairie Courts wanted stricter discipline in the classroom, but they were less concerned about parent and school patrols to supervise movement between schools. As they pointed out, it was natural for children to fight outside school. The teachers were what kept them from fighting while in school.

The situation, however, was more complicated than this suggests because of two other groups: the PTA in the Prairie Courts school, and the "Concerned Parents" who emerged shortly after the opening of the extension school. Both groups included almost exactly the same residents from Prairie Courts as were on the board of the extension school, but each group functioned differently. One would go to the extension board meetings where a very evasive language avoided any invidious comparisons and compromises were reached

From the City Beautiful to the Community Under Glass

more by endurance than by enthusiastic agreement. At the PTA,[7] the meeting would start with the pledge of allegiance, a reading of the minutes of the previous meeting, their invariable approval, followed by the principal's and vice-principal's reports. These reports would be approved, and there would be some announcements. Then we would adjourn for coffee. If you went to a meeting of the Concerned Parents, the scene would suddenly erupt in a series of loudly declared grievances, allegations, and protests. As it was explained to me, all this was very simple. The PTA was supposed to support the school; the Concerned Parents was the "fighting group."

A lot of these grievances had nothing to do with either school but were related as stories about past betrayals which I only later came to understand as parables to convey apprehensions about future betrayals.[8] In addition, there seemed to be a remarkable confidence in "Mr. Levin's" (one of the developers) ability to move mountains. The Concerned Parents often (not always) notified me of their meetings so that I could tell him their complaints and parables. Their confidence in "Mr. Levin" did not at all extend to me ("Jerry"), "Mr. Levin has money in this project and he controls it. You ain't got no say-so." On innumerable occasions, then, it was necessary to get "Mr. Levin" to come to the meetings to resolve an impasse on school policy or on any number of other issues: police harassment, traffic stops, crossing guards, parking spaces, the cross traffic from other public housing developments, etc. On many of these issues he was powerless, but only "Mr. Levin" could give them a definite "no."

The management of the school and interracial relations were complicated by the opening of the subsidized housing which attracted a preponderance of black children who had to be enrolled in

7. At first the PTA included only residents from Prairie Courts. I (or my membership fee) was recruited to this PTA before there were any students in the extension. The fact that I had no children was not at issue for very few of the members of the PTA had school-age children. Later the PTA came to include more members from South Commons.

8. For example, one story concerned how a swimming pool in one of the public housing developments had been located adjacent to an expressway, "so that whites could see how much they are giving these 'Niggers.' " This story was told at about the same time some children from Prairie Courts were allowed to swim at South Commons. There were lots of such stories, for example, the fence at Illinois Institute of Technology, the back room display of black products in one grocery store, the placement of a bus stop at Prairie Shores, etc.

the extension regardless of its racial or economic balance. Children and their parents from subsidized housing resented the fact that they could not swim in the pool at all hours unless they paid a fee. There were incidents between the children from Prairie Courts and those from South Commons despite a parents' brigade to manage the movement between each area. Under the best circumstances interracial relations were difficult in Chicago during the very early 1970s. We had just begun to adopt a rehearsed vocabulary in which Negroes were "black," black partronage was "affirmative action," intraracial crime was "genocide," and high decibel radios were "black culture." A particularly sore spot was the term "project." As the residents of Prairie Courts instructed me, "A project is a project until it is completed. Then it is a development. You live in a project. We live in a development."

A very few whites managed these disputed categories by becoming advocates for blacks, keeping one step ahead of them in vocabulary choices. Others simply played it very cool, saying little and letting their mute presence serve as tacit agreement. But South Commons had been engineered to bring people into at least casual acquaintance, and the whites recruited to South Commons found this an attractive feature. The housing had been promoted as a "suburb in the city," and the whites who first arrived there were neither "downtown cosmopolitans" nor active supporters of the black cause.[9] A few were quite religious, and several others were more than just conventional participants in their church. They were looking for a quiet neighborhood and a quiet interracial experience. The middle-income blacks were mainly people who saw in South Commons a housing bargain well within the familiar reaches of the South Side but not sandwiched into the half-cleared ghetto that reached from 35th to 47th Streets. Some did express a preference for integrated housing and schooling but they found demeaning the idea that whites might make some exceptional contribution through example or instruction. They also wanted a public vocabulary devoid of invidious comparisons between racial or income groups. Privately, of course, some middle-income blacks did confide to me a recognizable difference between themselves and those in public housing, but this did not extend to public talk. As the number of lower-income blacks increased in the extension, middle income blacks were just as quick to send their children to private schools.

9. Nor were they to any great extent from the suburbs.

From the City Beautiful to the Community Under Glass

For blacks this was a choice in favor of a better school. For whites it was a choice in favor of a whiter school.

Initially, it was possible to attract a high percentage of whites to South Commons by selective promotion (i.e., use the "white media"), but this did not expand to a secondary market through word of mouth. As more housing became available, the proportion of whites fell to 60 percent and declined thereafter both because the whites failed to replace themselves and new construction attracted a growing proportion of blacks. Within the space of eight years, from the opening of the first building, South Commons became 90 percent black, and the school extension was abandoned in 1979. Well before that time, the vast majority of middle-income black and white parents were sending their children to private schools.

These changing ratios and declining confidence in the school were not the result of outright confrontations between whites and blacks. Even during the urban riots following Martin Luther King's assassination, there was no notable change and the "Mother Ward"[10] was exceptionally quiet. The area had been so cleared of vestiges of exclusive white control that there were few targets left.[11] More important, many blacks, some of them from Prairie Courts, patrolled the street to insure everyone's safety. What gnawed at the whites' presence in South Commons was the quiet discomfort of insincerity.

By 1980, South Commons was no longer a project but, as the residents of Prairie Courts put it, a development. As it reached this stage of maturity it began to experience a number of difficulties. Almost two-thirds of the units were subsidized. Management had been routinized and tended to favor the less costly unsubsidized units. The costs of maintaining the subsidized units soared. Much of the commercial space was empty, and a restaurant that had turned into a bar had to be closed. The grocery store failed and remained closed for two years. There was no longer any attempt to obscure class differences, and the residents of the unsubsidized units—now called "luxury housing"—took exclusive possession of their "com-

10. Chicago's Second Ward which was the original electoral base for Oscar De-Priest's and William Dawson's successful entry into local and national politics (Gosnell 1935). Although vastly changed in appearance, there was some pride in its having given birth to the most durable and oldest black constituency in the nation.
11. Michael Reese Hospital and Medical Center and Mercy Hospital and Medical Center serve the black population and along with IIT are major employers.

mons space." Managers became less selective in filling the subsidized units. Some residents began to use the local alderman to represent their grievances to management. A previous tenants' organization had very nearly passed out of existence.

The management firm went through five local managers before finding someone who could regain control over the situation in 1985. A crucial step was to retain an investigative firm to screen tenants, especially those coming into subsidized housing. Another was to remove many of the on-site staff who had acquired a reputation for uncooperativeness and the "affirmative" issuance of maintenance contracts. A large investment had to be made in the repair of the subsidized units, including the removal of some "custodial" features (e.g., wired glass windows) that had crept into them. HUD had to be convinced to increase rent allowances and provide some funds for maintenance. A new grocery store manager was sought out and located in the shopping center. Rather than find another occupant for the restaurant, management began a search for its own operator. A portion of the community center has been taken over by a for-profit preschool program. Negotiations are underway with the Chicago Housing Authority to rent one floor in the center for a similar program for the children in the subsidized units. The "luxury units" have fewer children than ever,[12] but rental renewals have climbed to an impressive 90 percent over the last eighteen months. A small number of whites (about 5%) continue as residents, and they may be increasing in one of the buildings near Mercy Hospital so they can reach it without entering the rest of South Commons. In early 1984, there were over 150 vacancies, mostly in the "luxury units." in May of 1986, there were only thirty-one out of the total of approximately 500.

Anyone who walks through South Commons at the present time will see an attractive residential development, well treed and well groomed. The visible presence of security guards and a full-time roving security car give an added sense of safety. There has never been a serious problem of apartment break-ins, but cars are sometimes pillaged and purses snatched. The steel gratings on the windows of the grocery store and a sign inside that reads "No kids in this store without a note" is a reminder that one is still in the

12. Most of the children in the private preschool center come from outside South Commons.

Mother Ward. Residents in South Commons do not walk though the adjacent public housing, and excellent public transportation makes the area as much a bedroom community as any suburb.

South Commons, then, is an isolated island of "good planning." However, what was hoped to a "starter community" to stimulate adjacent development simply has not happened. Indeed, additional portions of the area have become vacant, and the shopping center in Lake Meadows remained closed for two years. Although there is a bit of media hype over gentrification in the "gap," a small area to the south, it is balanced by disinvestment elsewhere. Large areas of empty land and vacant lots make the area easily recognizable to anyone who has not seen it since 1970. Some people believe that the proposed World's Fair led speculators into the area, jacking up land values and pricing property out of the reach of other developers. Speculators did enter the area after 1980, but a land-use survey carried out just before its announcement (Suttles 1982) showed essentially the same pattern of inactivity.

South Commons may have been big enough to dominate its site, but its socioeconomic mix was just too extreme to overcome with casual good intentions. Too far from downtown to attract cosmopolitans, it cannot easily support its retail services. It faces the chronic problem of a shortfall in federal funding and requires an extraordinarily vigilant management.

The Instant Community under Glass:
Presidential Towers

Presidential Towers is a much more controversial housing development, and most urban planners would be appalled at my forthcoming argument that it has a better chance of spurring additional local investment than did South Commons. Some of the controversy is over its size; 2,460 units, all of them in four buildings and none larger than two bedrooms. Four massive forty-nine-story towers rise diagonally just five blocks from the Loop El on what was once the eastern end of Chicago's Skid Row but now better known as the site of Cleas Oldenburg's "Batcolumn." The buildings are joined at the third floor into a roofed area that covers two city blocks and is entered at a single lobby that opens up onto an atrium, bar, café,

From the City Beautiful to the Community Under Glass

Presidential Towers.

grocery store, newsstand, restaurant, and escalator that routes residents to a single security station where both an entry card and
phone-up system screen entrants through a second entrance.
House staff wear recognizable uniforms. Two-way radios cackle in
the background. A health club occupies much of the fourth floor,
and the roof provides a jogging track and regulation-size basketball
court. "Its awful," one critic told me. "Yuppieville!"

Still other critics object to the financing and regulatory exemp-
tion extended to the politically well-connected developers.[13] On
several occasions the developers obtained the direct intervention of
Governor Thompson, Senator Percy, and Representatives Dan Rostenkowski and Frank Annunzio. The project obtained the largest
insured federal low-interest mortgage ($158 million) ever commit-

13. The partners consist of Dan Shannon, ex-Park District president and former
business partner of Dan Rostenkowski; James McHugh, the brother and partner of
the president of the Park District board until 1986; and Daniel Levin, a cousin of Representative Carl Levin (D. Mich.), although the latter was elected to office after the
federal mortgage insurance was obtained. All had made contributions to Byrne's
campaign funds, but this is probably true of practically all Chicago builders.

ted. It was exempted from the requirement to include 20 percent subsidized housing and permitted accelerated depreciation. Both newspapers raised objections. The League of Women Voters was critical. But these well-publicized protests never aggregated or extended to a wider range of civic associations such as that which had opposed the Hilton Hotel tax break. One reason was that the bipartisan political support was just too awesome. Another was given by Annunzio: "My job is to bring federal funds to Chicago. I was protecting this project": that is, the distribution of the funds to Chicago rather than elsewhere (*Tribune*, 18 December 1983). But probably the more general reason for the scattering of opposition was that the developers had actually assembled their investors and supporters. The land had lain vacant for over ten years. No one could think of anything else that would be located in the area which was a mix of vacant land and underused commercial and industrial buildings. Presidential Towers might attract additional investment in the area that would create a more diverse mix of housing and commercial use. Concerted objection seemed hopeless in the absence of another alternative.

Once financing was obtained, the actual construction of the project went almost exactly the way it had been planned. Ground breaking occurred in August 1983, the leasing of the first tower began in January 1985 and the last of the towers was open for tenants in early 1986. A bar, café, newsstand, and grocery store were opened shortly after the residents arrived. All these services were subsidized or managed by the developers themselves on the assumption that Presidential Towers had to be an instant community, that the appearance of "community" had to be there from the start to reassure a cautious market. The first tower was 90 percent occupied within less than a year, the second and third about 40 percent occupied a few months later, and within thirty-six months Presidential Towers had 4,000 residents.

Most of the tenants have incomes from $25,000 to $30,000, but a few from the nearby futures market raise the average to well over $30,000. Most of them are young, childless whites in the early stages of their downtown careers and likely to move on as their income or family composition changes. During the 1986 season for lease renewals, about 75 percent renewed, a relatively low figure for Chicago, but Presidential Towers was built for high turnover. Most residents come from elsewhere in the city as young people rotate from slightly lower rent areas to a higher one or to apartments with new appliances.[14] A few elderly people have moved in, and they are said to especially like the intense security. At night the bar and café are a beehive of activity until 1:00 A.M. The vast skylights over the lobby define a huge urban space, filled with traffic, light, and bustle. The views from the diagonally spaced towers are among the most impressive in the city, with the Loop, parks, and the lake providing three layers of visual perspective. The project even came in at the expected cost.

On Mother's Day in 1986, a group of women picketed Presidential Towers demanding that its managers take Section 8 vouchers. Subsequently, the rental office was flooded with calls, roughly divided between residents alarmed that some of those vouchers might be allowed in and a host of others wanting to know how they could get on the list for Section 8 apartments. Although the developers were able to ride out this wave of criticism, they had to compromise by promising to provide some subsidized housing in a smaller, adjacent development they are proposing.

Reactions to this were mixed among the informants I questioned. Some thought that the number of proposed subsidized units was too small to diminish the area's attraction to private residential investors. What they pointed to was the readily visible evidence of loft conversions, the renovation of industrial buildings for office space, and new construction around the perimeter of Presidential Towers. Others, however, said that, while Presidential Towers had been critical in attracting investment into the West Loop, the threat of subsidized housing would essentially eliminate further residential proposals if they required federal mortgage insurance. Still, most thought that Presidential Towers had accomplished its aim. It was large enough to dominate its site, furnished with high-quality services from the start, its two-bedroom apartments would never require a school, and the security system was so obvious as to require no promotion. Presidential Towers may not be the City Beautiful, but it is a self-supporting piece of the landscape.

14. No one seems to know where the tenants for new rentals come from since the chain of movement is so long. Apparently young singles and couples cycle around the lakefront communities for years before buying a condo, or if they have children they purchase a home in the city or suburbs. There seems to be very little direct movement from the suburbs although some families formed while in the city may remain there if they can find the happy combination of a good school and a large enough home for children. The combination is rare and, therefore, expensive.

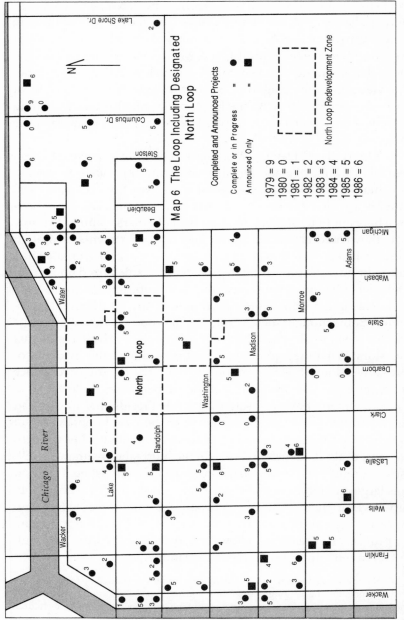

Map 6.1. The Loop, Including Designated North Loop

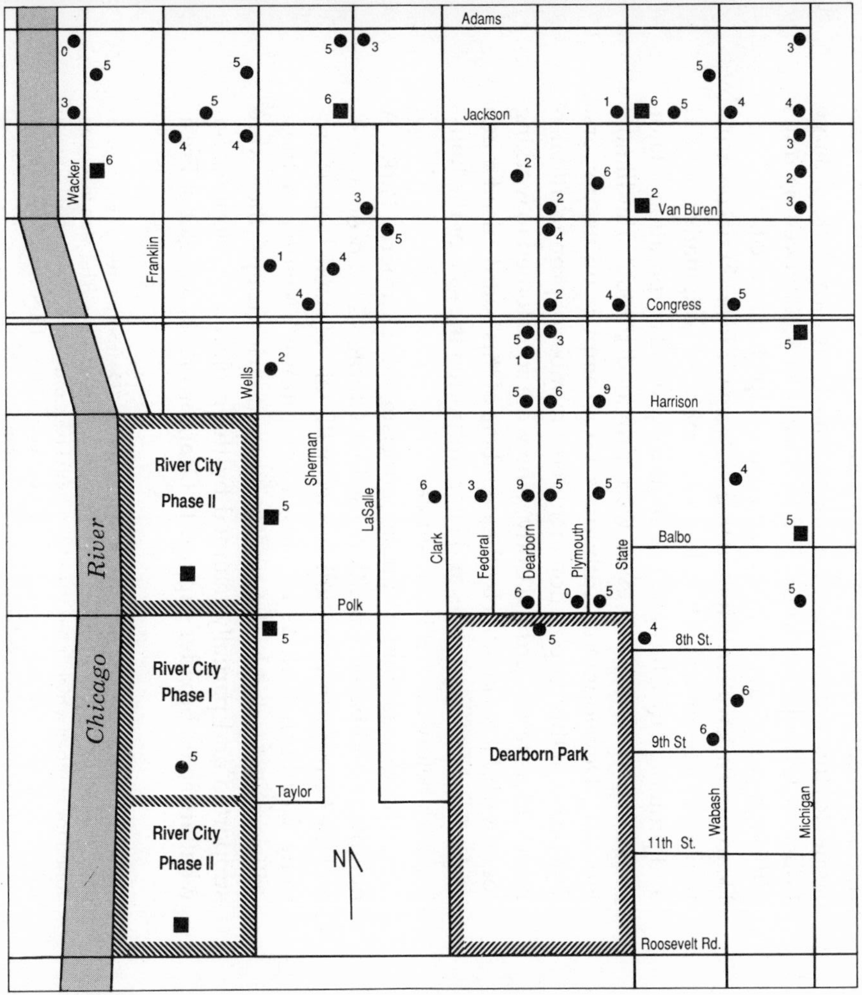

Map 6.2. The South Loop, or Burnham Park

Adams
Jackson
Van Buren
Congress
Harrison
Balbo
8th St.
9th St
11th St.
Roosevelt Rd.
Michigan
Wabash
State
Plymouth
Dearborn
Federal
Clark
LaSalle
Polk
Sherman
Taylor
Wells
Franklin
Wacker

Chicago River

River City Phase II
River City Phase I
River City Phase II

Dearborn Park

N

From the City Beautiful to the Community Under Glass

The Sentimental Favorite: Dearborn Park

The South Loop or Burnham Park has attracted far less criticism than Presidential Towers. The differences between the development of the South Loop and West Loop, however, are partly cosmetic but not for that reason unimportant.

At the outset the South Loop took on the appearance of preservation, and the role of private as against public investors has been better promoted. Lying south of Congress Parkway and extending to Roosevelt Road (see map 6.2) was an area of unused rail yards and declining industrial lofts. This existed until the late 1970s. The keystone to the area's redevelopment was Dearborn Park, a large housing development proposed to have over 3,000 dwelling units although "only" about 1,500 had been completed in the first phase. Dearborn Park was anticipated in the *Chicago 21 Plan*,[15] but construction did not begin until 1978. Land assembly was originally financed and promoted by Chicago 21, a limited dividend corporation. Major construction funds, however, were provided through the Illinois Housing Development Authority's tax exempt bonding powers. The board of this corporation included a number of prominent business leaders (and Cardinal Cody) who were accustomed to working together.[16] Firms headed by the members of this board raised much of the funds for land costs and later supported the sale of the housing with below-market interest rates.

There was minor public criticism of Dearborn Park. A neighborhood-based Coalition Against Chicago 21 did oppose it, and the Citizens Information Service of Illinois released a report profiling Dearborn Park as a "closed community." Neither of these criticisms extended to the city's important civic groups; they were supported and partially manned by the project's developers. But what attracted broader support to Dearborn Park, as against Presi-

15. First, as the "South Loop New Town," then as "Dearborn Green." Early plans make it look like South Commons with enclosed common areas. The plan was abandoned for another which interiorized common space much like Presidential Towers. This design, however, was replaced by a more conventional linear streetside development although it is accessible at only two entrances.

16. Thomas Ayers (Commonwealth Edison) was chairman, John Perkins (Continental Bank) was vice-chairman, and Philip Klutznick (Klutznick Enterprises) was chairman of the Executive Committee. Many of the other board members represented downtown firms, for example, Sears, Marshall Fields, Standard Oil, Arthur Anderson. The business leaders assembled were every bit as awesome as the political leaders assembled to promote Presidential Towers.

dential Towers, was its avowed purpose of introducing *family* life, school *children,* and landmark *preservation* into this mile-square tract at the southern boundary of the Central Business District.[17] The first phase would include 150 for-sale townhouses and over 1,000 condominiums, many of them with two or more bedrooms. Apparently, the developers also had control of much of the adjacent area which allowed them to promote its development as well. This included two blocks of industrial lofts, three landmark buildings, and still another large-scale residential development which would flank the river to the west. The old Dearborn Station, the last rail depot which might escape the wreckers' ball, would serve as a school.

From the start, then, Dearborn Park was a sentimental favorite. Daley supported it. Bilandic supported it. Byrne supported it. Despite this range of support, construction did not begin until 1978, largely because of the long queue for IDHA funds in a period of high-interest rates but also because an early physical design had to be scrapped. The general features of the plan, however, were modified only to give the buildings a more conventional appearance and include some subsidized housing for the elderly for which there was available financing.

Eight years later, however, there can be little doubt that the plan for Dearborn Park and its adjacent area are on track. Dearborn Park itself includes more than 1,500 dwelling units, almost all of them occupied, and the for-sale housing has appreciated in value. Practically all the loft space north of its has been converted to residential units, and similar conversions are occurring to the northwest (see map 6.2) among a scattering of "less distinguished" buildings. Those enthusiastic for historic preservation cannot be disappointed. Many of the old printers' buildings have been meticulously restored on the outside with fully occupied apartments on the inside. A church has located in a loft. One landmark building is to become a hotel. There is a growing number of retail establishments at street level, and the renewed facades and absence of projecting advertisements give the area an open feel while novel sidewalk attractions (seating and statuary) contribute to its sense of being inhabited. One can safely say that 99 percent of its 10,000 residents have moved in only after Dearborn Park broke ground. Local residents now support a neighborhood association with its own

17. Recall that "families" were to be the chief beneficiaries of all the plans published before Byrne's 1981 Comprehensive Plan which introduced the term "household" to accommodate gays and much of the black population.

a

b

South Loop, or Burnham Park: (a) Dearborn
Park; (b) Dearborn Station;   (c) River City.

From the City Beautiful to the Community Under Glass

c

newsletter, and there is an independent newspaper servicing the area. The racial balance is about 60 : 40 in favor of whites. A growing trickle of early theater-goers along South Michigan Avenue add to the evening foot traffic. In 1986, some conventional mortgages became available to people restoring older buildings. As one observer put it, "There are no bargains left in the entire area."

All this did not happen without interruptions and complications which draw out some parallels and contrasts with Presidential Towers. Unlike the developers of Presidential Towers, the developers of Dearborn Park did not use their own resources and managerial personnel to provide retail services to the new residents. The State Street Mall, two blocks north, was thought to be temporary alternative. But in Chicago one does not unhesitatingly go two blocks to pick up a loaf of bread if it means going past porno row and a mission hotel for the homeless. The developers did eventually lure in a White Hen Pantry and, later, independent entrepreneurs entered the area to provide a range of services. The lack of services, however, were a real source of complaint and one of the experiences taken into account during the development of Presidential Towers.

Also, as it turned out, the developers were able to gain control over the entire South Loop only by exerting themselves far more than expected. The principal challenge came from Bertram Goldberg, a prominent architect and developer who had been marginal to the original limiteda dividend corporation. Goldberg, however, had the backing of Chessie Resources and an established partner with a strong record of previous success. Goldberg was to develop the sliver of land that lay along the Chicago River, a prime site and one that would serve both as a boundary and an entrance to the west end of the community. Goldberg's "River City," however, alarmed practically everyone. River City was to consist of six "triads," each including three seventy-two-story buildings joined by service bridges at every eighteenth floor; altogether eighteen buildings, each with 1,000 dwelling units on forty-seven acres, or a density of 500,000 people per square mile.

For the other developers, this raised the specter of other hotly debated megablock development (e.g., Sandburg Village) in Chicago and simply undermined their promotion of a family centered community. A more quietly voiced concern was that over 3,000 units could open up each year, swamping the rental market and, if unoccupied, opening the possibility of subsidized tenants. Practically all the civic groups who had supported the earlier plan opposed Goldberg's addition to it. Goldberg replied by portraying himself as the innovator besieged by the establishment. As a student of Courbosier, he was being picked on. Who cared, he asked, if the rentals had to be subsidized? A family was not to be judged by its pocketbook. River City was the "democracy of architecture," and its pie-shaped rooms would return man to his primordial proclivity for tepees and caves (*Chicago Magazine*, December 1977).

Of course, lots of people did care about the size of Goldberg's buildings and the size of their tenants' pocketbook. The problem was that Goldberg had brought in one sentimental favorite to oppose another. What his opposition had to emphasize, then, was the chicken-warren appearance of Goldberg's buildings and their unsuitability for family living. Their argument prevailed, and once again it was the rhetoric of sentiment that won the day. A chastened Goldberg lost his financial backers. Then, in what seemed a remarkable grasp of the requirements of this rhetoric, Goldberg came in with a design tailor-made to its specifications. The new River City was to be a much lower, serpentine building that followed the river edge. It could be constructed in stages, the first including only 450 units. Although eventually to include 2,500 units, its great length makes the eleven-story structure appear remarkably low. The design does include spectacle; the serpentine shape, a yacht harbor, a

From the City Beautiful to the Community Under Glass

health club, and an interior street with a multistory atrium. All these elements are understated, and the room, neither pie-shaped nor circular, are only slightly oval. River City may never attract many families with children, but its low profile leaves that claim undisturbed.

Somewhat the same rhetorical requirements can be seen in the security system that has taken form in Dearborn Park. Far more passive than that of Presidential Towers, it is nonetheless impressive. Only one entrance admits automobiles, and a second pedestrian entrance was opened only after the residents settled in. Uniformed doormen, not guards, are stationed *inside* each high rise alongside a call-up system to *announce* visitors. An interiorized park is not visible from the surrounding streets. The postage-sized yards of the town houses are surrounded by *ornamental* iron fences. The headquarters of the Chicago Police Department is fortuitously just across State Street. These elements of social control are hardly visible in some of the early planning documents, but rental agents are nice enough to point them out to you.

While all this leaves unchallenged the image of family life, the effort to establish a local school is reminiscent of my earlier account of South Commons. The developers were at first assured of cooperation by the Chicago Public School District, and Dearborn Station was to be meticulously restored for this use. That proved expensive and then impossible as very few children arrived in Dearborn Park despite the number of bedrooms. The school district also underwent a change of management following Byrne's surprise victory, and the new school superintendent was quite unwilling to favor this relatively affluent population with an exceptional school. Then, as if reading the script from South Commons, the residents of Hilliard Homes, a public housing development a mile to the south, insisted on full access to the school. Not exactly the equal exchange that the residents of Prairie Courts had asked of South Commons but simply the demand that all their children go there. It was fine with them that the district call it a magnet school. As a temporary expedient the developers did obtain a Kg–2 school located in some town houses. But it was not until Harold Washington became mayor that the school district made a firm commitment to construct a local elementary school. Just how the continuing demand of the Hilliard Homes parents to send their children to this school will figure into its composition was still unsettled when I last interviewed in the area.

There are only about 300 school-age children in the area.[18] Many of the parents are reported to have already enrolled their children in private schools. For some of them, I am sure that it will be a better school and, for others, a whiter school.

Despite all these difficulties, Burnham Park must be considered a success. Dearborn Park, Printer's Row, River City, and the expanding area of loft conversions to the west are the kind of places you take visitors from out of town. Presidential Towers is a more contested addition to the Chicago landscape, and its appearance disallows the rhetorical advantages of Burnham Park. Yet, if one evaluates it against the experience of previous experiments—Pullman, Field's Garden Apartments, Rosenwald's Michigan Avenue Apartments, Lake Meadows, Prairie Shores, Carl Sandburg Village, South Commons, and a host of public housing developments—Presidential Towers must also be considered a success. Large enough to dominate its site, the overwhelming presence of middle-income residents insures a conventional moral order. A thorough and visible security system compound this impression. To put it in Oscar Newman's nutshell (1973), Presidential Towers is defensible space.

One could say more in defense of Burnham Park. It is not all rhetorical flourish. There is a great deal of for-sale housing. Adjacent development does provide much of the variety and visual appeal that we expect of city scapes. The landmark buildings set a standard for the present generation of designers. In the future, say two decades, Burnham Park may even attract an appreciable number of school-age children.

One can also document the success of these two experiments by the additional investments that have followed them. In a heroic effort, Mary Ludkin has recorded very nearly all the major investments (i.e., new construction, renovation, and adaptive reuse) occurring in the Central Area of Chicago (Ludkin and Masotti 1985). If one looks (table 6.1) at the level of additional investment occurring

18. As in the case of South Commons, there is continuing reluctance to accept the view that children and their parents must earn the opportunity to attend an exceptional school. The school district cannot be openly proposed or described as a meritocratic hierarchy contrived to promote the most accomplished. Magnet schools in Chicago survive primarily as neighborhood schools that accept selected children from other areas on their qualifications. Ironically, a meritocracy in which top athletes move to top teams is thoroughly acceptable throughout the city. Blacks respond marvelously to the athletic meritocracy and predictably to the absence of anything comparable in the remainder of the school system.

Table 6.1. Investment Following Construction of Dearborn Park in South Loop or Burnham Park (in millions of dollars)

Year	1979	1980	1981	1982	1983	1984	1985	1986	Total
New Construction:									
Complete or in progress						26 (1)	60 (1)		86 (2)
Announced								190 (1)	190 (1)
Renovation or adaptive reuse:									
Complete or in progress	1.5 (2)	7.9 (1)	19.7 (2)	0.4 (1)	35 (2)	8 (1)	188.4 (7)	55.5 (5)	316.4 (21)
Announced							51 (4)		51 (4)
Total	1.5 (2)	7.9 (1)	19.7 (2)	0.4 (1)	35 (2)	34 (2)	299.4 (12)	245.5 (6)	643.4 (28)

Note: Numbers in parentheses = *N* sites.

From the City Beautiful to the Community Under Glass

in Burnham Park following the time it broke ground, investments in renovation and adaptive reuse have steadily increased, amounting to over $315 million by 1986. Five new projects announced during 1986–1987 amount to another $241 million. It can even be argued (as Ludkin does, [see Ludkin and Masotti 1985]) that the development going on in Burnham Park has prompted investment to the north, between Congress and Adams Streets. As can be seen from table 6.2, investment in this area at first lags that in Burnham Park and then *very closely tracks it* (see fig. 6.1). Cumulative increments of investment in the North Loop are provided in the same figure to show that investment does not occur simply because an area (see map 6.1) is designated for new investment.

Before ground breaking for Presidential Towers in 1983, there was already some investment in the West Loop, all of it hovering very close to the Chicago River and adjacent to the Loop (see table 6.3 and map 6.3). What Presidential Towers seems to have inaugurated is the movement of investment westward, between it and the river; $475 million worth of additional new construction after 1984, and $137.2 million in adaptive reuse. Three projects announced during 1985–1986 are priced at $126.2 million. In the three years since ground breaking for Presidential Towers, the area has attracted

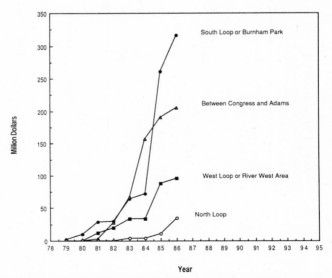

Fig. 6.1. Cummulative Investment in North Loop and Areas Adjacent to the Loop: Renovation and Reuse Only

Table 6.2. Investment between Congress and Adams (in millions of dollars)

Year	1979	1980	1981	1982	1983	1984	1985	1986	Total
New Construction:									
Complete or in progress		6.3 (1)			45 (1)	179 (2)		58 (1)	288.3 (5)
Announced								288 (1)	288 (1)
Renovation or adaptive reuse:									
Complete or in progress			2.5 (1)	24.8 (4)	40 (5)	89.5 (7)	34.4 (7)	14.9 (2)	206.1 (26)
Announced				55 (1)					55 (1)
Total		6.3 (1)	2.5 (1)	79.8 (5)	85 (6)	268.5 (9)	34.4 (7)	360.9 (4)	837.4 (33)

Note: Numbers in parentheses = N sites.

Table 6.3. Investment During and Following Construction of Presidential Towers (in millions of dollars)

Year	1979	1980	1981	1982	1983	1984	1985	1986	Total
New Construction:									
Complete or in progress					174 (2)		250 (1)	225[a] (2)	649 (5)
Announced							120 (1)		120[b] (1)
Renovation or adaptive reuse:									
Complete or in progress			11.5 (2)	8 (2)	13.9 (2)		54.2[c] (12)	8.3 (2)	95.9 (20)
Announced								6.2 (2)	6.2 (2)
Total			11.5 (2)	8 (2)	187.9 (4)		424.2 (14)	239.5 (6)	871.1 (28)

Note: Numbers in parentheses = *N* sites.

[a]Does not include several condos and boat slips and stacks in progress but for which no estimate was possible.

[b]Does not include a 1,000-place parking structure for which no estimate was possible and the proposed West Side amusement park.

[c]Does not include the renovation of Riverside Plaza in progress.

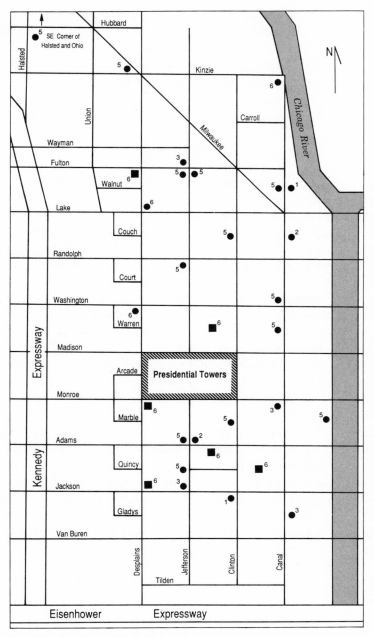

Map 6.3. The West Loop, or River West Area

From the City Beautiful to the Community Under Glass

$612.2 million in investment and $126.2 million in announced investment. Some people would dismiss the last investment because it consists largely of the new Northwestern train station. Possibly they are right, but the 4,000 residents of Presidential Towers make the Northwestern train station a lot safer for commuters than the commuters make life safer for the residents of Presidential Towers.

Conclusion

Well over a billion and a half dollars of investment with practically no disinvestment is not something Chicagoans are likely to dismiss. But before self-satisfaction sets in, they should recall how difficult it is to repeat the winning features of Burnham Park and those of Presidential Towers. There has always been a good rationale for building the big residential project in Chicago—so much remains vacant—but it defies a rhetoric of familialism and voluntarism. The result is that the essential pieces of social control are smuggled in through the back door. Well-connected developers occasionally accomplish it, but their efforts remain tainted, episodic, and unused in a comparative effort to build on experience.

The lesson, of course, is not totally lost. All across the city one can see elements of the community under glass (Paul Gapp's evocative phrase) being incorporated into new construction or retrofitted into older buildings. New high-rise apartment buildings along the lakefront have their uniformed doormen, TV monitors, and Kryptonite locks. Older buildings are sharply outlined by iron fences, first-floor windows are barred, basement windows bricked up. Enlarged house numbers insure a more specific police response. Ornamental lights supplement the street lights. Peepholes, infrared and ultrasonic burglar alarms, and whistle-stop programs ward off the more opportunistic. There are so many guard dogs that their feces dye the winter snows a Kennel Ration russet.

What we do individually, of course is forgivable. What we do publicly we disguise with sentimentality. Still another confidence game.

SEVEN

JUST A FEW GOOD MEN

Indefensible Venality

It was often said of Mayor Daley that, while he tolerated much petty corruption, he kept his distance from those involved and that little or no hint of wrongdoing touched him personally. Up to a point this seems to have been true, but like so much else written about Daley, it rests upon observations made before 1968, when most of the serious studies of his administration were completed. Afterward, he was the subject of many popular treatments (including the musical "Boss"), but the paradigmatic instance that was to stick in public memory was the Summerdale police scandal. Once several of the Summerdale District policemen were caught red-handed burglarizing stores, Daley acted vigorously to support investigators and promptly brought in an eminent criminologist to become the police superintendent.[1]

By 1965, however, there were already signs that this resolute response to public scandal was weakening. The most obvious instance was Daley's refusal to remove School Superintendent Benjamin Willis despite massive black protests against his continued efforts to segregate the public schools and his inattention to inequities between black and white schools. Admittedly, Willis was never indicted, and his segregationist policies were probably popular among most whites. But dislike of Willis was not restricted entirely to blacks, and Daley's failure to act decisively was among the most important reasons for a growing separation between black and white leaders *within* the Cook County Democratic party. The mounting salaries of schoolteachers without any improvement in educational quality and the frequent use of "Willis wagons" (mobile

---

1. Daley repeated this kind of housecleaning as late as 1965, when he appointed Vinton Bacon head of the Metropolitan Sanitary District following a number of scandals. Bacon was a highly regarded professional but removed from office by the MSD Board in early 1970, presumably with Daley's approval. Some of those responsible for firing Bacon were indicted and convicted in the 1976–1977 scandals.

Just a Few Good Men

classrooms) made Daley an object of ridicule among white liberals whose numbers were not large, but still count in close contests.

The police riot at the 1968 Democratic convention (Walker 1968), of course, was a great embarrassment to Daley and the Cook County Democratic party. At the national level, their endorsement became almost a liability. The trial of the Chicago Seven continued to focus critical mass media attention on the city as did that of Edward Hanrahan, the Cook County state's attorney who was accused of the murder of two members of the Black Panther party. At the local level it was, at first, easy to pass off these embarrassments. The national media coverage was such an unselective broadside that it only rallied local patriots to Daley's defense. The *New York Times* editorialized on the city of "small shoulders." Dwight McDonald announced that "Chicago has become our new Dallas" (1970, p. xiii), and John Lindsay bemoaned Chicago's crippling blow to democracy.

Such statements only drove the undecided to Daley's corner and helped juxtapose an "effete East" to an embattled Midwest for the next decade. This broader sense of regional defense, however, could not cover up the widening seams of disunity in the local Democratic party, and Daley's own subsequent electoral success was not shared by all fellow Democrats. When Hanrahan was indicted, Daly continued to support him until prevailed upon by other party members not to do so. He quickly returned to support Hanrahan after the attorney general was acquitted[2] despite the furious disbelief in his innocence among black voters. A coalition of blacks formed to oppose Hanrahan, and they were effective in defeating him. *It was Chicago blacks' first experience as exercising a successful independent voice in Illinois politics.* This sense of independence expanded incrementally in subsequent elections as blacks gained confidence and as voter registration among them began to approach that of whites.[3]

When the dust settled from the 1972 elections, the fracture lines were all to visible. A Republican was in the White House. An

2. When Hanrahan was acquitted, Daley said his previous withdrawal of support had been a "mistake." Hanrahan paid him back by opposing Daley in the 1974 primary.

3. Black voter registration increased very gradually at first, and as late as 1977 a study by the Urban League showed that blacks had to make up 75 percent of the residential population to elect a state or congressional representative. The growth in black voter registration was much more dramatic after Byrne's victory, which the media attributed—inaccurately, I believe—almost entirely to the black vote.

archenemy, even though a Democrat, was governor.[4] A Republican was Cook County state's attorney. Ralph Metcalfe, a very popular black state representative who had broken with Daley over his support for Hanrahan, had won by the largest plurality of any Democrat in the state despite Machine opposition and persistent harassment. In the suburbs, Daley's support had only redounded to the advantage of opponents.

The troubles of the Cook County machine, however, were just beginning. The Republican U.S. attorney general, James Thompson, was already hot in pursuit of a number of longtime officeholders. Former Governor Kerner (author of the "Kerner Commission Report"), often thought of as the "cleanest" Democrat in the state, was under indictment. Alderman Jambrone was indicted for bribery and conspiracy. Jambrone was a Republican, and Kerner, now a federal judge, was rather inactive in electoral politics. Their impending convictions did not especially single out the Democratic machine for ridicule. More important was widespread black pressure to remove Police Superintendent Conlisk over charges of police brutality and spying on prominent Chicagoans. Although these charges had more than a breath of truth to them,[5] Daley strongly supported his police chief. When in the same year twenty-five policemen were indicted (mostly for tavern shakedowns), his excuses began to sound a little lame.

In early 1973, Daley himself was touched with accusations of corruption when it was learned that several city departments had diverted insurance business to a firm connected with two of his sons. Daley at first flew into a pious rage, "If I can't help my sons, they can kiss my ass" (*Tribune*, 11 February 1973). Then, adding sentiment to righteousness, he declared, "What kind of world are we living in" if a man "can't put his arms around his sons" (*Tribune*, 11

4. Daniel Walker, who had authored the report (1968) on the "police riot" during the Democratic convention. Walker himself did not establish a high watermark for incorruptibility. In 1973, he won the Northern Illinois University students' contest for the "most crooked politician" well ahead of stiff competition from Richard Nixon, Richard Daley, and Spiro Agnew. Plagued by doubts about his campaign financing, three of his aides were eventually indicted. After serving one term, he returned to a career in business where he was indicted and convicted on charges subsequent to his term as governor.

5. In a nine-month period, Chicago police killed more people than police had killed in New York, Los Angeles, and Philadelphia combined. The police chief was eventually cited for contempt. Conlisk remained in office until late 1975, after at least another twenty-five policemen had been indicted and several convicted.

February 1973). Daley smothered the accusations with such memorable sentiment that it is often forgotten how seriously his troubles mounted over the next two years.

Table 7.1 attempts to give some gross impression of these difficulties as well as others which have followed Daley's death in December of 1976. I have included only those cases that led to convictions or instances (e.g., Swibel's removal and Byrne's allegations against Bilandic) that undeniably damaged the reputation of mayoral administrations. The more or less routine indictments of low-ranking city workers are excluded except for an occasional mass arrest of policemen (in 1972–1973, 1980–1981, and 1982).[6] Indictments with acquittals also have been omitted on the argument that an acquittal was as much a victory for local political leaders as an indictment was for their critics. Where indictments and convictions occurred in different years, however, I have listed them separately because this gives a better idea of the annual pall of corruption hanging over the city.

The year 1973 was a bumper year with the conviction of ex-Governor Kerner along with the former state revenue director, the indictment of two aldermen, the conviction of a third, the indictments of a Democratic committeeman (and ex-alderman) and a Cook County clerk, and the mass arrest of numerous policemen in various stages of prosecution. The most important of these indictments was that of Alderman Keane, Daley's floor leader in the City Council and a close family friend. The additional indictment of Earl Bush, Daley's longtime press aide, was also more embarrassing than that of the other city officials. Daley did remove Bush from his post, but his statement that it was "an unfortunate and sad incident" (*Tribune*, 12 August 1973) did not isolate the scandal from further press coverage. He was far more successful in rebutting the claim that special assistant police aide Clarke was his "eyes and ears" when Clarke's arrest was added to those above. Eventually, Daley also removed Keane from his post as floor leader, but this was

6. The police were not the only public employees to suffer mass indictments and firings. A large number of election judges were indicted following the elections in 1972 and 1982. In 1982 it was estimated that 10 percent of the vote was fraudulent (*Tribune*, 31 October 1983). A number of sewer inspectors were convicted in 1985, and several Streets and Sanitation workers were fired for altering work records in 1983. But it was the arrest of policemen that grabbed the headlines.

Table 7.1.   Selected Political and Legal Scandals in Cook County 1972–1986

1972

Federal Judge and ex-Democratic Governor Kerner under indictment
Ex-Alderman Jambrone indicted
25 policemen indicted

1973

Several city departments divert insurance business to firm tied to 2 of Mayor Daley's
   sons
Longtime press aide of Daley indicted
Democratic Alderman Keane, Daley's council floor manager, accused of conspiracy
   and mail fraud
Democratic Committeeman and ex-Alderman Kuta indicted
Special police assistant Clarke, once said to be Daley's "eyes and ears," indicted
Democratic Cook County Clerk Barrett indicted
Republican Alderman Potempa indicted
Republican Alderman Staszeuk indicted and convicted of extortion, mail fraud, and
   tax fraud
57 police officers charged by grand jury between March 1972 and October 1973
Ex-Governor Kerner convicted of bribery and conspiracy
Ex–state revenue director convicted with Kerner

1974

Alderman Keane convicted of mail fraud
Former press aide to Daley convicted of mail fraud
Democratic Alderman Wigoda indicted and convicted of tax fraud
Ex-Democratic Alderman Jambrone convicted of bribery and tax fraud
Cook County Clerk Barrett convicted of bribery
Circuit Court Clerk Danaher indicted for conspiracy and tax fraud but dies before
   trial
Secretary Zima of the Council Building and Zoning Commission indicted

---

1975

State Senator Swinarski (D. Chicago) indicted and convicted of tax fraud
Special police assistant Clarke convicted of tax fraud, perjury, and intimidation
Cardilli, assistant to commissioner of streets and sanitation, cited for contempt
   (Shakman decree)
Deputy Commissioner of Sewers and Democratic Committeeman Quigley cited for
   contempt (Shakman decree)

1976

Vice-President Janicki of the Sanitary District Board indicted
State Representative McPartlin (D. Chicago) indicted

1977

Former Vice-President Janicki convicted of bribery, conspiracy, and wire fraud
Former State Representative McPartlin (D. Chicago) convicted of bribery, conspiracy, and wire fraud

---

continued

Table 7.1. continued

Jane Byrne, commissioner of consumer affairs, alleges that Mayor Bilandic "greased" taxi fare increases. Bilandic begins appearances before grand jury

1978

Sun-Times and Better Government Association begin Mirage Tavern disclosures of bribery by city inspectors. Fire Commissioner Quinn, friend of late Mayor Daley, resigns
Jury continues probe of taxi fare increases

1979

Jury begins probe of false snow removal bills
State's Attorney Scott (Republican) indicted
Jury ends probe of taxi fare increase with no charges of wrongdoing

1980

Chief Kovic of Maintenance Division of police motor pool and five employees indicted
Byrne administration held in contempt for violating pretrial agreement in investigation of firing of 27 city employees
U.S. attorney begins investigation of local housing rehab program using HUD funds
Snow removal probe results in nine convictions but includes only one city employee

1981

Chief Kovic and five employees of Maintenance Division of police motor pool convicted of fraud
Swibel, head of Chicago Housing Authority Board and member of Library Board, ordered to pay back taxes
10 policemen ("Marquette 10") indicted as part of drug ring
Aide to Byrne's patronage chief cited for contempt of Shakman decree

1982

Chief of HUD insists on the removal of Swibel as head of Chicago Housing Authority Board over the objections of Mayor Byrne
Democratic Alderman and Committeeman Keener indicted
Democratic Alderman Farina indicted
10 policemen ("Marquette 10") convicted of conspiracy, racketeering, and extortion
13 policemen indicted (the fifth mass arrest of policemen since 1972)
State Representative Taylor (D. Chicago) and aide to Byrne found in contempt of Shakman decree

1983

Democratic Committeeman and Cook County Commissioner Tuchow indicted and convicted of conspiracy and extortion

continued

Table 7.1. continued

Democratic Alderman and Committeeman Kenner convicted of extortion, conspiracy, and tax fraud
Democratic Alderman Farina convicted of extortion and blackmail
Democratic Alderman Carothers indicted and convicted of conspiracy and extortion
State Representative Hutchins (D. Chicago) indicted and convicted of conspiracy and extortion
Mayoral advisor McClaine fired by Mayor Washington after criminal record revealed
Cook County Judge Murphy indicted ("Greylord")
Cook County Judge Olson indicted ("Greylord")
Former Cook County Judge Devine indicted ("Greylord")

1984

Judge Murphy convicted of racketeering, extortion, and mail fraud
Judge Devine convicted of racketeering, extortion, and mail fraud
Assistant City Corporate Council Canoff pleads guilty to racketeering, obstruction of justice, and fraud ("Greylord")
Cook County Judge LeFevour indicted ("Greylord")

1985

Judge Olson pleads guilty to mail fraud, racketeering, and extortion
Judge LeFevour convicted of mail fraud, racketeering, and tax fraud
Cook County Judge Holzer indicted ("Greylord")
Cook County Judge Reynolds indicted ("Greylord")
Former Cook County Judge Sodini indicted ("Greylord")
Former Cook County Judge Oakey indicted ("Greylord")
FBI begins investigation of bribery by bill collection firm

1986

Judge Holzer convicted of extortion, mail fraud, and conspiracy
Judge Reynolds convicted of racketeering, conspiracy, mail fraud, and tax fraud
Judge McCollom indicted ("Greylord")
State Representative Bullock (D. Chicago) indicted

both a personal and political loss. In the next year, as Keane approached his trial, Daley suffered a stroke.[7]

The next year brought several other convictions as well as that of Alderman Keane. By March people were already asking if the machine could survive.[8] Daley's stroke created too much sympathy for

7. See also John Daley's assessment of Keane's importance to the family (*Chicago Magazine*, June 1985). The Daleys remained loyal to Keane, one of them serving as executor of his will. This was to their credit. Chicagoans—including me—expect friendship to outlast a jail term.
8. George Togge, an editor of the *Tribune*, had already declared that "the Machine is finished" (25 March 1972). Guterbock's study (1980), which began about this time, is

the newspapers to pursue very far the revelation of a secret $200,000 trust apparently belonging to him and alleged to have done business with the city.[9] Nonetheless, two new indictments, one of a Cook County clerk and the other of the secretary of the building and zoning commission, kept alive the specter of vulnerability and occasional hints that the old man might be losing his grasp. Some suggested that he step down, but he did not and won handily in the next year over William Singer, a white reform candidate, and Richard Newhouse, a black who had broken with the machine.

Following Daley's victory in 1975, much of the speculation over the end of the machine abated. The secretary of the building and zoning commission was convicted, and State Senator Swinarski was indicted and convicted of tax fraud. The two Cook County Regular Democrats cited for contempt of the Shakman Decree (the prohibition of firings for political reasons) passed with relatively little attention. The decree was a recent ruling (mid-1972), and violations of it could be seen as "court tests" rather than criminal acts. I list it in table 7.1 mainly to foreshadow its subsequent importance and to anticipate Mayor Byrne's continued and self-destructive effort to violate it despite standing court rulings.

The blood bath slowed to a trickle in 1976, the last year of Daley's life. U.S. Attorney Thompson was off running for governor, and the new U.S. attorney, named in late 1975, had not yet found his direction. Only one major scandal was brewing, in the Metropolitan Sanitary District. The superintendent,[10] a vice-president of the board, and State Senator McPartlin were indicted in a long-running scheme of bribery and fraud, but there were no more major convictions for the entire year.

---

heavily preoccupied with the same issue, although he came to a more positive conclusion. Milton Rakove, who the press often used as their principal expert on the machine, stoutly defended its durability and by 1975 was arguing that the Chicago machine was a model of things to come in other cities (*New York Times*, 23 October 1975).

9. It did weaken somewhat his image as a modest man who received only a $35,000 salary. Daley had been dead almost three years before it was learned that he had also paid himself a secret $25,000 salary as chair of the Cook County Democratic Central Committee.

10. The superintendent was subsequently acquitted. When the others were convicted, the judge took the occasion to announce that they had little to fear from local law enforcement bodies (*Tribune*, 18 December 1977). Practically all of the indictments and convictions listed in table 7.1 were the result of federal action. After the machine lost control of the Cook County state's attorney's office, they were to be bedeviled by local investigators as well.

Yet, by the time of Daley's death (December 1976), a number of fateful steps had been taken. The Cook County Democratic party continued to be a liability in Washington. "Downstate" political candidates had only to oppose it to win the endorsement of good government groups. The Shakman Decree had held up in court. Unwilling to replace devoted followers, Daley was progressively unable to restrain them or protect them. And, on two out of three occasions, Chicago blacks had tasted political victory while opposing the machine.

The choice of Daley's successor was another fateful step. Rather than replace Daley with Wilson Frost, a cooperative black member of the Regular Democratic party, white members of the party maneuvered Bilandic into office. This was to rub salt in the wounds of the most loyal of black political leaders and to leave some of them (Metcalfe, Newhouse, possibly Washington) convinced that they could and should achieve political power at the expense of the machine.[11] Bilandic's rise to office also caused ripples of discontent elsewhere, especially among the Poles, some of whom thought that their numbers, their patience, and Alderman Pucinski's eminence deserved greater attention.[12] Pucinski promptly bolted the party machine to oppose Bilandic in the Democratic primary. Harold Washington followed him two months later. Although Bilandic pulled through with 51 percent of the vote, neither the Poles nor the blacks were fully reconciled to him. With 32 percent of the vote, Pucinski said he was considering a second run in the future. Wash-

11. And it was repeated by Daley's white successors (e.g., Bilandic's failure to appoint any blacks to visible positions and Byrne's refusal to meet black demands to appoint Sam Nolan as police superintendent). Unable to dominate black leaders and unwilling to co-opt them, white leaders in the party chose to torment them. It had all the wisdom of goading a tiger with a match stick.

12. To my knowledge, Pucinski is the only alderman who rose to national office in the last two decades. Poles were once the largest ethnic group in the city, but no Pole has ever been elected mayor. At the time of Daley's death, one of their most visible posts was that of city clerk. When Pucinski ran against Bilandic in the 1977 primary, Bilandic retaliated by dumping John Marcin, a northwest side Polish committeeman for that post, and replaced him with William Kozubowski, a Polish dependent of Irish political leaders on the Southwest Side. Byrne supported Marcin's independent run for alderman on the Northwest Side but turned against him when she reconciled with Edward Burke from the Southwest Side.

Byrne gained from the Polish revolt in her first election, but by the time she faced Washington she had alienated the Poles. They have frequently been divided by the selection of dependent candidates like Kozubowski in local elections. They do better in elections for national office (e.g., Rostenkowski) and state office (e.g., State Representative Lechowiecz).

ington, with only 11 percent of the vote, said much the same thing. Byrne's subsequent upset primary victory, only two years off, would owe almost as much to angered Poles as to the growing confidence of blacks.

Nonetheless, when Bilandic began his campaign against a sacrificial Republican, the general view was that the Machine had been restored. Andrew Greeley probably expressed the typical view: the working-class-ethnic-Catholics had won out over muddleheaded reformers who had fielded two candidates to divide their own vote. Bilandic himself could take further satisfaction in the fact that only two of his predecessor's appointments and colleagues were on their way to jail. Yet, by the end of the year Bilandic was in deep trouble. First, Byrne slapped him with the allegation that he had "greased" a large taxi fare increase. Just what "greased" meant was never clarified, but the term was so well chosen, so suggestive of inside knowledge, that a grand jury picked it up and Bilandic was soon trying to explain himself to the U.S. attorney. Then, in the beginning of the following year, the *Sun-Times* and the Better Government Association's disclosures on the proclivity of local inspectors to take bribes reached a national audience on CBS's "60 Minutes." Bilandic met that scandal by amusing the press when he appointed an investigatory committee consisting mainly of his own colleagues (*Tribune*, 14 January 1978).

Shortly afterward, Byrne was on the campaign trail, grimly shaking hands with voters and reminding them of Bilandic's tendency to favor downtown rather than neighborhood redevelopment. Bilandic obliged by running a campaign that consisted of little more than a slide show of downtown redevelopment. Then, in the dreadful winter of 1978–1979, Bilandic simply seemed helpless and inept. When he appeared on television to apologize, he had the same sweat pattern as Richard Nixon. It was fatal. By April, Byrne was mayor. She won essentially by capturing the "lakefront liberals" and the two areas that had previously voted heaviest for Pucinski and Washington. It was the fifth test of an independent black vote (i.e., following that of Hanrahan, Metcalfe, Newhouse, and Washington) and, if their confidence had suffered in two other contests, it must have soared when the press gave them and the snowfall almost sole credit for Byrne's upset victory.

Byrne entered office as a reformer and could stand above the current list of people serving sentences and under indictment. The

Just a Few Good Men

taxi hike investigation of Bilandic petered out.[13] The snow removal scandal resulted in several convictions but included only one city employee. The indictment of the Illinois state's attorney, a Republican, added to the general aroma of Illinois politics but could not touch Byrne. Even the 1980 police motor pool scandal reached well back into the Daley years. But if Byrne first presented herself as a reformer, she soon totally confused observers[14] and then sought to duplicate Daley's ironclad control over patronage. To do so she had to make amends with many of those she had opposed earlier. She cozied up to the First Ward organization, which some think equivalent to the Outfit. She brought on board as her advisor Charles Swibel, a man whom Daley had kept at a distance. Never indicted, Swibel has appeared several times before judges to explain back taxes and city ordinances that seemed to single him out with exceptional favor. She joined forces with Edward Burke and Edward Vrdolyak who had been largely responsible for maneuvering Bilandic past Wilson Frost in the selection of Daley's successor. She continued to stonewall the Shakman Decree only to lose each time she fired one of Richard J. Daley's precinct workers. And she accumulated an unprecedented campaign fund from firms doing business with the city.

Byrne may have been copying Daley also when she attempted to appoint several new people to government. Many of them were able and respected persons, but several quickly resigned or declined to serve once her standards of loyalty were clear.[15] The result was a "revolving door" of appointments that raised more doubts than those belayed by the outsiders she was able to keep.[16] An additional reversal occurred when HUD successfully insisted on the removal of Swibel from the Chicago Housing Authority board over Byrne's

13. Byrne explained, "I never said they broke a federal law—they broke the laws I had to administer" (*Tribune*, 23 January 1979).

14. See, for example, Masotti and Gove (1982, pp. ix-xii) and Granger and Granger (1980, pp. 217–232). Byrne was exceptionally visible in the mass media, and at least four books were written on her before she left office although one was purported to be fictional (Kennedy 1982), and another was little more than the usual authorized biography (Fitzgerald 1981).

15. Most local academicians either retired (Julian Levi), resigned (Louis Masotti and Dick Simpson), or declined to serve (Edward Levi and Norval Morris).

16. Most notably Blair, the fire commissioner; Love, the superintendent of schools; Brzeczek, police superintendent; Schultz, budget director; and Cartwright, commissioner of human services. All these people started with high credentials although Brzeczek and Love were the subject of some criticism. Washington axed them all.

prolonged resistance. Then Aldermen Keener and Farina, two of her supporters, were indicted. Farina, the "clown prince" of the City Council, was the chief sponsor of Byrne's Chicago song contest. Keener was what some people refer to as a "plantation black."[17] The indictment of twenty-three policemen and the contempt citation of Byrne's aides rounded out the year's legal encounters. Of far more importance, however, was the sixth occasion for blacks to exercise their political muscle. After an inept, almost laughable campaign,[18] Adlai Stevenson III very nearly won the governorship. Only a few thousand votes separated him from Thompson's victory and, upon analysis, it was clear that the black vote had almost carried Stevenson into office. It saved the Stevenson name for an equally inept campaign four years later.

By the time Washington and Byrne were facing off in the 1983 Democratic primary, Farina and Keener had been convicted and Cook County Commissioner Tuchow had been indicted. Tuchow had been one of Byrne's closest allies in her effort to unseat George Dunne (an old friend of Mayor Daley) from the Cook County board. Washington's victory, of course, owed much more to the stepwise growth in black confidence and voter registration.[19] But Byrne's complete abandonment of reform made Washington's claim to fill that role more plausible among the small (17 percent) white vote that went to him. The heated and racially polarized contest with Republican Bernard Epton was also to confirm an important (if shortsighted) political lesson: Washington could rally his black constituents almost to a man by provoking and enraging what was left of the leadership in the machine. Everytime they flew off the handle and obstructed his administration, canvassers went out to register more blacks. The only white voters he lost were those that had voted against him the first time.

Thus, for most of the remainder of 1983, Washington could watch placidly as Tuchow was convicted and two more "plantation" blacks (Carothers and Hutchins) were led off to jail. The U.S. attorney was soon so busy prosecuting Cook County judges (the

17. For example, he had turned against Ralph Metcalfe when the latter opposed Daley.

18. Among other things, he declared he was not a "wimp" before anyone else mentioned it. Four years later, Stevenson started his campaign by observing, "The sap is rising." It rose in the form of three La Rouche candidates who forced him off the Democratic ticket. He had to run as an independent.

19. As well as Jesse Jackson's uncharacteristic withdrawal from the race and his support of Washington.

Greylord investigations) that he had to queue them up over the remaining three years. Nonetheless, Washington suffered his first embarrassment that year when it was learned that one of his friends and aides, Clarence McClaine, had several convictions for keeping a house of prostitution and not paying his back taxes.[20] Washington fired McClaine and demoted him to an "acquaintance," but within little more than a year McClaine was to lead federal investigators to a promising trail within Washington's administration. The only questions was, When would the indictments arrive: before or after the 1987 elections?

Much has been made of the durability of the Cook County Democratic machine and its survival past that of "all others." But if one overlooks the massive amount of public attention that ornamented the Chicago machine, its life cycle compared roughly to what we might call the "standard American urban regime."[21] The Cook County machine was established and sustained for the first half of its life cycle by the fortuitous circumstances of the Great Depression which gave its members an overwhelming vote and opportunity. After the assassination of Mayor Anton Cermak (1933), this opportunity came into the hands of Ed Kelly whose mismanagement and corruption were so flagrant that Chicagoans voted in a reformer businessman, Martin Kennelly. Kennelly was apparently honest but ineffective. The machine very nearly expired

20. Washington himself had done time for tax evasion, but he profited from it so little that it was difficult to attribute his conviction to anything other than negligence. When he told his constituencies, "I've been paying my bills *slowly* all my life," even his opponents laughed. When he died, he left neither a will nor anything worth fighting over.

21. By this I mean a mayoral regime less dependent upon local political clubs than they are dependent upon the mayoral regime. Daley led his ticket, and local ward bosses depended upon him to gain office and influence.

It seems to me that most analyses of urban political machines rely too heavily upon the distinction between whether the vote is delivered largely by material incentives or originates out of some general proclivity for public regardedness (Banfield and Wilson 1963, pp. 234–242). In most cities, including Chicago, only a small proportion of the voters benefit enough from political favors to constitute a reliable vote (Guterbock 1980). The more important question, then, is whether or not a mayoral regime can capture enough of the remaining vote so as to oblige those who control the dependent vote to throw their lot in with the regime. Otherwise, one seems to get (1) a set of local baronies with a figurehead mayor, (2) a one term reform mayor, or (3) a regime so popular that it can ignore the dependent vote.

None of this denies the importance I later attribute to electoral rules. But I think it is these electoral rules rather than population composition that makes the dependent vote so important.

during the administration because of infighting.[22] Daley won office in a stiff campaign against reformer Robert Merrian, and his election as mayor was to save the machine. Without Daley, the Cook County machine would have been entirely unmemorable and unexceptional.

The way he rescued the machine has been documented many times (Bradley and Zald 1965; Banfield 1961; Banfield and Wilson 1963). He centralized patronage under his own control and was able to restrain venality and put an end to much of the party infighting. He made a series of impressive appointments by bringing outsiders into government. He was a vigorous facilitator who assisted private projects and investors. He approached the federal and state treasures with both hands for large and visible projects. If not an orator, he was nonetheless a pugnacious battler from the stockyards who could convey his affection for Chicago in well-orchestrated displays by party loyalists.

For ten years Daley rode the crest of national economic recovery, a growing federal budget, and increasing respect for this ability to turn out the vote. But by the end of those ten years, organizational rigidity had begun to take hold. Few new outsiders were drawn into government, and the Machine began to take the form of a closed club where the temptations of office were already beginning to leave some scars of scandal. Young men rose through the ranks where they were schooled in the dictums of defended venality and the slogan "Make no waves, back no losers." As the black population increased and as outside criticism mounted, the response was not to clean house and bring in blue ribbon appointees but to stand pat and draw up the wagons. Defectors were to be enraged even when they could not be quieted. As the fracture lines within the machine widened, it became more isolated from national and state leadership. The lessons of Daley's rise to power were reduced in collective memory to his ironclad control of patronage and the low price at which votes in Chicago could be harvested. By the time the machine chose Daley's successor it was as cautious and self-protective as the Soviet politburo. Well, if not that corrupt, then as corrupt as the two most recent Republican presidential administrations.

That is the way a lot of political regimes go through their life cycles. They are formed during fortuitous circumstances which give

22. See Masotti and Gove for a similar assessment (1982, pp. ix–x).

them a lead over the competition. They build their reputation around a single "great man." They ride an economic trend. They gravitate toward being a closed club, tolerant and cynical. When challenged, they respond with reduced and simplified formulas. The Chicago machine got started late, and its life cycle took it into the era of television when mayors must draw more heavily from show business. Otherwise, I am not sure that the Chicago machine differed much from other urban regimes, living or dead.

Visible Power

Louis Masotti and Samuel Gove recently repeated (1982, p. ix) the frequent observation that the sorry performance of Chicago sports teams has driven the residents to find equivalent entertainment in adversarial politics. Here I intend to document very nearly the opposite, that Chicago politics are sufficiently arresting to make professional sports appear as only a game played by oversized boys.[23]

As you can see in table 7.2, elections are heavily scheduled events in Illinois and Cook County. No year passes without some election, for many local or statewide elections are scheduled at a different time than the better attended national elections. Primaries frequently attract more attention than elections; Democrats often face the same kind of futility downstate as Republicans do in Chicago. Until recently, however, state legislative districts had candidates for four offices (three representatives and one senator) which was enough to arouse the hopes of even an enfeebled minority. Elsewhere, absolute majorities are required of candidates although primaries need not narrow the number of candidates to two. Runoffs are frequent. And, when someone dies or goes to prison, there usually has to be a special election. In most years there are two political seasons, one that just precedes spring baseball training and another that follows the world series by a comfortable margin.

The number of elections is compounded by the number of candidates. The ballot for one of the main events can be truly formidable, running well over a hundred candidates. In addition to the more familiar offices (mayor, governor, lt. governor, one state

23. Actually, there seems to be equal enthusiasm for both sources of entertainment. These enthusiasms extend to a common defensiveness in the face of wider ridicule.

Table 7.2.   Chicago and Illinois Elections: 1972–1985

1972

March: Election of ward committeemen, national delegates; primaries for governor, lt. governor, attorney general, secretary of state, state representatives, U.S. representatives, U.S. senators, U.S. president; and Metropolitan Sanitary District trustees (hereafter, general primary)
August: Special election for two aldermen
September: Run-off election following special elections
November: Election of U.S. president, senators, representatives; Ill. governor, lt. governor, comptroller, attorney general, secretary of state, house representatives; Metropolitan Sanitary District trustees, Cook County judges, and various suburban officials (hereafter, general election)

1973

February: Various suburban elections[a]
June: Special election in 4 Chicago wards
July: Run-off elections in 2 Chicago wards
November: Special elections in 4 Chicago wards

1974

March: Election of Cook Co. township committeemen and state central committeemen; primaries for U.S. House and Senate; state house and senate, Ill. treasurer, Metropolitan Sanitary trustees, Cook Co. assessor, Board of Commissioners and Tax Appeals, judges, sheriff, supt. of educational services, treasurer
November: Election for all those in March primaries

1975

February: General election for aldermen; primary for Chicago mayor, city clerk, treasurer
April: Election for mayor, city clerk, treasurer, and special run-off elections in 8 wards

---

1972

March: Election of national convention delegates and ward committeemen; general primary
November: General election

1977

April: Special election in 2 wards; special primary for mayor
May: Run-off election in one ward
June: Special election for mayor and one alderman

1978

March: Election of state central committee; general primary, excluding U.S. president

---

continued

Table 7.2.   continued

May: Special election in 2 wards
June: Run-off election in 1 ward
November: General election, excluding U.S. president

1979

February: General election for aldermen, primaries for mayor, city clerk, treasurer
April: Election of mayor, city clerk, treasurer; run-off elections in 10 wards
December: Special primary in one U.S. House district

1980

January: Special election in one U.S. House district
March: General primary
August: General election

1981

February: Special election in 1 ward

1982

March: Election of state central committee; general primary excluding U.S. president
June: Special election and run-off in 1 ward
November: General election excluding U.S. president

1983

February: General election of aldermen; primary for mayor, city clerk, treasurer
April: Election of mayor, city clerk, treasurer, and special elections in 14 wards
July: Special primary in 1 U.S. House district
August: Special election in 1 U.S. House district

1984

March: Election of ward committeemen, national convention delegates; general primary
November: General election

1985

February: Special election in 1 ward
March: Special elections for aldermen and committeemen in 7 wards, state central committee; general primary excluding U.S. president

aSubsequent reference to these elections is omitted from the remainder of the figure because information on them was so incomplete in the Chicago Municipal Reference Library. However, they are more likely to be held in April than February.

senator, three state legislators, state treasurer, comptroller, secretary of state, attorney general—any one of which may attract two or more candidates), there are county sheriffs, state's attorneys, assessors, treasurers, superintendents of educational services, commissioners of tax appeals, county board candidates and, for those enrolled, committeemen and national delegates. Beyond that there are city clerks, treasurers, aldermen and, in Cook County, the board of commissioners for the Metropolitan Sanitary District. In Illinois you also get to vote for county and state Supreme Court judges, initially when they are seated and thereafter to retain them. Outside the cities, there are township offices. In the suburbs, there are still other offices and elections referred to only as "various suburban elections" in the Chicago Municipal Reference Library. I have not included them in table 7.2, but trust me, there are a lot of them.

Now, very few Illinoisans know what these people do or, for that matter, who they are. Only professionals, newsmen, and political buffs can appreciate the subtlety and complexity of an Illinois election. Being able to do so does elevate one to the status of "expert," but most fans settle for a somewhat lower ranking, that is, they play the favorites, rally behind the home team, go with a longshot, depend on a crib sheet, or act on hunches.[24] I mean that they can vote for incumbents, pull the party lever, vote the rascals out, depend on the recommendations of some good government group, or adopt some mixed strategy which allows them to approximate rather inexactly the performance of these candidates.

Any of these strategies requires information. Even the most obedient Chicago Democrat must find out when the elections are scheduled, know what to do if a challenge has been casually dropped on his doorstep, or when to cross over for a Democrat masquerading as a Republican. (Members of either party can reregister in the other party and run in their primaries. Given the approximate level of knowledge, they sometimes win.) The mass media provide this information, and while it is almost impossible to give in-depth coverage to anything other than the principal candidates, politicians dominate everything but the sports and business section of the news.

To give the out-of-state reader some inkling of this, I coded a

24. The use of the vocabulary of athletics here is not frivolous. As John MacAloon (1987) shows, sports provide the metaphors by which Americans make politics memorable, accessible, and honorable. The language used above is more understandable to Chicagoans than that used by sociologists.

Just a Few Good Men

yearly sample of all those individuals referenced in the 1972–1985 *Chicago Tribune Index* who were designated as someone involved in public life. Not just politicians, but anyone who was said to be active in philanthropy, reform, business leadership, civic activities, union leadership, the management and support of nonprofits, neighborhood improvement, and so on.[25] In short, almost anyone credited with making a serious contribution to public life, although excluding those said to be contributing to popular and high culture as only performers. I did not include public employees who were not "appointive"; a tricky distinction in Illinois since virtually every public employee was "appointive" before the Shakman Decree. Essentially, I tried to apply the Shakman Decree to the sample of public administrators. I also excluded federal appointees except for judges and federal attorneys. Illinois federal judges and attorneys are not only drawn from those locally prominent, they have a tendency, like the present governor, to reemerge as bigger-than-life characters in Illinois politics or business as certifiable reformers. In the end, with some allowance for personal judgment, error, and vagueness, everyone could be classified as a leader in politics, law and the judiciary, labor, business, education, civic associations, and public administration.

Figure 7.1 gives the annual distribution of those in this sample. As the reader can see, politicians are always the largest group, ranging anywhere from two-thirds to two-fifths of the sample. No one else comes close. The practiced eye will probably detect some variation in the proportion of politicians mentioned and the level of electoral activity in the same year, that is, the slight dips in the number of politicians mentioned in 1973, 1977, and 1979 although not in 1981, the year with the least amount of electoral activity. There is also a slight trend downward in the proportion of politicians mentioned which is surprising considering the newsworthiness of the Byrne administration (1979–1982) and the Council Wars during the first three years (1983–1986) of the Washington administration. In large part, however, this is due to the growing

25. The sample excluded common and professional criminals, the victims of natural, supernatural, and unnatural events, novelists, entertainers, newspaper writers, actors, prisoners of war, beauty contest winners, sculptors, painters, athletes, the subjects of human interest stories, people who had died before the sample year, Nobel Laureates and other prizewinners, marriage notices, and obituaries *unless* some other item in the index indicated an active effort in public life for good or ill. All those included in the sample had to be mentioned twice or more; otherwise it became unmanageable. For further information on this sample, see Methadological Appendix.

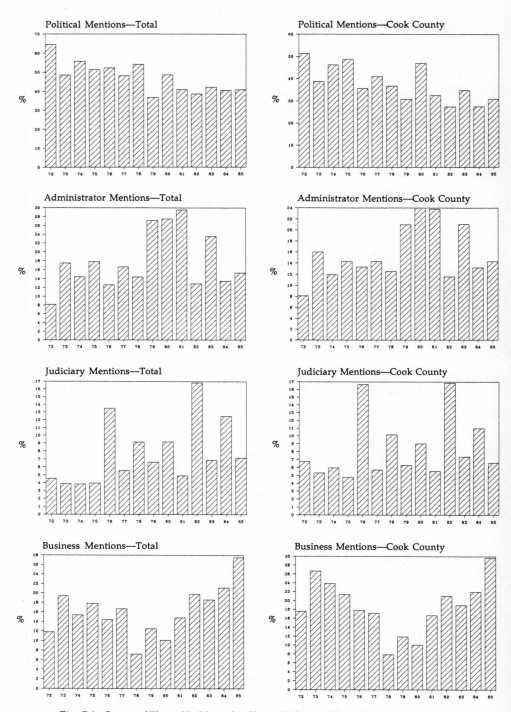

Fig. 7.1. Status of Those Visible in the *Chicago Tribune*, 1972–1985

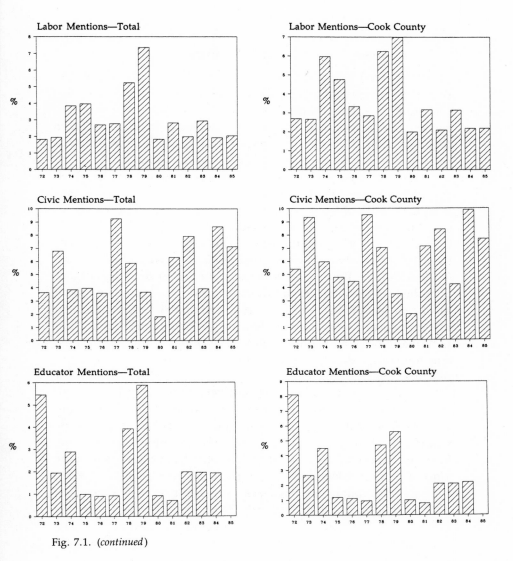

Fig. 7.1. (*continued*)

Just a Few Good Men

attention given to corrupt judges after 1979, and the Greylord indictments which began in 1983. In addition, there was a great deal of reporting on administrators during the Byrne years when she carried out her "revolving door" pattern of senior appointments. Taken together, then, the judges and administrators go a long way to even out this distribution for public officials over the years.

The reporting on businessmen also reveals the way in which the 1980 Census finally provoked a reexamination of the state's economy. Much of it was bad news after 1980—bankruptcies, mergers, buyouts, plant closings—something progressively avoided from 1972 to 1979 but not thereafter. The pace of publicized civic activism more nearly follows mayoral terms, a two-year honeymoon (1979–1980) for Byrne and a briefer one (1983) for Washington. Bilandic was a symbol of continuity and did not get a honeymoon. Most civic leaders in Chicago are reported on when they are trying to reform local government but, during the Washington administration, many black and some white civic groups became supporters, and the stories during the 1984–1985 period reflected this mix of responses.[26]

Labor leaders in Illinois are not very visible despite the concentration of heavy industry and fairly high levels of unionization. They seldom make up more than 5 percent of the sample. Some would expect this of the *Tribune,* but if you examine the stories before 1980, many of them focus on the role of labor leaders in some kind of helpful collaboration with the Chicago Machine. By 1981, they are most notable for paybacks, agreements to new work rules, and the modesty of their demands. One can almost sense directly the weakness of the Illinois labor movement from the decline in coverage after 1979. Indeed, there seems to be a kind of inverse relationship between reporting on businessmen and labor leaders. I do not think this is just an artifact of the *Tribune's* selective reporting but would guess that it resembles the more general tendency of Chicagoans to look to business for the initiative (or lack of it) that will rescue the region from economic backwardness. Certainly very few people are going to credit the labor union's paybacks for a revitalization of the region's economy.

Educators are even less visible than labor leaders. They seldom make up more than 2 or 3 percent of the sample. The peak of pub-

26. I did not read all of these stories on individuals, but I did read most of them. Still, I am making this and other judgments on the basis of general impression rather than an exact count.

Just a Few Good Men

licity in 1979 reflects Byrne's flirtation with a number of academicians whom she sought to bring into her administration. Most of
those who served soon left, and the others declined. A number of
academicians did enlist into the reform candidacy of Washington,
but that lapsed two years into his administration. Actually academicians in and around Chicago seldom become visible by serving in
public office. Six of those in this sample served in such a capacity,
but only four did so on a sustained basis for more than two years.
Three of these contributed to the "minority count" on different city
boards.

The other ways in which academicians become newsworthy is
when they announce some astonishing finding ("Chicago is the
most segregated city in the nation!" is an annual favorite), when a
Nobel prize makes one of them into a celebrity (Friedman, Stigler,
Bellow, Schultz, Cronin, and Chandrasekhar between 1972 and
1985), when they become newsmen themselves (Greeley, Sampson,
Rakove, Friedman), or when they run for mayor (Haider). My general impression from being one of them is that academicians are
reluctant to enter into the compromises of Chicago politics but that
this does not extend to utter avoidance. Both Andrew Greeley and
Milton Rakove took great delight in the foibles of reformers when
trounced by the machine, and Sampson is a predictable supporter
for the Washington administration. The more general pattern, however, is a willingness to talk but not to say too much unless one can
be "constructive." One reason I wrote this book was to see what
would happen if someone broke ranks.[27]

All of the above observations, of course, are based on the
Tribune's coverage of the entire state. State politics in Illinois can provide fascinating reading, but only an Everett Dirkson ("Mr.
Marigold") or Phyllis Shlaefly ("the sweetheart of the silent majority") can match the newsworthiness of a host of Cook County
politicians. Figure 7.1 also gives the proportions for Cook County

27. Of course, I am not the only one to have done so. Pierre de Vise frequently
breaks ranks with press announcements that are highly critical of city policy. Philip
Hauser also occasionally attacked city policy when he was more active. Morris Janowitz could not resist saying things that outraged people, but he got upset when
others did the same thing. Yet, more than anyone I know of, Janowitz tried to find a
language that could bridge academicians and politicians. The criticisms of others
(e.g., Orfield, Wilson) dwell on distributional inequalities or take the form of policy
analysis (Masotti). Only Donald Haider has taken the plunge to become a candidate
for mayor. The public statements of Greeley, Rakove, and Sampson are more as defenders of the people, Catholics, ethnics, and blacks, respectively.

alone.[28] Obviously individuals from Cook County make up the vast majority (78%) of those mentioned, not just because this is the primary market for the *Tribune* but because public life elsewhere in the state lacks equal drama or access to the national media. There are so many toy governments in Illinois—6,386 local units of government according to a recent count—that only a U.S. representative, state legislator, or especially venal judge can rise above the common herd of village presidents and county commissioners. The vast majority of these minor officials have their fifteen minutes of fame when they are slated, win or loose. Even a politician so durable as Robert Sobonjain (the fifth-term mayor of Waukeegan) shows up only occasionally in the *Tribune*.

Over time, however, one does notice some changes if we go beyond the data in figure 7.1 to see who is exceptionally visible. In the early 1970s, both U.S. senators (Stevenson and Percy) were closely connected with Chicago and very visible. The present U.S. senators (Simon and Dixon) are equally visible, but both are from downstate. There is also a growing visibility of people from DuPage County (for example, Lee Daniels). During 1985–1986 DuPage was said to be the fastest-growing county in the United States despite a general slowdown in population growth in the remainder of the region.

Otherwise the trends in Cook County resemble those throughout the state. The progressive decline in the reporting of businessmen after 1973 and its increase after the Census report in 1980 is especially marked. The slight downturn in the proportion of politicians mentioned is now a bit more pronounced but more obviously compensated for by the expansion of the Greylord investigations of judges after 1981, Byrne's "revolving door" for administrators for 1979 through 1981, and Washington's inability to get his appointees confirmed from 1983 to 1985. Taken together the proportions of mentions of politicians, judges, and administrators varies only by 2.2–5 percent between mayoral administrations.

All this, of course, is only to make the obvious inescapable. Of far more importance to Cook County voters are the names of political candidates. I do not mean who they are but simply what you can guess about them by knowing only their names. For example, there

---

28. A finer distinction between city and county is not possible or desirable for politicians, judges, administrators, businessmen, and labor leaders. Once in the political organization, one is active in the entire county. Residences and place of employment spread others about as well.

are the "on's": Thompson, Stevenson, Simon, Dixon, Washington, and Jackson; the governor, his most recent opponent, both U.S. senators, Chicago's mayor, and both the state's candidates for president; virtually the entire top of the political food chain in Illinois. An "on" is a good name in Illinois suggesting a certain WASPish (or Jewish) high-mindedness ("Too rich to steal," some would say), or obscuring the possibility of racial recognition. The full magnitude of this was revealed recently when three utterly unknown La Rouche candidates with names (Hart, Fairchild, and Jones) that could have decorated an especially reputable law firm, trounced Adlai Stevenson III's fellow candidates in the Democratic primary. "On's" have the additional advantage that they can pull votes from both ends of the state. In the total sample of "on's" ($N = 84$, 7% of the sample), two-thirds of the downstate [29] "on's" are politicians while a little over a third of the Cook County "on's" are politicians. In Cook County there are advantages to other, competing names.

Some of these names (5% in Cook County, 3% in the remainder of the state) begin with Mc and O'. Whites almost invariably assume them to be Irish, but many a Chicago black has been confused by a white Mc thinking it a black Mc. The Mc's and O's, however, are not especially concentrated (47% of fifty-seven individuals) in politics because a substantial proportion (32%) have become judges or administrators. Here they can probably avoid some of the hazards of electoral politics and, as the Irish have moved out of the city, a diminished role in local politics has been forecast for them. George Dunne, now restored as chairman of the Cook County Democratic party, recently remarked, however, that they do have one remaining asset: name recognition (*Sun-Times*, 15 March 1987). Even in Chicago, some of us have trouble remembering names like Bieschke or Bieszczat.

The suffix "ski" is much easier to evaluate regardless of what is in front of it. Essentially one can assume they are from Cook County (97% in this sample) and vote accordingly. Unlike the Mc's and O's, most of the ski's mentioned in the *Tribune* (87%) must still face the hazards of regular elections.

One could continue in this vein, with the indisputable Italians

29. In casual language, "downstate" includes everything outside of Cook County, including Lake County, up to the Wisconsin border. Increasingly people refer to the "Collar"—that is, the five-county area around Chicago—but my data do not permit such a breakdown for numerical analysis.

(e.g., -cci's or do's), Hispanics (e.g., -ez's), or Greeks (e.g., -tos'), but by now the reader must have a fairly good idea of how an Illinois voter carries out data reduction when going to the polls. What is more interesting is the way in which exactly [30] the same last name is shared by visible politicians, judges, and the remaining individuals in the sample. Altogether 766 individuals (61% of the sample excluding those sampled in more than one year; hereafter "unique individuals" or "unique sample") shared last names. As you can see from the pie charts in figure 7.2, politicians share the same last name about half again as often as do judges, and more than twice as often as any of the remaining groups. Educators and labor union leaders never share the same last name, although everyone shares some of the last names of politicians because there are so many of them. Labor leaders are as likely (33%) to share names with businessmen as with the much more numerous politicians. This is to be expected. Starting a business career in Illinois is rather like starting a union career: the first generation off the factory floor. The only individual in the entire sample who was killed professionally was Allen Dorfman, a businessman managing the teamsters' retirement fund. He could almost as easily have been classified as a "labor leader."

Administrators are especially likely (47%) to share a last name with a politician. One might think that the latter appoint the former or that one can move from being an elected official to being a better paid administrator. That is probably true in some instances, but one should not think of these shared names as indicating kinship.[31] Chicagoans think of them more as clan titles which can serve to promote one's own visibility if you have the right one. If you do not have exactly the right one, there are alternatives such as that followed by Representative Peter Piotrowicz Peters or Senator "Sweeney" Swinarski. Illinois women politicians are very frequently gifted with three names (e.g., Adeline Jay Geo-Karris, Peggy Smith Martin, Dawn Clark Netche) which give them two clan titles and/or provide a kind of rhythmic or mnemonic chant (Mary Margaret Decker, Aurelia Marie Pucinski, Mary Grace Stern). If this sounds a bit tribal, it is because we are approaching the deep structure of Illinois politics.

Publicity, of course, is not always an advantage, and fifty-eight

30. This excludes even minor variations in spelling, for example, O'Brian and O'brian.

31. I gave up trying to determine kinship although it certainly occurs, and my very incomplete count would concentrate it among politicians, administrators, and judges and, second, among businessmen.

(4.6%) of the unique individuals included in the full sample became better known because they were indicted. Most of those indicted (60% while being 45% of this sample) were politicians. Judges came in next (10% while being 8% of the sample), administrators third (14% while being 18% of the sample), and businessmen fourth (9% while being 17% of the sample). So few labor leaders (three out of forty) and civic leaders (one out of seventy-five) were indicted that one hesitates to bring them into the comparison. No academician was indicted, but one Chicago college president came close when it was discovered that he had lied about having a Ph.D.

One might think that some of these people became visible only because they were indicted. However, if one looks at all those indicted *after* 1972, almost all were somewhat visible before their indictment. In Illinois public life you have to be somewhat visible before an indictment makes you more visible. I do not know how many of these indictments eventuated in convictions. Some are still pending, but indictments in Illinois are more likely to be newsworthy than convictions. Indictments provide an element of surprise (some would say "hope"). By the time the trial has gone through the appeal process, it is old news and may move off the front page if it is only, say, an alderman. However, all three of the last six governors who happened to be convicted made the front page both when indicted and convicted.

This is probably a fairly high rate of indictments among American states, but it should not be surprising. Illinois not only has a lot of potentially indictable politicians, is has a lot of people looking to indict them. The intense adversarial character of local politics contributes to this, and indictments must be thought of as only another way of campaigning. The state also tends to produce an unusually large number of "apolitical" reformers. Some of the nation's most famous reformers (Jane Addams, Edith Abbott, Graham Taylor, Mary McDowell, Julie Lathrop, Grace Abbott, Lucie Flower, Charles Richmond Henderson, Florence Kelley, Clarence Darrow, Saul Alinsky, Sophonisba Breckinridge) had their peak years in Chicago. Until the last decade, Chicago had produced the nation's only saint. Watchdog and reform organizations abound: the Better Government Association, Independent Voters of Illinois, League of Women Voters, Committee for Political Honesty, Project LEAP, Business and Professional People for the Public Interest, Chicago Crime Commission, Illinois Public Action Committtee, Bar Association Screening Committee, Industrial Areas Foundation, and the John

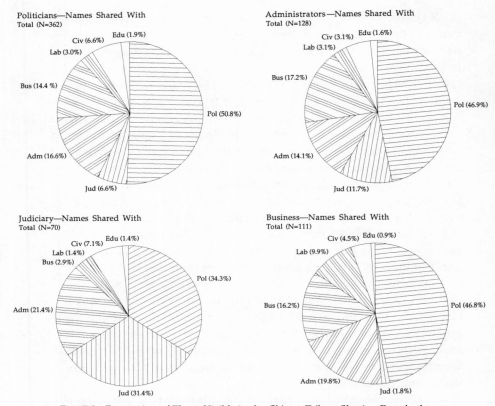

Fig. 7.2. Proportion of Those Visible in the *Chicago Tribune* Sharing Exactly the Same Last Name

Labor—Names Shared With
Total (N=33)

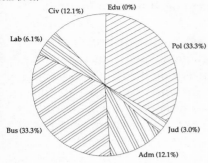

Civic—Names Shared With
Total (N=51)

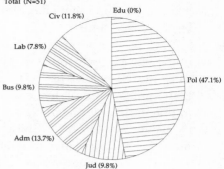

Educators—Names Shared With
Total (N=11)

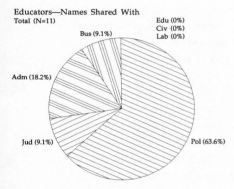

Fig. 7.2. (*continued*)

Howard Association are among the best known. Some of these groups occur in other cities, but Chicago must have an unusually large complement.

Chicago reformers and its crooked politicians provide each other with a growth medium. The reformers advance their career by catching the politicians.[32] The politicians gain credibility as pragmatic champions of the common man when compared to the impotent floundering of high-minded reformers. The irony of Paddy Bauler's statement, "Chicago ain't ready for reform," escapes many Chicagoans. They take it the same way Paddy meant it.

This symbiotic pattern is self-sustaining, but two self-proclaimed reform mayors in a row seem to have disarmed or confused many Chicago reformers. This is only slightly noticeable in the decline of mentions for civic activists during the early years of the Byrne and Washington administrations. But if one looks more broadly at a separate count (not shown) of independent aldermen, reformist businessmen and administrators, as well as civic leaders, the decline in visibility is notable. Norman Ross has gone to Durham. Marty Oberman chose not to run for alderman. Dick Simpson has become a preacher. Florence Scala runs a restaurant. Susan Catania is out of office. I am told that Ruth Moore Garbe left town. Ira Bach is dead, as is Edwin Berry. Most of the black reformers—Bobby Rush, James Compton, Al Raby—seem to have thrown their lot in with Mayor Washington as has David Orr, once an independent alderman.[33] Others—Gail Cincotta, Lewis Manilow, Alexander Polikoff, Terry Brunner—do still make news, but at a reduced level compared to say, about 1978. The new cardinal, Joseph Bernadine, is very visible although he seems much more a moral than a political reformer. One of the most prominent reformers remaining is Patrick Quinn, head of the Committee for Political Honesty. After 1982, he outdistanced all the reformers and civic activists other than Cardinal Bernadine and, in 1987, Washington made him head of the Department of Revenue. Washington fired him three months later because of "incompatibility." The Washington administration, however, makes a difficult target for reformers. Blacks should have their

32. The Better Government Association of Chicago was so optimistic about the availability of scandal that it signed a contract with CBS's "60 Minutes" to produce one on demand.

33. The Washington administration may live to regret this. Apparently Orr has authored a very strict ethics ordinance for aldermen, and they may not be able to remove all its teeth before passage.

Just a Few Good Men

chance and, as the newspapers put it, "He's no worse than ———— (fill in with anyone but Richard J. Daley)."

Newsmen and reformers, however, should soon regain their direction and find their target. The vulnerabilities of Illinois politics and those of the Washington administration are too tempting. As reformers and newsmen move in this direction, racial sensibilities are apt to be high. Almost three-quarters of all the Cook County blacks mentioned in the *Tribune* sample are politicians (54%) or administrators (20%), thus likely targets. During the first three years of the Washington administration, blacks have become more visible among the Cook County sample, making up 20% of the whole, about double what they were in previous years. Not all the news is favorable if one reads a sample of these stories, but increasingly blacks need not feel they are being held to a lower standard.

There is no similar increase in the newsworthiness of Orientals or Hispanics during the sample years. Only one of the former occurs, and the latter are very rare (less than 1%). Women do show a modest, incremental gain of visibility over the Byrne and Washington years, from about 8 percent to 12 percent ($N=98$) of the Cook County sample. If one examines the stories about them, they are almost uniformly positive, except for Byrne herself.[34] I do not think that this means that women are being held to a lower standard. The women sampled in the *Tribune Index* are only slightly less concentrated (59%) in politics and administration than the men (65%) but not a single one was indicted, and I cannot think of another source mentioning the indictment of an Illinois women politician between 1972 and 1985. Women administrators and politicians often emerge from reform or civic groups, areas in which they are overrepresented (by a 4 : 1 ratio in this sample). To survive in Illinois politics, women must be made of stout moral fiber.[35]

Women are not alone in providing this kind of dramatic, almost inverse, contrast to the general pattern of easy virtue among Illinois politicians, judges, and administrators. The state does pro-

34. Byrne was the most newsworthy of anyone who fell into the sample, outdistancing everyone, including the governor, for the years she was mayor. All four mayors and the governor fell into the sample. Comparisons of mentions across mayoral terms are not really possible because of some variations in the way the *Tribune* index was kept. But the number of mentions for Byrne simply falls off the scale no matter how you try to standardize it.

35. Mayor Washington's affirmative efforts on behalf of women may have been less selective. In 1987 at least two of the women among his supporters were under investigation.

duce people of remarkable talent and integrity. If one looks away from the modal pattern drawn from the *Tribune Index,* the performance of some Illinoisans over the same period is truly distinguished (see table 7.3). Again, it is as if rising above the temptations of mediocrity and the adversities of cynicism produces people of ability and hardened morality. Of course, many of them find their calling at the national rather than the local level.

This sort of glaring, but recurrent exceptionalism is probably one reason that Daley has remained so fixed within the local mass media as the standard for his successors to follow. He was a national figure among big city mayors, if never a national candidate.[36] People from out of town admired him, even academicians. Thus, after he was medically dead, Daley lived on in our sample to overshadow most of his opponents who were medically alive (table 7.4). Daley did not become as fixed in the public mind as did John F. Kennedy or Martin Luther King, Jr., but no other local person seems to have achieved equal immortality. Even Ernie Banks, "Mr. Cub," is mentioned less frequently although his number was not retired until 1982. We have yet to retire Daley's number. He is still number one.

Still, one might want to search these newspaper accounts for some signs of change. To get some sense of this, I coded separately all those people picked up in the *Tribune Index* who were mentioned seven or more times during the recent 1982–1985 period.[37] As can be seen from table 7.5, the vast majority (79%) of these people came into visible public life during the Daley years (i.e., before 1977). This is especially true of the politicians, 91 percent of whom were at least somewhat visible before 1977. Just about the same percentage (88%) of judges and prosecuting attorneys date from that period. There is some sign of change among administrators, only about 60 percent of

36. Mayors of U.S. cities seldom survive their office to become national candidates or, for that matter, much of anything else. The last ex-mayor I can recall receiving the nomination to run for president was Hubert Humphrey, and he arrived at this nomination through the senate. Kotter and Lawrence (1974, p. 239) comment that *"not one"* of the mayors they studied, many of them of proven ability, *"achieved his post-mayoral objective!"* (emphasis on original). Involvement in local American city politics just seems to be fatal.

37. There seemed to be a "natural" discontinuity at this point, and all but one of those mentioned this frequently were mentioned in two or more years. One might say that they have become fixed in the memory banks of the media and probably in that of the general public as well. The 1982–1985 period coincides roughly with the beginning of the Washington administration. The *Tribune* index for this period was compiled by the same firm while the previous years were compiled by a different one.

Just a Few Good Men

Table 7.3.   Some Eminent Illinoisans (1972–1985)

John Paul Stevens (Supreme Court justice)	Robert McCormick Adams (director, Smithsonian Institution)
Edward Levi (U.S. attorney general)	Norval Morris (head, Law Enforcement Assistance Administration)
Philip Klutznick (secretary, Department of Commerce)	Clayton Yeutter (U.S. trade representative)
George Schultz (secretary of state)	
Kenneth Dam (undersecretary of state)	Daniel Boorstein (Librarian of Congress)
Michael Bakalis (undersecretary of education)	Beryl Sprinkel (chair, Council of Economic Advisors)
Donald Rumsfeld (secretary of defense)	Peter G. Peterson (secretary of commerce)
John R. Block (secretary of agriculture)	
Paul Heron Robinson (ambassador to Canada)	

whom date from the Daley years. About the same is true of businessmen (there is only one businesswoman). Labor union leaders, educators, and civic leaders adhere to Michaels' iron law.

Those reaching visibility in the Daley years are notable for their longevity. The Bilandic years (1977–1978) are notable for the comparative absence of any new names that have endured into the Byrne and Washington years. The Byrne years are most obviously the period in which her "revolving door" introduced new men, some of whom lasted into the Washington years. There are very few new faces appearing in the first three of the Washington years. This may surprise some Chicagoans, but in the main Washington seems to have revived the careers of blacks and some whites who were visible during the Daley and Byrne years. A few blacks have achieved exceptional visibility in the Washington period, but most have been around for some time. Seventy-nine percent of the blacks reaching the level of visibility measured in table 7.5 were visible in the Daley years, and 97 percent of them were visible by the end of the Byrne years. Women are somewhat less likely to have been visible in the earliest years. Sixty-nine percent of those fixed in the public media in the period 1982–1985 were visible during the Daley years. Most of the remainder entered public life during the Bilandic and Byrne (27%) administrations.

There are some differences between the roles people occupy and their longevity that bear interpretation. The politicians have the greatest longevity, which is understandable because visibility is their stock in trade and, once they have it, they usually survive until

Table 7.4. Number of Mentions of Daley, His Election Opponents, and the Immortals: *Chicago Tribune, 1976–1985*

	1976	1977	1978	1979	1980	1981	1982	1983	1984	1985
Primaries:										
R. J. Daley	335[a]	49	31	22	12	10	3	5	15	12
M. Kennelley	1	1								
L. Daley			5[a]							
W. Singer	10	24	2	5		1	2	1	2	2
R. Newhouse	11	10	7	10	6	11		2	4	8
E. Hanrahan	6	56	3	5	10	2	1			1
B. Adamowski	1	1			2		1[a]			
R. Merriam	1	1								
General election:										
T. Sheehan	4	1	2	2[a]						
J. Warner	15	5								
R. Friedman	1	2		2	3					
J. Hoellen	1			1		1	3		1	18
W. M. Reid	1		1	1						
J. Arvey	3	8[a]								
Immortals:										
J. Kennedy	35	24	31	34	9	12	10	23	20	9
M. L. King	15	19	38	27	6	11	17	40	15	14
E. Banks		6	1	1		4	1		1	1

[a]Year of death.

Table 7.5. Relatively Visible Individuals during 1982–1985, and the Earliest Year They Became Visible in the *Chicago Tribune* (cumulative percentages)

	Daley Years					Bilandic Years			Byrne Years			Washington Years			Total
	1972	1973	1974	1975	1976	1977	1978	1979	1980	1981	1982	1983	1984	1985	
Political	64 (89)	77 (17)	86 (12)	89 (3)	91 (4)	91 (0)	94 (5)	97 (4)	99 (2)	99 (1)	99 (0)	99 (0)	100 (1)		138
Admin.	20 (10)	40 (10)	52 (3)	60 (7)	60 (0)	66 (3)	70 (2)	82 (6)	86 (2)	90 (2)	94 (2)	98 (2)	98 (0)	100 (1)	50
Judges and prosec. atty.	30 (10)	61 (10)	73 (3)	79 (7)	88 (3)	88 (0)	88 (0)	88 (0)	97 (3)	97 (0)	100 (1)				33
Business	37 (21)	51 (8)	56 (3)	60 (2)	63 (2)	68 (3)	70 (1)	75 (3)	82 (4)	84 (1)	93 (5)	98 (3)	100 (1)		57
Labor	60 (6)	60 (0)	80 (2)	80 (0)	90 (1)	90 (0)	90 (0)	90 (0)	90 (0)	100 (1)					10
Education and civic	47 (7)	60 (2)	67 (1)	73 (1)	73 (1)	73 (1)	80 (1)	87 (1)	93 (1)	100 (1)					15
Males	48 (134)	65 (46)	73 (22)	78 (13)	80 (7)	82 (6)	85 (7)	89 (12)	93 (10)	95 (5)	97 (8)	99 (5)	99 (1)	100 (1)	277
Females	35 (9)	46 (3)	54 (2)	62 (2)	69 (7)	69 (0)	77 (2)	85 (2)	92 (2)	96 (1)	96 (0)	96 (0)	100 (1)		26
Whites	46 (120)	62 (42)	70 (20)	76 (15)	79 (8)	81 (5)	84 (8)	88 (12)	92 (10)	94 (5)	97 (7)	99 (5)	99 (2)	100 (1)	260
Blacks	53 (23)	70 (7)	79 (4)	79 (4)	81 (1)	84 (1)	86 (1)	91 (2)	95 (2)	98 (1)	100 (1)				40
Total	47 (143)	63 (49)	71 (24)	76 (15)	79 (9)	81 (6)	84 (9)	89 (14)	93 (12)	95 (6)	97 (8)	99 (5)	99 (2)	100 (1)	303

a

b

c

d

e   From Cairo to Chicago: (a) the magnificent miles of Illinois; (b) going north; (c) entering Chicago from the south; (d) somewhere in Chicago; (e) "aus" at the Wisconsin border.

Just a Few Good Men

death or imprisonment. Judges are appointed essentially for life and exit mainly when they die or there is a siege of reform such as the Greylord investigations which began in the early 1980s. Labor, civic, and educational leaders are basically similar; they have tenure because there is no career line that leads to their replacement or rotation in public life.

Administrators and business leaders are the exceptions. Only about two-thirds of them date from the Daley period. Their replacement begins in the Bilandic period and continues through the Byrne and Washington administrations. The notable thing about administrators and businessmen is that they can be fired. Their fortunes are those of whichever firm or organization they preside over. Notwithstanding the changes that have occurred at the very apex of Chicago's political leadership, then, it appears that the heaviest turnover by 1985 may have been among public administrators and business leaders.

From Cairo to Chicago

Illinois has more local governments than any state in the Union. Outside of the Chicago region, it is a great glacial plain speckled with small towns like Dixon or Savanna where Ronald Reagan grew up. The formative experience of those who rise to public life in these towns carries with it all the compromises that advance one in politics and business and all the dreams embodied in the Fourth of July, the basketball team, and the homecoming queen.

Within Chicago and its suburbs the differences are less than one would expect. Most of the city and its suburbs are cut up into wards, parishes, defended communities, ghettos, and urban villages. They also have their main street, their basketball teams, and their homecoming queens. The places that fall away from this pattern are so few as to be almost universally recognized: the Gold Coast, the "lakefront liberals," the Hyde Park "pinkos," and the North Shore. Evanston is the largest of the suburbs and two decades ago, Cicero, another suburb, was the second largest city in the state. Outside of Chicago, only four places (Rockford, Springfield, Peoria, and Decatur) surpass the size of these suburbs.

For all its appeal to that special sentiment which attaches to the bucolic and the urban village, Illinois is the crossroads of the nation. The state possesses more interstate expressway mileage than any other. It has been the rail capital of the nation since there were railways. And it lies athwart four of the five great migration routes that settled the country. All these ways of passage have left the state overlain by a strange mix of people. The southernmost section, Egypt, combines blacks and whites from the Mississippi Delta alongside a population of coal miners who resemble those from West Virginia. Moving north, a section of "Hoosiers" define what was once called "the Sucker State." They mingle northward with a German and English population which in turn merges with an admixture of Scandinavians at the Wisconsin border. Chicago itself is built up, layer by layer, zone by zone with the passage of New Englanders, Germans and Scandinavians, Irish and Italians, Eastern Europeans, blacks, and now the Mexicans.

Illinois, then, contains within itself virtually all the divisions, rivalries, and animosities of the nation. This does not make it typical but extreme. It harbors almost all the difficulties that are experienced more modestly elsewhere. Yet its political structure, its urban forms, and its own choice of self-presentation would lead a stranger to think that it is only a kind of enlarged village. So far as its political forms are concerned, this impression is not simply a matter of cultural lag or midwestern populism. For over a century the long ballot, the off-year elections, the elected judges, and endless list of local

While, on the Michigan side of lake. . .

governments have been designed so as to favor the politically obedient. There is not even much effort to disguise it.

Despite their plainness, political manipulation, and congestion of animosities, Illinois and Chicago can extract from some
people an exceptional loyalty and rather extraordinary burst of
creativity as writers, poets, journalists, and public servants. It is not
like the South where you have to defend it so often that you get to
believe what you say. It is more like Mencken's "Middle Empire."

The Spirit of Chicago—1929.

EIGHT

MENCKEN'S MIDDLE EMPIRE

When the Chicago Bears won the 1986 Super Bowl, the public response was so awesome as to be excessive. Undoubtedly, everyone was starved for a championship, but the most impressive part of the downtown reception was the recognition of *how* the Bears had won the Super Bowl; they had gone through the offensive line of the New England Patriots like shit through a goose. Tons of shredded paper were dumped from the buildings along LaSalle Street. At least 300,000 fans simply overcame the mounted policemen in the near zero weather. Some of the Bears emerged out of the top of the buses to sample flasks brought by generous fans. Even Mayor Washington was out there "giving them the finger" to the consternation of some image-conscious journalists. They were the "Grabowskis" said Mike Ditka, not the "Smiths" you find in Los Angeles.

A certain amount of grossness is essential to Chicagoans. It is their way of assuring one another of their genuineness, their lack of pretense, their membership in Mencken's "Middle Empire." Chicago emerged out of post-Jacksonian America when the common man of the nation's posterior had reached a level of numerical and political power unequaled by symbolic recognition. Above all, there was no place, no city, to measure up to the claims of our eastern cradles of nationhood and continuing kinship to the better parts of Europe. For a while, Cincinnati, Louisville, and Lexington carried on a fierce rivalry to approach the standards of the East (Wade 1959). But all their efforts were overshadowed when it was discovered that Chicago could be made into a much more interesting iconoclast. Not simply a weakened imitation of the East, but a mockery of imitation itself; "not London and Harvard . . . not Paris and buttermilk," but American "in every chitterling and sparerib" and "alive from snout to tail." Mencken (1917) saw it clearest, helped give it form, and then let us deceive ourselves by saying it was simply there without journalistic hype.

Admittedly, Chicago had many attractions to draw this kind of selective attention. Situated on a mud plain, named after a foul-smelling plant, it was full or foreigners, squalor, dust, boisterous politicians, and greedy businessmen. Of course, all these ingredients were available in other American cites, but in Chicago they were to be made exemplary. What was common elsewhere could be made here into a statement about America: a defiant disclaimer to the borrowed images of eastern hierarchy. If Chicago had not existed, some other foul-smelling place would have had to be invented.

There was no lack of self-consciousness in this creation. From the outset the small town at the southern end of Lake Michigan had found itself at the periphery of national attention, especially from the country's capital. To compensate, Chicago's political and business leaders practically besieged the federal government for canals, railroad right-of-ways, and contracts. No claim was too brazen, no scheme too base, if it would overcome this sense of disfavor. As early as 1850, the city was host to what was then a huge gathering of 20,000 people to complain of federal neglect of their region. Many of the city's earliest and most prominent residents were from upstate New York or nearby New England (Jaher 1982, pp. 454–456), and some of them seem to have harbored a standing grudge against familiar rivals in New York City or Boston.[1] The emergence of political promoters like Stephen Douglas, "Long John" Wentworth, and "Deacon" Bross gave direction and shape to this sense of being cut loose from the ordered and borrowed world of *New* England. Chicago was a newspaperman's town before it was a writer's town, and "the windy city" was at first a political, not a climatological description.

This shameless insistence on being noteworthy and being different did not go unchallenged. The first generation of Chicago writers—Chatfield-Taylor, Juletta Kinzie, E. P. Roe, Henry Fuller, Will Payne—misspent their talent trying either to disguise the crudity of their contemporaries or to shame them into a more refined appearance (Duncan 1964, pp. 5–10). By the time of the Columbian Exposition this show of gentility, however, was on the wane, and the "newspaper gang" of Edgar Lee Masters had seized the local

1. A thorough schooling in the compulsive competitiveness of New England village life may have been of equal importance. Harris observes in his study of P. T. Barnum (1973, p. 10) that "the passage from Puritan to Yankee involved psychological as well as economic changes and the Yankee type was forged in the furnace of village animosities."

readership from Chatfield-Taylor's "Little Room Group." From 1893 on, the city's novelists, journalists, and promoters built layer upon layer of popular and high culture that spoke with unanimity about the character of Chicago and the nation's "middle empire:" Its overt love of money, its shameless fascination with everything big, its polyglot population, its preoccupation with production, its unmasked intolerance, its willingness to compare poets and hogbellies.

At present this inventory is so repetitive and so mnemonically connected (Suttles 1984) that it has almost a life of its own. This inventory does not stand apart from daily life but colors much of its experiential content and transforms the remainder so that it has a selective meaning. Chicagoans do not start the day by a raw encounter with their environment. Instead many—perhaps most—start it by reading Mike Royko, Bob Green, or Bill Granger. When they ride, say, the El to work, they can review the latest graffiti to see which gangs have penetrated the neighborhood. As they make the final walk to work, they can recall who has run for election for the last five to ten years by examining the posters still plastered on the light poles. Work is not usually carried out in some austere, neutral cubical but occurs within buildings made conscious of their designers; rooms and offices decorated with signs of ethnic or athletic pride; and work mates bearing their own personal messages of loyalty and disaffection on their chests, hats, behinds. During the ride home they can survey the vanity plates and bumper stickers to find yet more local loyalists or critics. At home they can begin the long voyage to Dallas, Miami, 47th Street, Atlanta, or other places including Chicago which have become sets for formulaic dramas that freeze urban places into commercial simplicity and contrast.

Although Chicagoans are literally showered with reminders of who they are and how they differ from others, underneath it all there seems to be a current of doubt about whether or not Mencken's "abbatoir by the lake" can make its way unchanged into the next decade. Some of this uneasiness must arise from the regional setback. How long can "that toddling town" lose population without confessing maturity? And hogbutcher? That has been a figure of speech for forty years. The steel industry is being robotized and turned over to technicians who dress like laboratory scientists. U.S. Steel is now USX Corporation. International Harvester is Navistar.

Mencken's Middle Empire

The biggest growth industry is the futures market, a series of increasingly glitzy buildings, where high rollers can go to avoid the more common neon of Las Vegas. Gay Chicago is probably larger than what remains of Polonia. And there is not a brewery left in town.

Sometime back it was circumstances like this which drove Mike Royko to poetry.

CHICAGO

Hi-Rise for the World
Partygoer; Stacker of Stereo Tapes
Player with Home Pool Table and the Nation's Jets;
Dapper, slender, filter-tipped,
City of the Big Credit Card:
They tell me you are wicked, and I don't believe them; for
I have seen your painted men tossed in jail every time
they try luring the farm boys.
And they tell me you are crooked, and I answer; Yes,
it is true, but now you steal with the ballpoint pen
and contract, and that's no fun.
And having answered so I turn once more to those who
sneer at this my city, and I join in the sneer and
say to them:
Come and show me another city with razor-cut head
singing so proud to have a Mustang and a white
turtleneck and reservation for dinner.
Fierce as a poodle with tongue lapping for dog yummies.
Wig-headed,
Skiing,
Spending,
Twisting,
Purchasing, discarding, repurchasing,
Under the big restaurant canopy, burgundy sauce
all over his mouth, giggling with white capped teeth.
Under the terrible burden of Consolidated Monthly
Payments, giggling as a disk jockey giggles.
Chuckling even as a smooth salesman chuckles who
has never lost a sale.
Bragging and chuckling that on his wrist is a
battery-operated watch and under his ribs a moroccan
leather belt.
Giggling!
Giggling the silly giggle of the fourth martini
at lunch: half naked, but not sweating, and if
sweating, not offending; Proud to be Hi-Rise
for the World, Partygoer, Stacker of Stereo Tapes,

Player with Home Pool Tables and Jet Handler to the
Nation.
(San-Fran-York on the Lake, 1968)

Of course, intrusive anomalies like these can be overcome as Royko
does with suitable mockery. What really seems to unsettle the town
is not the fear that it has lost its neon soul, but that it might have to
embrace a higher destiny: *Chicago might have to become a world-class
city!* People began talking about it almost as soon as Mayor Daley
died. For example, when Mayor Bilandic married Heather Morgan,
he moved from Bridgeport up to the Gold Coast and, no sooner
there, he wanted to build a world class library and to start a world
class marathon.[2] Governor Thompson built a world class State of Illinois building. Previously, if you wanted to put up a building in
Chicago, all you had to say was that it would be the tallest, biggest,
or have the most parking spaces of any in the world. Now it has to be
"world class."[3]

What really gave momentum to this elevation in municipal
longing was an article by Andrew Neil in the *Economist* (Spring 1980)
where he said that "Chicago has the right credentials" to "reach for
the world" and become a truly world class city. Coming from a European, a Scot at that, this was a compelling charge. The city, however,
was not totally unprepared. There were a number of people quietly
waging a campaign for another world's fair, something to top the
last two and launch Chicago into the next century ("The Age of Dis-
covery"). Neil's article gave them courage (Branden, 1984), and they
went public with their mission before they knew what it was. Still
another group, mostly North Siders, were sponsoring something
called "The Bright New City." They wanted to restore night life in
the downtown with unanxious tourists. Some people even spoke
shamelessly of "Manhattanizing" the downtown by bringing in full-
time residents. They would go to a world class stadium just to the
south along the river, attend a world class performing arts center at
the southern end of Grant Park, and contemplate a new world class
symbol of Chicago out in the lake (*Chicago Central Area Plan* 1983).

2. We got the marathon.
3. This aspiration for "class" has not totally replaced local pride in sheer volume. A
recent promotional brochure included at least one page extolling the city's "number
one" rank in the production of many items (e.g., bolts, nuts, rivets, washers, metal
barrels, drums, pails, etc.) as well as a series of "Chicago Firsts" (e.g., the world's
"highest restaurant"). I note, however, that the list of "Chicago Firsts" no longer includes the nation's largest parking lot.

Chicagoans responded to all these improving schemes in various ways, and one of them was with confusion.

Borrowed Glory

Not entirely familiar with what is a world class city, one tendency was unselective borrowing from cities like Baltimore and Detroit. Waterfront festivals are an "in thing" in America, but it was not until Mayor Bilandic that Chicago got its own. Called "Chicagofest" and situated on Navy Pier, it attracted hoards of people who strolled along the sunlit pier, sipping light beer, girl-boy watching, eating pizza, listening to rock bands, and swapping jokes in front of the porto-potties. The crowds were remarkably well behaved. Whites came. Blacks came. Children and suburbanites came. Even people from Wisconsin came to sip St. Louis beer. It was Mayor Bilandic's fondest, tearful memory in his farewell address as mayor.

Not everyone, however, approved of this idle show of good nature, and there were those who spoke of it as "bread and circuses." Jesse Jackson disapproved. Reverend Jackson did not seem to mind all the beer drinking and consumerism, but he was thoroughly roused by the number of jobs and contracts given whites. He started a campaign against Chicagofest, and when Byrne came into office she said she would put a stop to the event. The public reaction was almost wholly negative, and she promptly reversed herself. Jesse Jackson was unrelenting, however, and called for a black boycott of Chicagofest. The effects of the boycott were disputed,[4] but when Washington came into office he felt honor bound to end Chicagofest.

---

4. Some black entertainers declined to perform, and black attendance was down. But some say that only increased suburban attendance. Still, attendance at Chicagofest had become a "racial statement" as so frequently happens in Chicago. Despite the prevalence of black athletes on Chicago sports teams, none of the teams are closely identified with the black community. When the Bears won the Super Bowl, the team was still described as belonging to the immigrants (the "Grabowskis"). As Stephen Chapman (*Tribune*, 2 January 1986) pointed out, the media hype bore little resemblance to a team that includes Walter "Sweetness" Payton, Gary Fencik, a Yale Yuppie, and Mike Singletary who sets his nerves for a game by listening to baroque music.

Chicago sports teams have low black attendance, and their owners seem more inclined to move to the suburbs than to give blacks a piece of their team's identity. The "Cubbies," of course, have always had a following among the more genteel and are beneficiaries of a "gay cheer"—a raised fist with a limp wrist.

At first Washington tried to replace this festival with local, ghettoized minifestivals, and while people did not seem to mind drinking beer in their own neighborhood they did not produce the contracts and jobs Reverend Jackson wanted. Gradually, then, there has been a restoration of the lakefront festival in the expansion of the "Taste of Chicago," an event (modeled after the one in New York's Central Park) originally held on North Michigan Avenue where one could obtain tidbits of food from the city's better restaurants at modest prices. The food now comes from less select eateries, is served in larger portions for still higher prices, and the light beer has been replaced with regular brew. Essentially, it repeats gastronomically the city's ethnic mix.

There is also an International Folk Festival where one can find groups like the Belorussians who may not have a neighborhood in Chicago but who are still lobbying to restore a nation elsewhere. Some of the politically more significant groups in the city get a lakefront festival of their own. When Byrne was mayor, budgetary reports on these festivals conveniently listed expenses by ethnic groups. Washington's budgetary reports made a point of listing expenditures by turf or community area. One exception to this procession of ethnic groups is Mike Royko's lakefront event where people compete to concoct the most formidable barbecued ribs. It is truly open to world competition, and in 1985 a confessed Yuppie took first honors. Recently, Royko even relented and let vegetarians enter the event. It is one of the few self-supporting lakefront events, receiving nothing from the motel-hotel tax fund which is supposed to promote the city.

All these festivals offer far more latitude for consumerism than do the more traditional State Street parades, and the latter are now less well attended and frequently moved to another location. The festivals are unburdened by political speeches and shows of party loyalty or Americanism. Thus, they genuinely reflect the fragmentation of the city. At the same time, they are well attended and have a diverse participation. It is apparent that Chicagoans like to get out of their neighborhoods and have a low-risk encounter with people unlike themselves. Shows of nationhood also are not totally missing, and the best attended of all festivals is a July 3 fireworks extravaganza where people bring their own food and listen to the Grant Park orchestra raise the "1812 Overture" to new decibel levels. Recently, that festival has been merged with Taste of Chicago so that you can support the local ethnic (and fast food) eat-

Mencken's Middle Empire

eries. Some people see these events as publicly sponsored pigouts, but they can also be seen as an experience of tolerance for each other's more local loyalties. And, of course, an evasion of the expression of wider ones.

When Mayor Byrne was still in office, she was especially captured by the enthusiasm for lakefront events. She made expeditions to Baltimore, Atlantic City, New York, and even Paris to see if they had anything worth bringing to Chicago. One thing that really caught her eye was a downtown Grand Prix race which would have moved Chicago into the same league as Detroit, Charlotte, and Indianapolis. It would have run a right-angled course enclosing Grant Park "to showcase our city to the rest of the world" (*Sun-Times*, 24 September 1980). Park District officials said their only problem was how much money the promoters would pay the district. The local museums took a different view, saying that it would close them down along with a quarter of the north-south traffic in the city. Byrne was insistent, but her promoters eventually backed out saying that people were just too "concerned about picnics and bird-watching" (*Sun-Times*, 24 September 1980). Byrne proposed, as well, a casino like the ones in Atlantic City so that people could spend money closer to home. It was never a popular idea. In a city

Primitive commensalism: "We're Havin' an Eat Wave."

already world class in its organized crime, people seemed to think that something might go wrong with a casino.

Mayor Washington also made expeditions to other cities to advance Chicago. He adopted Shenyang, China, as Chicago's sister city although the relationship seems more instrumental than familial. Shenyang is the location for the Illinois Trade Office on mainland China. Some British journalists have volunteered Liverpool as "Cook County, U.K." but no Chicagoans have laid claim to this sister city. Nor is there any response to Toulon, France, where racial strife has led the citizens to christen the dockyard area "Little Chicago." Despite these signs of recognition in faraway places, an eager airline consultant told Mayor Washington that the city simply has no image. Washington, himself, said that he wanted to "reimagize" Chicago, and his administration has coined the slogan "The City that Works Together," but many people believe that it speaks better to something absent than something present.

The for-profit sector has not been altogether backward in the search for new collective representations. Some leading businessmen established a "Chicago Business Hall of Fame" in which local entrepreneurs can be installed just like football players are in Canton, Ohio. The Cook County medical examiner was far less successful when he proposed a murder museum to display some of the city's more gruesome killings. It attracted a hail of criticism although others agreed that it would have been as impressive as London's Black Museum and would have drawn many more tourists than the Business Hall of Fame.

If some of these events seem a bit desperate, it must be remembered that most of them were borrowed from other cities. Chicago is not alone in its graceless democratization of consumption, its avoidance of serious self-examination, and its inability to find symbols of collectivity larger than those of ethnicity, race, and neighborhood. Waving the flag is now a partisan act given over to one political party. There are almost no military uniforms visible at such events and, in Chicago, the servicemen from Great Lakes Naval Base and Fort Sheridan come in civvies.[5] Yet tolerance or apprehension extend to an absence of critical comparisons. In 1986 about the same-size crowd attended the July 3 Taste of Chicago as attended New York's

---

5. Except, of course, young people in camouflage battle fatigues waging their endless war of independence.

restoration of the nation's most famous tourist trap.[6] From the news accounts, the two events seem almost the same, a kind of primitive commensualism unsure of its deservedness.

Marketing Nostalgia and Modernity

Local boosters can still be heard to say that Chicago is the youngest of the world's great cities, but their statement no longer carries the weight of Sandburg's poetic license to replace all its existing buildings. Preservationists and developers now carry on an internecine struggle that sometimes breaks out into guerilla war. One day in the spring of 1978, for example, people arriving downtown noticed that workmen were hacking away at the ornamental exterior of the Troescher Building (designed by Adler and Sullivan). Sure enough, a demolition permit had been quietly granted the owners. Preservationists tried to intercede and demanded public hearings. By the time they succeeded, six months later, the building had been made unsalvageable.

The threat of destruction is so critical that preservationists must mount a twenty-four-hour watch to see that someone does not run off with another building. Landmark status itself is not always sufficient. The owner of Rinker House (Chicago's second oldest) bulldozed it "by mistake." He had another house in mind, and the workmen just picked the wrong one.

Those trying to preserve some portion of Chicago's architectural past, however, are no longer dismissed as cranks and antiquarians. Very large segments of the American population now find themselves able to openly appreciate ornamentation (Harris 1983). Modernism had produced its own wars, inequalities, unlivable spaces, and bad press (Wolfe 1981). In Chicago, however, this desire for preservation draws support from more than just a change in taste. Architecture is Chicago's most visible and monumental achievement. Its conservation is as much a part of the convention trade as is the Sears Tower, "Big John" (Hancock Building), or "Big Stan" (Standard Oil Building). Others pressing for some kind of conservation are moved by a sense of group honor or past

6. The one effort at serious reflection reported by the *New York Times* (7 July 1986) was that of a panel that drew the conclusion that "liberty" means "community." If community means restraint and collective service, then the panel may have obscured more than it revealed.

accomplishment. Catholics from the suburbs are sometimes jarred into action when they hear that "their" parish church in Chicago is to be torn down. They struggle with an embarrassed archdiocese that has too many churches and too few parishioners. Other buildings have no certifiable architectural merit. Nonetheless, they are the headstones where some group of people remember their ancestors.

Frequently, the preservation of existing structures also becomes another weapon in more general debates over land-use changes. The landmark designation of the Loop El was as much a way of undermining the Franklin Street Connector and subway as a way of retaining this "vaguely italianate" railroad track. The designation of residential districts and tax relief for their owners is more an invitation to gentrification than architectural appreciation. Knowing this, some "lakeside liberals" (including the governor who sponsored the bill) already living in gentrified areas have piously reversed themselves in extending the same tax relief to other areas lest it lead to "displacement." Yet on more than one occasion civic and political leaders have "threatened" entire city blocks with landmark status to get the local merchant's associations to exert some restraint in outdoor advertisement and density of development.

These various strategies make for improbable opponents. Arthur Rubloff, who wanted to destroy practically every landmark building in the North Loop, locked horns with Potter Palmer III when all he wanted was to build a funeral home at the Rosehill Cemetery where some of Rubloff's kinfolk are buried. Members of the Union League Club still oppose the reuse of the Goldblatt building as a library because libraries, they say, "should be like cathedrals." The City Club fought a losing battle to restore the Chicago Theater to its original use as a film palace for suburban nostalgia buffs while its current restorers see it primarily as a live theater for contemporary productions.

Preservationists are divided into several camps: those who are just nostalgic, purists who insist upon exact restoration of appearance and function, those who want to clean up the city's history and impress outsiders, those who want to hype the infamous for the tourist industry, and those who want to combine an exterior of nostalgia with an interior of modernity. There is both fascination and commercial possibilities with places and people celebrated in criminal history. Despite all the Van der Rohe look-a-likes, the city still has the sort of "grainy," highly textured appearance that moviemakers like to include in criminal drama. Thus, under the leadership of Lucy Salenger, Chicago has become an important site for film locations. Its gritty appearance, the screeching El, the rows of six-flats, and the wind-whipped garbage give plausibility to a scale of lawlessness that just could not occur elsewhere.

This renewed attention to the past is combined with a growing interest in the avant garde. The Art Institute now includes so many modern pieces that the segmentation between its patrons and those of the Museum of Contemporary Art has become problematic. Local artists also now find it possible to sell their works without having to go to New York first to establish themselves. Collecting art from elsewhere is well established in Chicago; it combined a growth investment with social recognition. Investor confidence now extends to local artists. The less-collectable arts, such as ballet, were never well supported until recently. Indeed, Tallchief's ballet may have failed, but the Hubbard Street Dancers' boisterous mix of tap, gymnastics, and comedy seems to have thoroughly won the local taste for athleticism.

Chicago's public sculpture has gone through an even more radical about-face. Prior to the 1960s, Chicago sculpture consisted almost entirely of figurative pieces which celebrated group honor and heroic accomplishment: a modest number of pieces that asserted the city's inclusion in the grand Western Pagan-Judaic-Christian tradition (e.g., goddesses, virgins: 12%), a regal bestiary (e.g., lions, eagles: 10%), the Nation's founders (e.g., George Washington: 6%), regional discoverers (e.g., Marquette: 5%), native sons (e.g., Lincoln: 15%), the captains of industry (e.g., Marshall Field: 14%), and ethnic advancement (e.g., Kosciuszko: 27%).[7] For the most part, they took the form of personification and were occasioned by some notable event: the conclusion of a war, the construction of an expensive public building, the assertion of ethnic presence, the end of a riot. They are easily recognized. Plaques explain their meaning and give the names of those represented or honored. They are popular art as well as high art and meant to stir one's attachment to place and group.

One of the earliest thoroughly modern pieces was Calder's

7. The percentages refer to the distribution included in Bach and Gray's *Chicago's Public Sculpture* (1983). Bach and Gray's choices for inclusion are neither exhaustive nor representative in the statistical sense. However, their list is authoritative and what Chicagoans are directed to appreciate. See Riedy (1981) for a very similar selection.

"Red Petals" commissioned by the Arts Club of Chicago.[8] By the early 1960s, a few large apartment houses and office towers incorporated modern sculptures at their entrances or in their lobbies, and the University of Chicago had commissioned several for its campus. These were private organizations, and their precedent made little impression until the public commissioning of Picasso's "Chicago" in 1967. A doubtful Mayor Daley and a reluctant Picasso were convinced to situate the 50-foot, 160-ton[9] Cor-ten steel figure on the plaza of the new Civic Center. Picasso declared that Chicago was his kind of town, and Daley himself unveiled the thing. It was the source of instant controversy and publicity. One alderman wanted to deport it and replace it with a statue of Ernie Banks. Ten years later a local architect was still campaigning to replace it with a memorial to Daley. By then, however, city boosters had recognized Picasso's promotional power, and from that time on the art critic Franz Schulze could say with confidence that "public art [in Chicago] is by now modern art with virtually no exceptions" (Bach and Gray 1983, p. xiv). A Calder, a Chagall, an Oldenburg, a Miro, and a Dubuffet, each on a grand scale, have been added over the years. Public buildings now include an institutional provision (Illinois percent for art program) for yet more sculpture. A small park has been set aside for sculptural adventures that can be displayed for one year, and Judy Chicago has appropriated the city's name to promote her own outspoken approach to the vagina. The Picasso is said to have become "the most instantly recognized symbol of Chicago" (Riedy 1981, p. 253).

Dozens of other pieces dot the city's landscape with three dimensional puzzles, overscale spoofs, and a new bestiary of bumpers. They are an invitation to the new city of consumption, entertainment, and showmanship.[10] When seen together, they bring into clearer awareness the funerary aspects of previous sculptures.

All this attention to the promotional value of high art extends to new audiences and new media. The Chicago Symphony Orchestra, long appreciated by local loyalists, now receives mass attention. The press counts Sir George Solti's Grammy Awards as if they were

8. It was commissioned in 1942 but not placed on public view until 1951.

9. Ridey says it weighs only 132 tons but 160 is the figure repeated most often.

10. There are exceptions to this—for example, Kelly's "I Will," a celebration of local achievement, and McCullogh's "Our King, Dr. Martin Luther King, Jr." But most are well described by Schulze's statement that they are "seldom definable as somebody or something" (Riedy 1981, p. xii).

sports trophies, and some writers refer to the "CSO" as casually as others do to the "U of I" football team. Mayor Washington recently said that the orchestra was the city's best ambassador in attracting business and industry. In 1984, the Lyric Opera made the cover the telephone book white pages on its thirtieth anniversary.[11] The Chicago Pro Musica brought home a Grammy to general applause for its first recording. The Biograph Theater, Dillinger's last air-conditioned resting place, now shows art films, and a Chicago Film Festival is scattered across the North Side each year. In 1986, the city hosted its first International Theater Festival.

Chicago's artists and their supporters are surprisingly far in advance of the official agencies directly responsible for local promotion. In the last year of his administration, Daley did establish a committee to attract outside investors. Tom Ayers of Commonwealth Edison was made chairman and essentially continued that firm's program to increase the number of energy users. The committee's main product was a couple of booklets with rather dreary black and white photos, maps, and tables emphasizing the city's central location, transportation access, and ample space for industrial expansion. Under Bilandic's administration, a number of glossy brochures were produced with upbeat slogans ("Chicago says let's talk business," "The city that works can work for you," "Chicago's got it"), and the thematic emphasis extended to downtown cultural activities.

By the time of the Byrne administration, the promotional efforts of nearby Wisconsin ("Escape to Wisconsin!") and Michigan ("Say yes to Michigan!") were so apparent that local business groups found themselves in the peculiar position of having to convince political leaders that things were so bad that a special effort had to be made to deny it. ("Illinois, you put me in a happy state" and "The Magnificent Miles of Illinois" were the antidote.) Since then both the city and state have created substantial budgets for promotion. Byrne's efforts were captioned by two slogans, "Chicago, my kind of town" and "Chicago: One town that won't let you down." That campaign soon fell victim to allegations of political favoritism (Lochin 1986). Like Bilandic, however, Byrne's print

---

11. The local museums made the cover in 1983. This is a new promotional trend for Chicago's most visible book. In the 1950s and early 1960s the covers usually featured a telephone company employee. In the 1970s it usually portrayed a tall building or familiar downtown cityscape.

material emphasized more the city's cultural events and extended to mention the region's colleges and universities.

The Washington administration was slow to establish a clear direction for promotional activity until 1984. Washington, himself, first emphasized the corruptibility of his predecessors and adversaries and then promised to clean up the city's "rat-a-tat-tat" image. Later, the administration settled on the slogan "The city that works together." Print material includes all the themes of previous administrations and attempts to extend the notion that Chicago is a city of diversity and wide choices. This permits a more positive statement on the city's ethnic and racial mix. It also provides the opportunity to tell prospective residents that there are parochial and private schools as an alternative to the public schools.

In all this promotional material one is struck by the constraints of the official public boosters. They seem to be walking a fine line between very upbeat showmanship and a sober effect to prove that they are "bottom of the line" realists. Little is made of the city's past. The only memorable accomplishment so far was a state-sponsored TV commercial featuring a very attractive Ms. Patty Rooney relaxing in the snow and inviting viewers to spend Christmas "where it's hot in winter—Chicago." One staff member told me that she would love to run an ad featuring Al Capone with the caption "Come to my city or else," but the opportunity eludes her.

Freedom from these constraints is probably one reason that private individuals and firms are so far ahead in their showmanship. Artists, actors, and performers know by training and experience that controversy, outrage, and novelty are essential to catch the public's attention. They also seem to grasp almost intuitively the need to link new symbols to old ones so that what is familiar can help to bring to mind what is new (Suttles 1984). One does not purify a city's past, then, without losing some capacity for recognition and association. Even when the past is only an anachronism, it can be "museumized" to create this kind of connective tissue between the familiar and the new. For example, when Studs Terkel grumbled that the Biograph Theater would no longer have "the smell of Dillinger around," owner Larry Edwards, an ex–real estate entrepreneur, obliged with a fifty-year anniversary showing of "Manhattan Melodrama," Dillinger's fateful choice.

The practitioners of popular and high art have always had to hustle in Chicago. There are not that many angels around, and they usually supported an established product like the Art Institute or the Chicago Symphony. Still, there has always been just enough opportunity to entice experimentalists.

Still an Outlaw's Capital

One of the likely reactions of a city which is being upstaged by new places like Houston is to look to its past for guidance or solace. This return to an urban past seems particularly intense in Chicago because there is a sense of being unanchored to familiar geographic and demographic features. Even in my own university press, one can see something of this turn from the present to the past.

Between 1962 and 1979, the number of original, contemporary studies of Chicago or Chicagoans published (table 8.1) was roughly the same as the number of historical studies published. From 1980 to 1986, the number of historical studies climbed sharply while only three books were published on contemporary social conditions.[12] The decline in contemporary studies, of course, did not start promptly in 1980 because the lead time for preparing such a book can be several years. Guterbock's 1980 book began in 1972. Barr and Dreeben began their research in 1969 and the manuscript in 1979. Taub et al. began their principal survey in 1977. This lapse in scholarly attention to local social conditions, then, probably started much earlier.[13] The inaccessibility of much of the city's population, and the tendency to gather data by more indirect means or from less hostile sources are a two-decade-long practice. The familiar approaches of live-in ethnography, face-to-face interviews, and casual observations are more difficult to take and to publish without giving offense.

The University of Chicago Press, of course, tries hard to be unrepresentative. Yet, if we look at the Subject Index to *Books in Print*

12. Choices for inclusion in table 8.1 required some close calls. For example, none of Paley's books are included although they concern her preschoolers at the University Laboratory School. She reports on them as children, not as Chicagoans. Similar close calls at other periods or according to topic would just about even out across categories. I also doubt that many of these differences are due to University of Chicago Press policy. There has been no major change in Press management, and my own observations as a member of the Press board suggest no obvious change. Of course, I say this with all the biases (and privileged information) of a member of the board.

13. It may also be temporary. William Julius Wilson is undertaking a major study of Chicago minority households. Dennis Hogan and Evelyn Kitagawa have an ongoing study of teenage parents. Robert Dreeben is continuing his work in Chicago schools which now welcome researchers.

Table 8.1. Books Substantially Focused on Chicago or Chicagoans: Published by the University of Chicago Press, 1962–1986

Year Published	Contemporary Topics	Historical Topics
1962	Essien-Udom, *Black Nationalism* Wilson, *The Amateur Democrat*	Thomas, *John Dewey* McDonald, *Insull*
1963	Bogue, *Skid Row in American Cities*	. . .
1964	. . .	Condit, *The Chicago School of Architecture: 1875–1925* Wade, *Graham Taylor*
1965	Short and Strodtbeck, *Group Process and Gang Delinquency*	Siegal, *Chicago's Famous Buildings*
1966	Keil, *Urban Blues*	Storrs, *Harper's University* Byrd, *A Bibliography of Illinois Imprints, 1814–1858* The University of Chicago Press, *Catalogue of Books and Journals: 1891–1965* (75th anniversary volume)
1967	Oaks and Lehman, *A Criminal Justice System and the Indigent*	Spear, *Black Chicago*
1968	Suttles, *The Social Order of the Slum*	. . .
1969	. . .	Findlay, *Dwight L. Moody: American Evangelist 1837–1899* Mayer and Wade, *Chicago: Growth of a Metropolis*
1970	Zald, *Organizational Change* Rees and Schultz, *Workers and Wages in an Urban Labor Market* Ryan, *Don't Smile Until Christmas*	Hyman, *The Lives of Sidney Benton* Wells-Barnett, *Crusade for Justice* Faris, *Chicago Sociology*
1971	. . .	. . .
1972	Suttles, *The Social Construction of Communities*	. . .
1973	. . .	Condit, *Chicago 1910–1929: Building, Planning and Technology*
1974	Bidley, *Radicals in Urban Politics* Kornblum, *Blue Collar Community* Hunter, *Symbolic Communities*	Condit, *Chicago 1930–1970: Building, Planning and Technology* Karl, *Charles E. Merriam and the Study of Politics*
1975	. . .	Kantowitcz, *Polish-American Politics in Chicago*
1976	Cuban, *Urban School Chiefs under Fire* Peterson, *School Politics, Chicago Style*	Murphy and Bruckner, *The Idea of the University of Chicago* Duis, *Chicago: Creating New Traditions*
1977	Jacobs, *Stateville*	Darling, *Chicago Metalismiths*

continued

Table 8.1. continued

	Hughes, *Behind the Wall of Respect*	Joachim, *Art Institute of Chicago French Drawings and Sketchbooks of the 18th Century*
1978	Anderson, *A Place on the Corner*	Block, *Hyde Park Houses*
1979	Kellam, *Mental Health and Going to School*	Hines, *Burnham of Chicago*
		Harrison, *A Times Affair*
	Goodwin, *The Oak Park Strategy*	Holt and Pacyza, *Chicago: A Historical Guide to the Neighborhoods*
	Buroway, *Manufacturing Consent*	Joachim and McCullogh, *Italian Drawings in the Art Institute of Chicago*
1980	Guterbock, *Machine Politics in Transition*	Darling, *Chicago Ceramics and Glass*
		Wright, *Moralism and the Modern Home*
		Lewis and Smith, *American Sociology and Pragmatism*
1981	. . .	Lane, *Chicago Churches and Synagoges*
		Bennett, *Oral History and Delinquency*
1982	. . .	Darling, *Decorative and Architectural Arts in Chicago*
1983	Barr and Dreeben, *How Schools Work*	Bach and Gray, *A Guide to Chicago's Public Sculpture*
		Block, *The Uses of Gothic*
1984	Taub et al., *Paths of Neighborhood Change*	Connors, *The Robie House of Frank Lloyd Wright*
		Bulmer, *The Chicago School of Sociology*
		Kurz, *Evaluating Chicago Sociology*
		Rossen, *The Art Institute of Chicago Museum Studies, vol. 1, no. 1*
		Smith, *Chicago and the American Literary Imagination: 1880–1920*
1985	. . .	Rossen, *The Art Institute of Chicago Museum Studies, vol. 1, no. 2*
		Schulze, *Mies Van Der Rohe*
		Rossen, *The Art Institute of Chicago Museum Studies, vol. 1, no. 1*
		Peterson, *The Politics of School Reform: 1870–1940*
1986	. . .	Harrington, *Mies Van Der Rohe: Architect as Educator*
		Slayton, *Back of the Yards*
		Rossen, *The Art Institute of Chicago Museum Studies, vol. 1, no. 2*
		Provine, *Sewall Wright and Evolutionary Biology*

Mencken's Middle Empire

(1986), the disproportionate number of historical studies of Chicago as against contemporary ones is even more extreme over the last fifteen years (table 8.2). This listing is an indication of which books have been kept in print (i.e., their marketability) rather than all those published, but it is still revealing. Contemporary studies published prior to 1970 and still in print outnumber historical studies about two to one. Historical studies published afterward and still in print outnumber contemporary ones by the same margin. Either there were a lot more historical studies of Chicago completed during the last fifteen years or the recent historical studies are being kept in print much longer than contemporary ones.

Most (65%) of the contemporary studies published after 1979 are scholarly or serious journalistic efforts, but this proportion is still higher (89%) among the historical studies done in the same period. As one might expect, most of the contemporary studies published in the 1920–1939 period are associated with the Chicago School of Sociology, and the majority were republished in the late 1960s and 1970s. The lapse in contemporary studies still in print over the next three decades (1940–1969) is probably due to a decline in that school. During the 1970s, however, there does seem to have been a

Table 8.2. Nonfiction Books on Chicago Listed in *Subject Guide to Books in Print* by Original Year of Publication[a]

Period	Contemp. Studies		Historical Studies		Consumer Guides	
	(N)	(%)	(N)	(%)	(N)	(%)
Before 1900	8	9	5	4	—	—
1900–1909	1	1	—	—	—	—
1910–1919	3	4	3	3	—	—
1920–1929	6	7	—	—	—	—
1930–1939	14	16	4	4	—	—
1940–1949[b]	2	2	2	2	—	—
1950–1959	2	2	—	—	—	—
1960–1969	3	4	4	4	1	2
1970–1974	8	9	12	11	1	2
1975–1979	12	14	26	23	25	43
1980–1985	26	31	56	50	31	53
Total	85	100	112	100	58	100

[a]5 percent could not be classified because of missing dates or because of inappropriate categorization, e.g., maps, bibliographies, quizzes, etc.

[b]Over 90 percent of the books originally published before 1950 had been reissued at a subsequent date. Almost all of them had been reissued during the very late 1960s or 1970s.

slight revival of a similar approach, and seven of twenty titles incorporate ethnographic reports. Four of the titles are by University of Chicago students, however, and I know they started before 1970. As with the University of Chicago Press, additional ethnographic studies essentially disappear after Guterbock's 1980 manuscript.[14] By contrast, the number of consumer guides outnumber these contemporary studies. If Chicago scholars find it difficult to contemplate the present or to approach it on intimate terms, they will find it easy to locate alternative distractions.

Chicago's journalists and writers of fiction are presented with a more difficult dilemma. The most generous estimate would put the city's middle-income population at below 50 percent, and at either extreme there are large numbers of people who can be better defined by what they consume than by how they get the money to do it. Since the favored and most convincing style is one of relentless exposure, it requires both great familiarity with one's subject and a willingness to go for the jugular. Chicago literary characters are never simple moral figures but gain their plausibility from their failings, and they draw our interest because they are "acquisitive, transgressors who overreach themselves [to serve our] literary fix of fraud, con toughness and even slaughter. It's a form of Disneyland, or better, it's a national Oberammergau played with real nails and real blood."[15] To make believable narrative out of such material, one cannot simply pick any available moral weakling and flay him with merciless prose. Chicago heroes must fall from some height even if it is only the elevation of self-deceit.

But in a city where 20 percent of the population is on welfare and black, it seems wantonly cruel to torture them with further disclosure. One can always have fun at the expense of politicians and petty bureaucrats, but that is too easy. The political machine is so crippled that one is moved to sympathy or, more often, nostalgia. Still another portion of the city's population, the trendies, the yuppies, the singles, the gays, and airline stewardesses, the bunnies (the last, already history), and the TV personalities call for literary

14. Undoubtedly, there is a good deal of arbitrariness in what the editors of this volume include under the topic "Chicago." Neither Taub et al. nor Barr and Dreeben were included, possibly because these are both very recent publications. Almost all other studies familiar to me were included, and I was able to locate many more consumer guides than serious studies that had been omitted.

15. Quoted, with some license, from Richard Stern's "The Chicago Writer's City." I am indebted to Stern's paper and his commentary on it in one of my own courses. A version of this paper was published in his *The Position of the Body* (1987, pp. 21–29).

Mencken's Middle Empire

treatment, but it is hard to mold them from the vocabulary of an Algren, a Ferrell, or a Sandburg. Chicago writers do not wholly neglect them, but they usually remain remote counterfoils to the "real" people who preceded them. Of course, not all these "real" people have vacated the city. There are still ethnic pockets, petty crooks, con artists, street toughs, and whores. Dope dealing is more rampant than ever, and the sales rights to some corners are said to go for $10,000. The spoken word has not improved over Daley's example, and only a handful of the city's seventy-five high schools reach the nation's low average.

All these losers and winners ought to be proseworthy. What is left of the "real" people, however, seems like an atavism or something to put on the culture bus route for tourists. The others speak with a less familiar tongue. And they are often of an unfamiliar color.

It is hard to write convincing narrative about a population that, on the one hand, is seen as remote and plastic and, on the other, sessile and damaged. One of the most obvious casualties in the effort to do so was Nelson Algren. After his novel, *A Walk on the Wild Side* (1956),[16] critical success failed him. Algren's stories became progressively desperate for effect, as if he thought his reader numb from the previous encounter. The prose poem *City on the Make* is undoubtedly an evocative work, but if one reads it from the distance of thirty years, it becomes noticeable how little of it can be projected into the present. There is a splendid paragraph toward the beginning. "It's still an outlaw's capital—but of an outlawry whose colors, once crimson as the old Sauganash whiskey dye, have been washed down, by many prairie rains to the colorless grey of the self-made executive type playing the percentages from the inside. Under a pale fluorescent glow."

Throughout *City on the Make* Algren effectively uses the image of Chicago as a portage, a place of passage. But beyond this image and one compelling passage, Algren's imaginative powers remain rooted in pre–World War II Chicago. The sections on Chicago in *Who Lost an American?* (1960) attempt to bridge this gap, but manage only to sound like someone who has heard of and disliked the place from a reading of *Playboy* and *Town and Country*. Several years ago Algren left Chicago saying that it was too boring. In this 1983 introduction

16. *A Walk on the Wild Side* is actually a reworking of a 1935 shorter novel, *Somebody in Boots*. The last original work to have critical success was *Chicago: City on the Make* (1951).

to *City on the Make,* Studs Terkel denied Algren's lack of affection for Chicago or the weakening of his descriptive powers. At Algren's death in 1981, Mike Royko said that Algren was doing what he was always doing. Moving on. But I think that Algren was right about himself and Chicago. In the mid-1960s I spent a drunken night with him wandering about the West Side. Our ramble took the course of an homage to those places he had been before. He was so occupied with telling me what they were "really like" that neither of us could notice what was going on. As he stood, absorbed, before an empty lot where his mother had run a boarding house, unmindful of the traffic around him, it came over me that he was trying to reink a dry pen. It was the second and last time I ever saw him.

Terkel, himself, is a veritable genius at representing the past, making it seem like the present. Almost daily on the radio, tape recorder and mike close at hand, he would seem the embodiment of contemporaneity. Yet, once Terkel's subjects are rendered into print or edited script, a nineteen-year-old can sound as if he just walked out of the Great Depression and, like Terkel, never recovered from it.[17] Royko remains the most effective of the city's "public wits" (Williams and Duffy 1983) for he has a special talent at revealing his own weaknesses through overstatement while needling those of his juniors. His competitors are more defensive of their own turf or home range. Bob Greene must turn the 1960s into a moral age to question the present one of consumerism. Bill Granger, now pushed to the back pages of the *Tribune* by Royko, tries to convince us that the boys from the suburbs can talk tough too.

The most durable observer of Chicago, of course, is Saul Bellow. Undoubtedly his characters can survive into the next century. They are modern men who have escaped the tribalism of Chicago (Kazin 1985). But even Bellow has expressed his growing bafflement about Chicago.

> It has always been my opinion—the opinion of an amateur "urbanologist"—that the Immigration Act of 1924 entirely changed the character of the city. No more carpenters, printers, street musicians and small entrepreneurs entered the country from Greece, Serbia, Pomerania, Sicily.

17. See, for example, *Division Street* (1967, pp. 98–101). Along with Hans Mattick and Frank Carney, I once helped Terkel interview a number of gang members on the West Side. When the recorded program was finished, they sounded as if they had come out of the 1930s Chicago Blues period. It was not simply the editing that did this but that Terkel's presence, his mike, and his questions seemed to prompt such a response.

Such trades were *infra dig* for the descendants of earlier immigrants. They improved themselves and moved upwards.
The neighborhoods they left were repopulated by an internal immigration from the south and from Puerto Rico. The
country people, black and white, from Kentucky or Alabama, brought with them no such skills and customs of the
European immigrants. Assembly-line industries had no
need for skilled labor. What we have now taken to calling
"ethnic neighborhoods" fell into decay. The slums, as one of
my friends once observed, were ruined. He was not joking.
The slums as we still knew them in the Twenties were,
when they were still maintained by European immigrants,
excellent places, attractive to artists and bohemians as well
as WASPs who longed for a touch of Europe. The major consequences of the devastation of these neighborhoods,
invariably discussed on these occasions—the increase in
crime, the narcotics addiction, the welfare problem, the
whole inventory of urban anarchy—I will spare you. I will
appease the analytical furies by mentioned only three side
effects of the change; the disappearance of a genial street life
from American cities; the cultural mildew rising from the
giant suburbs, which are still growing; the shift of bohemia
to the universities. But I will stop with that. ("A Kind
Friend," pp. 9–10).

   In Hyde Park near the University of Chicago the faculty lives peacefully enough in its sixflats but a few blocks in
either direction are the Black slums. A different sort of life,
in Woodlawn and Oakwood, tears apart the sixflats and
leaves them looking shelled. They are stripped of salable
metals, innards torn out, copper cable chopped to pieces
and sold for scrap, glass all smashed, and finally an emp-
tiness. Sometimes there is no one at all in these devastated
streets—a dog, a rat or two. The grassplot fences are torn
up. True they were inelegant, shapeless lumber, four-by-
four rails set on an angle, the sharp edge upwards to dis-
courage lounging. But even these have been stolen, burnt.
The grassplots themselves have been stamped into solid
clay. (Pp. 12–13).

   Among school children you look in vain for resemblances with the past. The public schools are now 76
percent black and Puerto Rican. Chicago's teachers have the
highest salary scale in the country. They are not paid to keep
order; that is a matter for the security guards. What they
teach is hard to determine. *Whom* they teach is even more
mysterious. There are classrooms the pupils walk about
knocking out rhythms on the walls, listening to the tran-
sistor radios they have brought with them; in which no one

seems to grasp that the room has a center, that one focuses on a teacher, in which there is no structure. The ungrasped despair of the children, seeking to express itself, presses on your heart and viscera for many days afterwards. They are like little Kaspar Hausers—blank, deformed; they do not know the meaning of simple words; they live in turbulence, convulsively, in darkness of mind. They are unlike poor innocent Kaspar Hauser in that they have a demonic kind of knowledge of sexual violence, of drugs, or vices which they do not see as vices, of intricate and sophisticated relationships on the streets.

Look at them as they stand before Judge R's bench, and they are incomprehensible. You can no more know what they are thinking and feeling, than they can know what you are feeling and thinking. I am speaking, please notice, of a subclass and not of Black Chicago as a whole, the orderly churchgoing Black working class or the middle class doing its best to come out of chaos. These struggle to maintain themselves in a disintegrating city and to protect themselves from guns, rapes, drugs and street violence and their children from beatings in school playgrounds and assaults in the hallways and toilets. No one goes out for a breath of air in the streets at night. Those who go about freely are black princes, bold and leonine, in high costume and probably armed. (Pp. 14–15).[18]

Like Bellow, Richard Stern has written about Chicagoans who could live at other times and places. But, like many of us at the University of Chicago, Stern's characters do not go far north of 47th Street or south of 61st Street without finding themselves in a different city of country. One of Stern's most attractive volumes is *Packages* which David Mamet (*Tribune*, 12 October 1980) has described as:

a collection of short stories that concern essentially the immigrant experience. The experience is written by someone to whom that experience is second hand . . .
    There is a certain tone of longing that can be created by a writer writing in a beloved second language. We can be struck by the force and originality of his poetic idioms and by his inability to master or mimic those that already exist;

18. These paragraphs are from the second of Saul Bellow's Jefferson Lectures, "A Kind Friend Worried about My Soul . . . " Delivered at the Drake Hotel, Chicago, 1 April 1977. Shortly after Bellow delivered this talk, which is still unpublished, someone from *Time* or *Newsweek*, I do not remember which, called and asked me what Bellow had meant. I think I said that he was expressing our bafflement at Chicago's new population. Well, maybe I did not say "our" bafflement. I do not know why they called me. I have never met Bellow.

Mencken's Middle Empire

he both speaks of and embodies the problem of assimilation.

Then, speaking of the two favored stories within the collection, Mamet goes on:

> . . . together and especially in juxtaposition, they manifest for me what Stern . . . is expressing in his work; a view of the end of the immigrant experience.
> . . . though his stories are an *homage* in style and tone to the unique sentimentality of the immigrant writer, Stern's vision is finally not the vision of an immigrant but someone who longs for and can never have the vision of an immigrant—he is a generation too late.[19]

Mamet, himself, is the newest and most recognized voice in speaking of postimmigrant Chicago. In *Glengarry Glen Ross* and *Sexual Perversity in Chicago,* his characters speak with a homegrown North Side idiom known first hand. Ex–ad man Alan Gross (*Lunching*) brings to his work some of the same gift at recreating the dialogue of these "naturalized" Chicagoans. Indeed, the city's younger writers, writers-to-be, and articulate observers seem to be overtaken with a fascination for the theater. Tiny, undersubscribed, often poorly attended, there are probably over a hundred live stages in Chicago where young playwrights, actors, and directors struggle with the spoken word. The Second City Playhouse has produced more talent or aspiring talent than the city can consume, but this does not dampen the flow. Some of this surplus must be because of the city itself, the sort of thing that made the Second City Playhouse possible and unique in the first place.[20] In a city where public confidence in official culture is never more than an inch deep, reality has to be created anew each day.[21] Politicians hustle from one media show of power to the next. Judges spend much of their time trying other judges. Promoters unveil, demonstrators perform, and mayors "reimagize." Where public appearances provide such thin disguise, the imagination is free to create yet other illusions, and there is very little difference between the stage and political podium. Both play to an audience uncautioned by the reflective and solitary

19. Mamet's reading at first seems eccentric. One almost has to have read his review to then discover in Stern's stories what Mamet is saying. But once read, it is hard not to come away from the stories without the same feeling.

20. It is no longer unique. There are branches on the West Coast and in Canada.

21. Although Andrews (1982) *Chicago in Story* is long on homage and short on critical analysis, he is probably right in characterizing Chicago literature of the 1970s as the "decade of disbelief" (p. 325).

experience of the reader. There is the occasion for contagious belief in wild exaggeration. Appearance, presence, spontaneity, extemporanity, and recovery all count for more on either kind of stage. "Chicago should be reviewed on the drama page as well as the political ones" (Stern 1987, p. 7), and increasingly it is. Roger Ebert and Gene Siskel are the city's most famous TV personalities, and Walter Jacobson's recent conviction for TV libel exceeded the legal, not the local, limits of imaginative reporting. Bob Sirrott's move to New York left him missed here more than he was appreciated there.

This punctuation in the material available to the solitary reader is not so much one of quantity as of type. The number of historical studies since 1970 would supply a small library. There are two recent books on the Chicago novel (Smith 1984; and Andrews 1982). There are more books on Bellow's books than books by Bellow. Three recent books examine the city's journalists (Schaaf 1977; Demuth 1980; Williams and Duffy 1983). Books on local architects and architecture are a growth industry (Hines 1974; Condit 1974; Bruckner and Macauley 1976; Block 1978; Lowe 1978; Applebaum 1980; Wright 1985; Schulze 1985). Novelists still return to the scene of the city's more recognizable crimes (Brashler 1976; Stein 1983; Von Hoffman 1984). There is juvenilia for experienced Catholics (Powers 1975) and sexual fantasy for inexperienced ones (Greeley 1982). The suburbs have finally come in for serious attention (Guest 1976; Atlas 1986) rather than serve as only icons of monotony. The number of guidebooks is astonishing. There are guidebooks for where to eat cheap, where to eat well, even guidebooks for where not to eat much at all. There is a guidebook for where Jewish princesses can order out. These guidebooks will direct you to almost anything: famous buildings, sculptures, festivals, the sites of authenticated gangland killings, (1,008 of them at the most recent count), gay bars, landmark buildings where to find a typical Chicago bungalow, where to find the airline stewardesses, where to find the future winners in the futures market.

But if Chicago theaters, theatricality, and guidebooks allow us to knowingly approach one part of its consuming public, it has left the other half only dimly seen in our apprehensions. It is hard to write about people on welfare. Unremitting pity is patronizing or empty now that some seem to regard welfare as much a part of the fixed environment as the public parks. No one seems to worry much about the Orientals. Their silence, their lack of complaint is eloquent. It assures us of their harmlessness. Even the silence of the

Mexicans does not bother us much. They keep opening restaurants and bodegas. They stay out of public housing. They are family oriented, house-proud Catholics and cautious that they not bring attention to their friends and relatives who are illegal aliens.

It is the blacks one wonders about. They, more than anyone else, are going to run this city in the future. Are they as violent as we fear? Bent on vengeance? Bound to the precedent of their worst oppressors? Are there any signs of self-discipline and self-examination? The black journalists carried by the local papers are as humorless and affirmative as a deacon's bench. Blacks are unique, they say, and yet no different from anyone else. Leanitia McClain was much more self-revealing, but she killed herself a few years ago. The sociologist William J. Wilson and the humorist Aaron Freeman often break ranks with other blacks but have been roundly condemned for doing so. More than anyone else, they provide white Chicagoans with a window into a more complicated black community with its own divisions and self-doubts. For all their efforts, however, it still must be the novelists, journalists, or poets who create some imaginary place where we can exchange identities, even colors. The city does have black writers. State Poet Laureate Gwendolyn Brooks, however, now confines herself to inspirational pieces such as her recent *Mayor Harold Washington and the "I Will" City.* Leon Forrest (1977; 1983) deserves a wider reading, but his Forrest County, Illinois, sounds more like Yoknapatawpha County than Cook County. Others like Ronald Fair (1970), David Quammen (1970), and Iceberg Slim (1970) continue to reveal blacks as only a damaged people, too close for comfort.

What is interesting about Bellow's *The Dean's December* is his effort to talk about all this empty space between Chicago's blacks and whites. The book is not about blacks. It is about a white man, Albert Corde, ex-journalist, now a college dean; Hugenot and Irish by extraction; more a Midwesterner than a Chicagoan. Corde has an articulate inner life and a gift for verbal malice that extends to himself. An attentive husband, he is in cold Bucharest with his wife to stand vigil at her mother's death.

Before leaving Chicago, Corde has caused a lot of trouble. He has been a zealot in helping to hunt down the black killers of a white student to the embarrassment of his provost. To make things worse, he has relapsed into journalism by publishing some articles in *Harper* which have gotten too close to even Chicago's dulled sensibilities. We are told all this from the distance of Bucharest, a city run by grim Stalinists, while Chicago is recalled for us as a city run by jovial crooks. This sense of distance is enlarged by Corde's keeping most of the story to himself. It is strained through his memory, seldom shared, even with his wife. A few letters and telephone calls interrupt his sense of solitude but only often enough to make it more apparent. The white student's killers remain remote and unfathomable figures even with Corde's descriptive powers. His nephew, an acquaintance of the black killer and an unremitting apologist for all blacks, describes them to Corde in that mimicry of black speech that college students affect. Corde is doubtful of his little crusade for justice. He has tried to enter the black community to see it for himself. He has discovered a black reformer warden in the County Jail and an ex-hired killer now running a cold turkey detox center. He receives a letter from the warden who has been cleared of the charges of brutality but left with a ruined career. Corde's articles in *Harper* may have helped to do both things.

Corde is helpless to do anything at this distance. The black running the detox center occupies his thoughts: a shell of a man, a full-time ex-addict. Corde's inner debates are jarred momentarily by two encounters with blacks in Bucharest. There is a black American diplomat, a cultivated and kindly man. "Your kind of black," his nephew might say. Two passing African students with their clipped British accents remind Corde that Rumanians do not like blacks either. The real practice of communism in Bucharest brings to mind the recreational Marxism of U.S. campuses. The college campus is a world apart from the black community with its casual crimes without passion. Corde cannot return to academia. He is a journalist.

Bellow does not need to contrive this sense of distance between Chicago blacks and whites. Rather the feeling of wintry remoteness is inescapable if he is to write honestly about someone trying to write about blacks. Of course, there are many Chicago whites who gain a certain familiarity with the black community. Some almost disappear into it. Some marry into it. A lot of them know just enough about it to make the rest of us feel backward, timid, and prejudiced. Indeed, I suspect that there are more acquaintances, friendships, and marriages between Chicago blacks and whites than ever before. This is almost certainly true because of the increasing presence of blacks in the workplace and because most of the whites who religiously avoided them have gone to the suburbs.

But individual acquaintances, friends, and spouses are always exceptions. Social psychologists overemphasize them as a solution to racial stereotypes. Stereotypes apply to those people we do not know, and there are always plenty of them, black or white. It has become unreflective convention to say that we want only to be treated as individuals, judged on our own merits. We want much more. *We want to know strangers.* They are always types. They can be as simple as those conveyed in the formulaic dramas on TV or the ads for Black Velvet Scotch on the side of Chicago buses. In literature, however, they become something more: Articulate, complicated, full of doubt, opportunistic, self-revealing—double-edged people whose imperfections count for as much as their virtues.

They are not just the lineup for awards during Black Pride Week. Important as all these shows of heroism may be, it is in literature that we must find the most believable strangers. You can say things on the pages of a book that you could never say face-to-face. Not everyone reads it that way. Not every novelist writes it that way. But those that do, count. As Richard Stern puts it, "Chicago writers have done as much as anyone to create this city."

One detects in much of the writing about Chicago both the devolution of a genre into formulaic repetition and a groping effort to find new forms and new characterizations still linked to a memorable past. This sense of change and challenge is widely recognized but nowhere better stated than in Bellow's conclusion to his Jefferson lectures.

> This is our Chicago condition, our American and universal condition as well. Because we are *between* the categories, so to speak, because no case is quite covered by them, we enjoy a rich but also painful freedom of spirit. It is painful because the setting is one of ugliness, cruelty and suffering. It is rich because we are at liberty to go as far as mind and talent permit to satisfy our hunger for the essences, to make sense of this mystifying mixture, our individual and historical legacy, our great given. (1977)

From Production to Consumption

Chicagoans' pride and awareness of their material productivity has been thoroughly objectified in the city's collective representations. These icons and artifacts give proof to the satisfying assertion that a city of unlettered migrants and immigrants can gain distinction unassisted by patrician guidance. From the turn of the century to the 1960s, local high culture and popular culture ran along parallel courses, sometimes becoming tangent to one another (e.g., Sandburg, Field, Lardner). Where popular culture often veered toward unrestrained boosterism, the city's novelists, journalists, reformers, and scholars provided their own brand of rough exposure and ridicule. They spoke of the same things, and the language was understood on both sides.

As Chicago enters the new era of urban consumption, many of its most articulate observers appear baffled or empty-handed. The requirements of the new city seem only those of indulgence or undiscriminating tolerance. The city's new industries, its large dependent population, its festival mood, its burned-out buildings, its stunning lakefront, its half-literate schoolchildren, and its Nobel Prize winners just do not add up. There is no lack of elegance and high fashion. But as you trot down North Michigan Avenue, that "Magnificent Mile," you cannot help notice the bag ladies grown so large from the detritus of American fast food that they seem preparing for an especially long Chicago winter. Or go down State Street, that "Great Street," where beggars disguised as street musicians play to empty pools of sidewalk circumvented by noonday office workers. Outside some of the best pizza parlors, you can catch a glimpse of an old man slowly using his tongue and saliva to lather an authentic "Chicago deep dish pizza" crust through his toothless jaws. In San-Fran-York the cultivation of consumption may be more forgivable or thought anterior to the informed appreciation of museums, plays, musical performances, and skilled table talk. But once you have the language of Chicago in your craw, you see it with a different eye.

Many scholars and writers, of course, have now retreated to topics that are safely historical. What is so jarring about Bellow's *Dean's December* is its departure from this form, what Towers (1982) called its strain "against the constraints of fiction," and what Lehmann-Haupt (1982) complained of as its lack of "a preponderance of poetry." Bellow rubs our noses in some social facts.

Yet, I do not agree with Bellow about the ruination of our slums. I think it occurred in the late 1960s when the urban riots paralyzed a tenuous passage between blacks and whites. When I first came to Chicago in 1961, most ethnic and racial groups had their entertainment or bohemian zones and that included blacks. One went there for something especially American: jazz, the blackest of humor, and the eroticism of the tenderloin.

Undoubtedly, what I observed was a much diminished version

The Spirit of Chicago—1981: Ellsworth Kelly's *I Will.*

of what one could have seen during the Great Depression when William F. Whyte (1943) roughly divided the youthful residents of his slum into college boys and gang boys. By the time Gans (1962) and I (1968) got there, the college boys were gone. Neither of us thought even to mention their absence.

What destroyed Bellow's slums was prosperity. What destroyed mine were the riots of the late 1960s. I do not doubt the value of the great Civil Rights Movement of the 1960s. But there was a cost. Native sons and articulate observers lost common material if not their tongue. When they tried they sounded like lobbyists, promoters, or TV anchormen.

Yet, slowly I sense that there is a growing rapprochement between Chicago whites and blacks. It is not much, but it fits into something that has happened before. In Chicago, culture has always had to pay its way. Popular culture and high culture, then remained on speaking terms. They faced the same market test. They still do.

NINE

THE ELEVENTH TASK OF HERCULES: POLITICAL REFORM IN CHICAGO

The Darwinian Solution

In 1965 Wilbur Thompson estimated that it takes about two decades for a large American city to shift from a declining economic base to a substantially new one. He quickly added, "Of course, this is the very kind of knowledge which, once revealed, might effect changes in the developmental pattern and might even shorten the period of response" (p. 21).

Over two decades after Thompson's revelation and a decade and a half after Chicago's regional decline became detectable, there is little evidence that this kind of knowledge informed the city's slow and incomplete recovery by 1987. What we might call the city's or region's urban information system remains primitive and inarticulate. To a large extent, one can describe the region's slow transformation as a "Darwinian solution": the marked attrition of sunset industries and the much slower replacement of them by sunrise industries, the faltering careers of established political leaders and the appearance of successors who have only partially consolidated a regime, an uncertain mass media poised between the assertion of permanence and the recognition of change, the wavering position of civic groups who progressively found themselves in conflict and are still unable to recruit widely from new elites, the arrest and conviction of unprotected politicians, the aging and decline of familiar business elites, the challenge to existing images of boisterous pride—all without obvious replacement.

This Darwinian solution starts with the decline of business firms and advances to the destruction of public confidence in political and elite leadership; it extends to the disappearance of apparent unanimity among civic groups, and gradually invades the entire range of images and assumptions that previously gave a sense of certitude about what was allowable if not always desirable. Seen in this way, Chicago's transformation is essentially a subsocial process, a market phenomenon which has crept beyond the marketplace itself to alter, piece by piece, the city's political, civic, and cultural life. This market model writ large fits our most evident experience so splendidly that one is tempted to leave it at that. Ogburn, with his notion of "culture lag," would be delighted. Even those who adhere to an oversimplified, subsocial version of the Chicago School of Sociology would not be disappointed. But if one reflects upon the fuller account I have tried to provide, it is not that simple for, if thoughtful planning did not replace trial and error, neither was it only an atomistic process, each person going his own way without authoritative guidance.

Cultural Lag

One reason for saying this is that Chicagoans worked very hard not to recognize their region's decline. Coming from New York in 1976, it seemed patently obvious to me. What was more observable, however, was a scarcely disguised pleasure in that eastern spendthrift's pauperization and much self-congratulation on having managed Chicago's civic household with frugality and hard work. Daley's death in that year created momentary alarm, but Bilandic's succession quieted those fears and reassured others of Daley's more complete restoration in the person of his son. The wounds to Wilson Frost and other blacks were thought to be fatal rather than provocative.

Byrne's upset victory released the hopes and criticism of some reformers and some blacks, but she soon returned public opinion to Paddy Bauler's maxim, "Chicago ain't ready for reform." The same things were allowable (some would say more allowable) if not desirable. Not until the 1980 Census report and a change in city rank was this brave front punctured to the extent that regional decline was recognized and a mostly Midwestern "rust belt" replaced the more easterly "frost belt" in public discourse. Still, Byrne and other Illinois politicians spent more time threatening to forcibly reopen the steel mills than to prepare their workers for a change in employment opportunities.

Not until Harold Washington's second victory—eleven years after Daley's death—were hopes for Daley's restoration abandoned and replaced with the recognition that a new, largely black machine must be dealt with on its own terms. At about the same time, the

Political Reform in Chicago

Civic Federation went public with its talk of disarray, the attrition of past leadership, and the failure to attract new elites.

Chicagoans worked so hard to avoid the obvious that many passing watersheds went partly unrecognized as such. Kahn and Major's book, detailing some of these failings, simply went unreviewed by the local media.[1] Mayors Bilandic, Byrne, and to a considerable extent Washington tried to fit themselves into the same mold, attracting criticism mainly when they diverged from it. The theatrics surrounding the expansion of McCormick Place were treated as a bad example of planning rather than a typical instance of big project entrapment. The end of the world's fair was explained as a shortage of money rather than as an inability to articulate it as anything other than a site plan on the cover of the telephone book. When Mayor Washington tried to throw the residents of public housing on the doorstep of the federal government, it was an exceptionally bad case of CHA management, not the standing practice of mayoral administrations for the last thirty years.

Perhaps the most important of these careful omissions was the failure to recognize the weaknesses of the black labor force and its systematic avoidance by local firms. The number of vacated plants only increased when threatened by affirmative action. The weaknesses of the black labor force were externalized as racism, 400 years of slavery, or some other claim that only imposed upon them the image of a damaged people. Those who detected among them a pattern of shared poverty where income and public benefits were no longer a separable good ran the risk of being bigots.

I do not mean by this that on one recognized these events or conditions for what they are. Practically every informant I talked with "confided" some of them to me. Their observations, however, did not usually extend to public talk. Put the same person in front of a TV camera or on the podium of a community meeting and the rhetoric of mobilization and racial etiquette became unpracticed speech. There were exceptions, and a wide stream of cynicism ran just below the surface of public opinion.

Public opinion, however, its not meant to be descriptive but to be strategic. The chief normative requirement is that one be constructive and helpful. The alternative is to run the risk of being a

1. Admittedly, Kahn spends the first three quarters of the book praising Daley before getting around to the regime's collapse after the 1968 Democratic convention. The book was favorably reviewed in the *American Political Science Review* and axed in the *Journal of Politics*.

Political Reform in Chicago

crank, bigot, or cynic. To call this boosterism is only to recognize that the strategic aims of public opinion can become so transparent as to become largely ineffective. "Responsible" public talk must sustain the impression that collective effort already exists and that group honor has been enlisted in these endeavors all along.[2]

Changes in such a responsible rhetoric seem possible only when some sharp, qualitative divide has been passed, making the obvious inescapable: a change in city rank, the third consecutive defeat of a political regime, the mass arrest of alderman and judges. Strategic public talk can change on these occasions because there is some realistic basis for thinking that popular opinion (aggregate individual opinion) has been sufficiently shaken to warrant a change in public opinion (responsible public talk). After Daley's humiliation at the 1968 Democratic convention, Bill Singer's challenge for the office of mayor did provoke open criticism of Daley and what turned out to be a reckless anticipation of change. Jane Byrne's upset victory as well as Washington's first election brought reformers out of the closet with momentary, strategic statements of potential change. As these hopes faded, the public rhetoric of responsibility did not quite return to its previous form but was partially replaced by more open expressions of cynicism and mounting exposés. Chicagoans are now being treated to the disclosure of more scandals than at any time since the Kelly administration. There is less and less pretense of an unbroken record of mobilization and group honor. The form it takes, of course, is familiar; like Avis, second city observers try harder.

The absence of a new public rhetoric to replace a failed one was not exactly what Ogburn had in mind when he introduced the concept of cultural lag.[3] He would also find irony in the fact that the most telling efforts to overcome this self-deception occurred among individuals clearly sited in cultural positions. The Second City Play-

2. This notion of strategic and responsible public opinion is sufficiently similar to Gramsci's concept of cultural hegemony as to be misleading. There are crucial differences. The concepts that make up the vocabulary of public opinion are "concepts at risk" (Sahlins 1985) for the obvious can become inescapable. Also, as I wish to argue below, this sort of self-deception is correctable by institutionalized methods of self-examination.

3. Actually, most of his examples draw upon instances where one piece of physical culture (paved roads) lags the introduction of a complementary one (fast automobiles). The main drift of his argument, however, is to say that culture is weak and cultural ideas especially so (Ogburn 1964, pp. 167–173). Yet, at the same time, Ogburn was the nation's leading advocate of social indicators. Ogburn himself was more complicated than his theories.

A WINNING SEASON

Department of Cultural Affairs
Annual Report
1984–1985

City of Chicago
Harold Washington, Mayor

Department of Cultural Affairs
Fred Fine, Commissioner

A promotional Picasso.

house probably has the longest running record in stripping away the guise of boosterism although it provided little in its place. David Mamet has populated the city with new persona every bit as tarnished as the familiar ones. Saul Bellow, the novelist, delivered an especially unsettling account of the city in his still unpublished Jefferson Lectures. He tried again with *The Dean's December* only to have reviewers treat it conventionally as a piece of fiction or biography. The city's sculptors and their patrons have turned almost entirely to the new city of consumerism, entertainment, and showmanship. They even possess some sense of self-mockery. Chicago's Picasso is not just big. It's super big. Gross to the max.

There were also some newsmen who did more than float trial balloons to test the shakiness of popular opinion. Richard Christiansen wrote consecutively about the almost complete turnaround in the city's performing arts.[4] By 1980, R. C. Longworth kept reminding readers that the region's economy had reached the point of no return and that the city's public college system was not even an effective remedial high school. Mike Royko, the least objective newsman in town, persistently needled liberals whose notions of social cause did not include individual responsibility. By comparison, most mainline social scientists were more "constructive" or, if critical, inclined to discover distributional inequalities as if we were still in Galbraith's age of affluence. A few Marxists passing through town threatened the city with revolution, but that seemed about as credible as Galbraith's age of affluence. Most businessmen and civic leaders sheltered behind a "heritage of involvement" until 1986 when they went public with their tale of woe.[5]

Clearly, the Chicago that remains after this final burst of self-examination is not the same as the one that was said to work as late as 1979. But is it ready for reform?

"It's Our Turn Now"

Chicago, indeed the State of Illinois, has been so carefully crafted to register the influence of the politically obedient that it might take as

4. I neglect the electronic media since it had a time perspective that reached back only to yesterday.

5. The Chicago Association of Commerce and Industry did openly complain of the lack of cooperation by the Washington administration during his first term. These complaints were disavowed by other business groups.

long to undo the system as to have constructed it. Even if one or a few of these political arrangements—the long list of candidates, the off-year elections, the number of voting districts, the special elections and run-offs, the election of judges, the casualness of voting challenges, the uncertainties of political affiliation—could be changed, the remainder might be so effective as to preclude any noticeable difference. Piecemeal change in such a well-devised system would require sustained public enthusiasm in the absence of early and obvious results.

In Chicago, sustained public support for political reform is doubly difficult to achieve because it appeals primarily to those whose leaders are out of office. A one time that included a large number of blacks and new minorities, a condition that is now reversing itself. The chants of black voters during Harold Washington's political rallies—"It's our turn now"—do not auger well for political reform. What was once an obstacle to their political representation is now the instrument to perpetuate it.[6]

This is no reason to give up on political reform in Chicago or Illinois. Movements for political reform, usually occurring after an unbearable string of scandals, are the main way in which people of great talent and integrity have been lured into public service. They not only cautioned the magnitude of local corruption, they helped keep this fertile crossroads of the nation a promising enough place that those with the talent to leave it did not. The challenge to sustain this promise now revolves onto new shoulders.

Blacks now occupy the apex of political power in Chicago. Numerous other groups have preceded them with quite uneven records of opportunism and public service. The transition from opportunism to constraint was never automatic; that is, creeping respectability. Already blacks approach this task with too much help

6. This was written before Washington's death and the subsequent valorization of him as an unrelenting reformer. There were differences between the Washington regime and the one following it. Washington's supporters were heavily concentrated in local community organizations and nonprofit organizations which, for the most part, stood outside the previous ranks of the politically obedient. Thus, Washington did shift patronage toward a new population, but also one that showed strong signs of forthcoming obedience.

The regime that followed under Eugene Sawyer was based on the fragmented remains of the old Cook County Democratic party. It was a collection of decentralized baronies with very little capacity to constrain venality or to "make patronage work." The change in regimes was very similar to when Cermak's death passed the mayor's office to Kelly.

from whites who would ride to moral victory by portraying them as a damaged people whose excesses are always excusable. To their advantage, however, most remaining whites in Chicago will be less patient; the distance between public opinion and popular opinion is no longer that great.

A much more formidable obstacle for Chicago's black leaders is the presence of a large and undisciplined population among their constituents. Like some other primordial groups in Chicago, for example, the Irish and Italians, it has been hard for blacks to tell when some of their members are simply thugs or patriots striving for freedom and equality. The great Civil Rights Movement of the 1960s further obscured this difference, and many of the weaknesses of the black community were elevated to the status of black culture. Sometimes this went so far as to suggest a kind of mystique of Negritude, another chosen people as isolated as those portrayed by the southern white poet, Will Percy (1941).

But this mystique did not go very deep in Chicago. Respectable, hardworking blacks in Chicago never quite lost control over their social movement, and the whites who ran ahead of them often found themselves running alone. Even when he let his hair grow natural and dressed in a dashiki, Jesse Jackson was a preacher and a Christian one, too. Now he is the best-dressed presidential candidate in the country. Harold Washington traced his political origins right back to the practical politics of his father. Elijah Muhammad was not Malcolm X, and his relatives show an altogether American spirit in how they wish to divide his legacy. Louis Farakahn alarms white liberals, but he alarms black mystics more. Some whites think he is more like a Mormon than like a Muslim. Aaron Freeman tells jokes that whites laugh at, too. Even black crime in Chicago is getting more organized and, as Chicagoans know, organized crime helps drive out disorganized crime. One might not go so far as to agree with Jesse Jackson that Chicago blacks have neighborhoods and New York blacks have nothing, but Chicago blacks never let whites define their lot as one of complete dependency on white paternalism.

Chicago's black leaders show many resemblances to their white predecessors. Some of them are already in the same jails. Increasingly, they have the means for asserting a traditional form of social control in their neighborhoods: the manipulation of patronage to empower residents with a natural interest in a quiet neighborhood. The Shakman decree, of course, has somewhat weakened the arsenal of public employment, but affirmative hiring agreements in the private sector have more than outstripped the loss. The distribution of these benefits, however, has to be very selective if they are to favor those who have some standing in their neighborhoods and will serve to maintain order if not official morality. Often these people are not directly dependent on the political food chain but resourceful enough to have established an independent livelihood: undertakers, tavern owners, organized criminals, and preachers, for instance. They are well liked, feared, or influential, sometimes all three. You cannot just rush them to the public trough. They become effective guardians of public order when they can exercise some control over the distribution of patronage. Mutual advantage sometimes assures their willingness to do precinct work and may promote their visibility to practical politicians. They can deliver the vote and identify the deserving. But their enlistment is not automatic, and frequently they are displaced by patronage employees who have little standing in their neighborhoods but must do something for their job. Even those who start with some standing in their neighborhoods may not outlast a changing population.[7] Keeping the peace with patronage is problematic. It takes self-conscious selection.

The same argument extends to Chicago's private sector and is all the more important since it makes up so much of the city's reconstituted patronage. Chicagoans never gained their deserved reputation for hard work because of some mysterious "work ethic" that outlived pietism.[8] Employers took on employees who were well recommended and, if they worked out, let them help recruit and train additional employees (Bonney 1974). Recruitment, of course, tended to stop at ethnic or racial boundaries. Indeed, it was very hard for an outsider to get trained even if he could get a job. Federal insistence on "universalism" and affirmative hiring has been useful in breaking through these boundaries, but they do not insure that exceptionally effective minority workers will discipline new hires and report their willingness for hard work. This does not occur automatically but hinges upon self-conscious selectivity combined with the

7. Kornblum (1974, pp. 141–160) provides further distinctions among Chicago precinct workers. During the Daley years, some of them became so nearly strangers in their neighborhoods that he required them to face competitive elections.

8. The proportion of able-bodied who participate in the region's labor force has typically been 2–5 percent higher than in comparable regions.

kind of social pressure that demonstrates a "work ethic." In short, a reversal of the current pattern of statistical discrimination.

Far more problematic is Chicago's public housing which undercuts even the most credible claims that blacks might have to being an orderly and hardworking people. Privatizing public housing in Chicago is extremely difficult because support for it is very nearly the litmus test of one's liberal and antiracist sentiments, especially among whites. It is admirably appropriate for such a test because no instrumental reason, neither cost effectiveness nor social control, could ground such faith. Those who defend public housing speak with the faith of Job.

Aside from the fact that public housing is an inhuman way to warehouse people, it imposes a very high overhead cost on blacks who might gain from reversed statistical discrimination. Once you are a resident of public housing, you can sensibly leave it only by some heroic effort guided by a vision of windfall mobility. When turned into patronage it becomes visibly coercive: well over 100,000 blacks too sessile to be Americans. Even if it is deconcentrated and run by a religious order, public housing is changed only from the warehouse to the poorhouse, something for the dangerous classes.

Blacks and their leaders have a good deal more to gain from privatizing public housing than do whites, but there is little indication that they appreciate this. It is still a test of one's liberal faith. But the absence of forthcoming federal funds and periodic self-destruction do provide occasions when one might have to privatize it one piece at a time. Involuntarily, of course.

There are a number of other items of liberal faith which pose similar political risks: providing housing for the cursed Yuppie, furthering the Chinatown strategy for ethnic commercial centers, assembling large tracts of land where developers can provide a mix of renovation, landmark preservation, and a variety of new construction. Each of these courses of action is strewn with political risks. Even someone courageous enough to put condoms in the Chicago public schools might pale at the prospect of meeting them head-on. How could one make them politically expedient?

Making Patronage Work

If patronage is not its own guarantor of performance, what conditions have occasionally inclined it in that direction? The simplest answer is that, after some extended period of corruption and the mass arrest of Chicago public officials, reformers have aroused a movement of sufficient strength to actually threaten political incumbents. The newspapers ran sustained exposés. Local intellectuals, civic activists, and a few public administrators engaged in tangible cooperation. Some persons of prominence and independent standing offered themselves up for high public office. Studies were mounted. Chief executives joined civic associations rather than send the public relations man. Private universities threatened to leave town. Prosecuting attorneys made a name for themselves.

The result of all this in Chicago has never been massive change throughout the political system. Instead, the tendency has been for some visible changes in personnel at the top of the ballot and reform from within. Political regimes saved themselves by constraining venality and by making patronage work. One reason that Daley stands so tall in Chicago's collective memory is that he started by appointing some blue ribbon candidates and manipulated patronage to provide a kind of city planning. It was not a Prussian bureaucracy, of course, and it aged badly after 1968.

The machine that Daley rescued bears many parallels to the current one being put into place. The machine that began with the election of Cermak rested on long-abused ethnic pride. It was nearly invulnerable for two decades despite growing scandals and reform movements. The election of the reformer Kennelly did little to improve government but did seem to frighten machine leaders enough to give Daley the power to carry out his reform from within.

The emerging political machine in Chicago may be as invulnerable as the previous one for it rests upon the well-remembered outrage of blacks. Can we afford to wait for two decades when it might become sufficiently weakened to be sensitive to newspaper campaigns and the complaints of intellectuals and preachers? It is conceivable. For many of the city's business leaders it may be possible to move most of Chicago to DuPage County. Many universities are already establishing extensions there.

But the model for Chicago need not be Detroit. Chicago is still a headquarters city. Some of its sunrise industries are downtown. Its cultural institutions and its convention trade provide for a viable tourism. Suburbanites even go to watch its baseball teams.

By themselves, however, these strengths are insufficient just as conventional reform movements alone are insufficient. What seems to be needed is something more, an institutional base that would not only set a standard for regional performance but create a new level of public discourse informed by something more than the hope of being constructive. Some inkling of how this might come about is provided in Clark and Ferguson's book (1983). As their studies show, local political regimes can accomplish vastly different things with similar resources. There is an implicit standard in their findings, and they embolden one to think that this standard rather than strategic opinion alone might become the basis for public discourse. For this to occur, however, it must be greatly extended and elaborated in public and private institutions.

Public Planning as Constrained Collective Behavior

At this point it is useful to think about the parallels and differences between our controls over regional and national economies. Much of what is said openly about the national economy by the president and Congress is transacted through the media. It consists largely of selective facts, accounts, and proposals which aim to shift the burdens of responsibility, lobby for legislative or regulatory packages, rally the faithful, and attend to group pride. It is not that they seldom disagree. They often do so, but within a set of counterclaims that assert that the solution to economic problems lie within the reach of existing leadership. Their alternatives are the alternatives worth talking about—those worth reporting in the media.

To "make" public opinion, however, one must somehow round the corner to create the impression of critical necessity and virtual commitment. This may involve an initial round of promotional claims followed by episodes of brinkmanship and an escalation of the benefits asserted to belong to one or both outcomes. A sense of urgency is conveyed by both sides and becomes newsworthy. Well-known authorities, people who can walk on water, will be enlisted to give testimony. More important, other decisions will advance on the assumption of the one under consideration. The costs attributed to irresolution climb as do the benefits claimed for resolution. The situation, then, is transformed from one of deliberate choice to one where the costs of irresolution are nearly those claimed. The crisis has become real.

Now, this is very similar to what happens in Chicago. News releases, leaks, and plants are instruments for mobilizing popular opinion around existing images of "the city that works." There is

Political Reform in Chicago

plenty of disagreement (Mayor Washington, "Chicago is on a roll"; Alderman Vrdolyak, "This is not Poland!"). And there is variation. A few trial balloons are lofted and quickly abandoned. Some projects achieve commitment before overcommitment. But the general pattern, the pattern that traces out the scenario for the "big project" is one of overcommitment. Promotional statements rapidly escalate. Water walkers are brought to center stage. Side best begin to accumulate. The seed money has already been spent. Site plans announced. Federal funds committed. The investors may back out.

What is involved here is both more and less than a self-fulfilling prophesy.[9] It is a process of escalating promotional claims and crises construction which, on the one hand, oversells the value of a given project and, on the other hand, becomes progressively vulnerable to adversarial criticism. The process works smoothly only when there is a political regime (like Richard J. Daley's before 1968) so thoroughly entrenched that almost all expert opinion can be orchestrated and fed into the media with unanimity. Once adversarial politics take hold, the decision-making process becomes more nearly one where luck and rhetorical advantage are decisive. The specific merits of a project (i.e., costs and benefits) fade into the background as the issues enlarge to include the appearance of venality and cronyism, the distribution of jobs to minorities, the exceptional protection of underdogs, and that special appeal embodied in city slogans. Even where some of these valuative arguments might have instrumental objectives (e.g., job training for blacks), they are likely to be phrased in a vocabulary that narrows to questions of distributive equity and the defense of sentimental attachments. Progressively, it becomes less an issue of increasing or maintaining the economic base of the city than of dividing up the spoils. The project is no longer an investment, but a transfer payment.

It is very hard for the mass media to rise above this rhetoric of justice and sentiment to reassert the primacy of the city's economic base, the retention and training of its labor force, the maintenance of its physical plant, and its competitive position in attracting sunrise industries. The media are very nearly confined to the data provided

9. It resembles somewhat Smelser's value-added theory of collective behavior (1962) but owes more to Park's idea that the media are the most available instrument for the construction of public opinion as a means of social control (1967, pp. 249–267). For Park, the South Sea Bubble and cases like it are only failed instances which differ quantitatively rather than qualitatively from the general run of fictions upon which our everyday expectations float.

them. Only in the event of flagrant overstatements can they quickly shoot down trial balloons. Otherwise, they too must be constructive, providing "both sides" of the story, repeating the claims for social justice, acknowledging the special sentiment invested in families, underdogs, and heroic images. Almost without noticing it, the issues shift from those of political economy to those of welfare economics. Who prevails, then, depends more upon who has a gift for the theatrical than upon deliberate and reasoned judgment.

In one respect, I believe that public discourse on the performance of our national economy does include some constraints which buffer the extremes in the strategic use of public opinion and occasionally compel us to give priority to the national economic base rather than just distribution. In the last sixty years, a host of economic indicators have been institutionalized and are regularly reported on by the Federal Reserve, Departments of Commerce and Labor, the General Accounting Office, and the Office of Management and Budget (see Whitnah 1983 for a full list and brief histories). The most impressive thing about these reports is their standardization, the routine timing of their announcement, and the widespread acceptance of them as a global assessment of the performance of "our economy."[10] They do not fully define the national interests, but they do establish a minimal standard against which presidential and congressional regimes are held accountable. Others may question their validity (Block and Burns 1986), but I would emphasize more their reliability; they are as unavoidable as a child's report card. Undoubtedly there is an element of magic and faith in these numbers, but it is constrained magic and faith. Even a presidential administration that believes in voodoo economics and astral signs is limited in what it can claim and what it can promote.

The presence of these national accounts has made it possible for economists to emerge as an independent and authoritative discipline which can second-guess political promoters. The performance of the economy is no longer a state secret. Uncertainties continue, of course, but when faced with them, the media are as likely to turn to independent "experts" as to political promoters. The credibility of the latter rests in some measure upon the independent evaluations of the former. There are still left-handed and right-handed economists, of course, but they work within a methodology that has a

10. I hope to provide some evidence on this in a forthcoming article, "Front Page Economics in 1929 and 1987."

central tendency and a hierarchy that places the opinion of some above that of others.

Embedded in these accounts is a concept of the nation as a single unified household or *oikos*. The concept is so implicit that it escapes easy recognition. But the consequences are to rivet our attention on the collective product of economic activity rather than only the "shares" that "belong" to one sector or one group. To a considerable extent one can think instrumentally first and sentimentally next.

Nothing like these national accounts exist at the regional level, and certainly not in Chicago. True, there are federal statistics on, say, employment, income, and housing starts at the level of the state and SMSA, but even these are seldom represented in a comparative framework which would measure local performance against some standard. Nor are they well suited to this purpose. The samples are too small to reveal anything about areas smaller than the Chicago SMSA and, in any event, these accounts are not selected with the objective of evaluating local investment strategies. There are essentially no measurements of local investment and, of course, no selective focus on outcomes which might be linked to these measurements.[11] The result is a kind of hit-or-miss, case-by-case review where informed opinion is the best the media can seek out. Frequently, the best informed are themselves promoters of one or another investment strategy and their views tainted by a conflict of interest. The review, then, easily unravels into a debate over a division of the spoils.

Even the concept of the region as a single, interdependent economy is hard to sustain. Partly this is because of the paucity of information on the way in which different economic sectors interact to create a collective product and partly it is because there is no routine effort to assess import-export relations among regions. Even if the fit of current regional input-output models is only approximate, they can help to fix peoples' attention on their shared, instrumental household before turning to the questions of income transfer. Chicagoans sometimes act like the members of a family who want to divide up the wages of the breadwinner before finding the breadwinner a job.

11. Private firms, some public agencies, and an occasional scholar may undertake such evaluations. Sometimes they may reach the press. But they lack the ponderous regularity and fatefulness of the quarterly announcements made by, say, the Department of Commerce.

Political Reform in Chicago

The media have no capacity for this kind of analysis nor is any expected of them. Thus, even the most able newsmen must write about the local political economy much in the way they would have written about the national economy sixty years ago. Expert and independent authority cannot be consulted routinely because there is not much they can draw upon to give a credible statement. The lack of any deadline for the routine announcement of standard statistical reports does not create the public apprehension and expectancy a newsman can rely upon to provide the drama aroused by scheduled anticipation. The debate remains pretty much in the hands of those with a direct interest in the spoils.

What prevails, then, is a peculiar mixture of selective permissiveness in the "free market" and uncertain campaigns for the "big project."[12] This kind of unashamed promotionalism cannot be eliminated nor would one want to do so. It is one of the reasons that one can say that Chicago is one of the most—and best—planned cities of the modern era. The problem is how this promotionalism can be constrained within instrumental boundaries and build public confidence rather than undermine it. How can one erect a new level of public discourse that would not be so vulnerable to cynicism and disclosure?

The most obvious answer, I believe, is some system of regional accounts that would enable "experts" to second-guess these investment schemes and pass their evaluation on to the media. Regional economies, of course, are different from national ones, and I am not suggesting that we simply copy the latter for regional use. The actual means by which Chicago's local economy might be subject to effective monitoring is a long way off and will have to go through an experimental stage. One can be fairly sure, however, of some of the criteria such a system must satisfy. First, the institutional base for such a system of reporting cannot be located at the level of city or state government. No one would trust it, and it is doubtful that genuinely eminent people could be induced to serve. A trustworthy and politically secure base for this kind of monitoring could be noth-

12. This mixture is noticeable in Chicago's man-made landscape; a vast number of vernacular pieces of uneven quality and every conceivable design and a much smaller number of monolithic pieces of uniform design and frequently of high quality. Wilbur Zelinsky recently observed that the hodge-podge of vernacular design is what makes Chicago especially recognizable.

ing less than a regional institution, one that would include several states, possibly the entire Midwest.

This scale of regional monitoring satisfies a second objective, the requirement that its reports be comparative. Regional science is a relatively immature discipline. It has no absolute standards, but within the Midwest there is great variation in the comparative performance of urban subregions. Comparative analysis of this kind will not provide obvious remedies, but it will heighten media attention to each subregion's standing and possibly a more thoughtful examination of niche exploitation and the efficiencies of public spending. It is even possible that the diffusion of successful policies would be debated and the recognition of failed policies less subject to artful caveats.

Third, any effort at this scale of regional monitoring must develop a time perspective that extends beyond the most recent business cycle or some preferred point of electoral victory. Otherwise, one will be faced with the usual excuses of local strategic opinion making which seek only to shift the blame or protect group honor.

An institutional mission of this scale does not come into existence *toto caelo*. Only the desperation of late 1929 led to the first steps toward our present system of national economic indicators. For this reason, local universities will have to nurse along regional accounting until some other crises create the proper historic moment.

In the Chicago region there is some growing interest along these lines: a focus on regional economics at Northern Illinois University, an expanding Committee on Policy Studies at the University of Chicago, and the established Urban Studies Center at Northwestern. There are also private groups which occasionally link up with the universities, primarily the Metropolitan Planning Commission or groups growing out of it. No one of these programs is large enough to accomplish much by itself. They lack a common regional unit on which to report. Their reports are too episodic to really whet the media's appetite. The universities find it hard to give tenure to those who specialize in routine reporting. But universities have a way of plodding along. Granted the lack of confidence in other local institutions, their kind of fact-finding may win over public opinion in the long run.

These ideas are not original, and they must come as disappointment to anyone expecting something better than a more defensible venality. They smack of technocracy. They are self-serving for the universities. They make for duller newspapers. But shared ignorance and political expediency are not to be confused with democracy.

Something more is possible. But for that kind of self-examination, we must look beyond the university.

Chicago: 1987

Chicagoans share with other Americans the exhaustion of the New Deal and the cultural era of which it was a part. Just when they thought they could take pride in hard work and productivity, they find themselves most recognizable as consumers. It is not that they have stopped working but that the mirror through which their image is reflected seems only to capture them at leisure. There is the loss of tangible products: bolts, nuts, rivets, washers, sausages, surgical equipment. There is the growth of the convention trade, tourism, white-collar work, restaurant going, and health clubs. And there is welfare.

How does one valorize the possession of a BMW or teenage motherhood? It cannot be done. One must look beyond the surface and dig into the recesses of life that are inaccesible to the glass eye of television and images scripted for the Anti-Defamation League. Several generations of Chicago writers and journalists did go below the surface, so much so that some critics faulted them for their realism. And, indeed, they have produced little of that form that goes directly from the academy to the conservatory. Their work, however, preserved for us a healthy skepticism about the value of form over content, the word over the deed. Seeing was believing. This skepticism still makes Chicago a place of literary possibility. There is an imperfect heart ticking down there somewhere.

METHODOLOGICAL APPENDIX

Going Downtown

One day in early 1977, Morris Janowitz stuck his head in my office, stared at me for a nanosecond, and said, "Let's go. I want to show you something." I did not argue. Sometimes Morris had the authority of a three-star general.

As we drove to downtown Chicago, Morris did not elaborate on what he was up to. And we seemed almost purposefully to avoid talking about the flawed planning projects we had both had a hand in since 1967 when I first arrived at the University of Chicago. This time, I sensed, Morris had bigger game in mind. And I was right.

Before I really knew what was happening, Morris and I were sitting around the conference table at the Chicago Metropolitan Housing and Planning Council[1] with a number of people examining proposals for land-use change in the city, in this instance the development of Dearborn Green. It then dawned upon me what Morris was up to. He was bringing me into contact with some of the most knowledgeable people in the city, people who collectively seemed to know what was happening to every plot of land in Chicago. Morris was also farming out to me one of his many roles, but I was to learn that later as I replaced him on the local planning committee of the MHPC.

The discussion was frank, and those present moved quickly from an evaluation of the strategic value of the project to the question of how it could be sold to various publics: the media, watchdog groups, blacks, a new mayor, good government groups. Even the

---

1. Now the Chicago Metropolitan Planning Council. I still remember a long session at the council in which some funders told us that "housing" was a red-letter word they could not afford to have listed on their contributions. The word "housing" was eliminated from the agency's title shortly after I left it. I think it was a good choice. The term "housing" overly committed it to welfare goals and frightened away funders and supporters who wanted development rather than the more controversial topic of "affordable housing," that is, a low-rent district.

name of the project, Dearborn Green, suggesting the suburbs, was changed to a more conventional Dearborn Park. Eighteen of Chicago's seventy-seven community areas have "park" in their name. There are no "greens."[2] Many of the parks, of course (like Hyde Park), do not exist.

It was clear that two quite different things were going on. First, there was the evaluation of the project, primarily in terms of alternative investments and their costs and benefits to the city. Second, there was the search for a language that would give it moral worth to various publics. The match between these two rhetorics was problematic, unachievable in some instances, awkward in others.

The meeting was an eye-opener for me. I had spent most of my research life on Chicago's street corners talking to the rank and file. To them "city planning" was a chartered conspiracy among the enemies of the people. I knew there were limits to this point of view, but city planning still seemed to me a black box. I had read the conventional works on city planning, but much of that literature strikes one as retrospective rhetoric rather than convincing description. Only Banfield's *Political Influence* (1961) had impressed me with its descriptive accuracy. Daley, the facilitator, however, was dead. In any event, he was supposed to be a freak exception, the last of the bosses.

What I had observed was a group of knowledgeable and influential people quickly—in almost thirty minutes—arrive at an evaluation of a quarter of a billion-dollar project and spend something over an hour figuring out how to market it to someone else. What knit together the language of this second discussion was an appeal to "fairness" or, better yet, a communitarian ideal, rectifying known injustices and affirming shared aspirations. Words like balanced development, mixed use, family housing, diversity, and choice crowded their way into this discussion. I was so impressed that I kept notes on the meeting, as if I were doing fieldwork.

Over the next seven years, almost monthly, I was to observe repeatedly this vacillation between a deliberate language of instrumental planning and another that embraced the latest in moral appeal. The Local Planning Committee of MHPC became my most strategic post for these observations, and all the large downtown

2. That is, none other than "Cabrini-Green," Chicago's most terrifying public housing project. Actually its formal name is Frances Cabrini and William Green Homes. But one might want to avoid any hint of association, however mistaken.

projects included in this book were reviewed more than once during its meetings. Not until I was well into the first year of these observations, however, did I begin to keep systematic field notes. I did so without telling anyone.

By this time, something else had struck my eye. Planning, at least planning in Chicago, was much more nearly a retrospective process than a linear design that began on paper and proceeded through a determined set of stages to brick and mortar completion. Proposed projects often postdated city plans, some of them a decade old (like the Chicago 21 Plan), and they were crowded into these plans like makeshift pieces in a jigsaw puzzle. In turn, new and extensive land-use plans were more nearly a way of packaging existing projects than preconceived guidelines for development. This was especially apparent to me in the 1983 Central Area Plan where I had an opportunity to follow portions of its construction from the beginning, although this time in the firm of Skidmore, Owings and Merrill rather than the MHPC.

City planning, then, was a way of aggregating together a lot of independent projects so as to give them an appearance of unity in purpose and public acceptance. City planning takes the flotsam and jetsam of public and private land users and regroups them as a rational construction of "the public interest." The process, of course, was not simply one of passive acceptance. Many more projects are proposed than reach completion. The selective process, however, relies less on textbook planning than upon some construction of public interest. It was a package deal that could mobilize supporters and disarm adversaries: a deal that could grandfather in orphans from the past, invite new births that had not occurred, and wrap it all up in a bundle labeled "already agreed upon."

It was only later, by about 1981, as I began to absorb the lore of those attending these meetings and others like them, that I became aware of why it is that contemporary city planning cannot achieve public acceptance as simply a professional activity in which available means are used to arrive at collective ends. By now, following different land-use proposals had become something of an obsession with me, and I accumulated an enormous file on practically every major proposal that required public action (rezoning, City Council approval, federal financing, or court action). I went to public hearings, press conferences, unveilings, ribbon cuttings, and topping-off ceremonies. I had developed a detailed scenario for each downtown project and eighty-nine additional projects along Chicago's

North Side and in the North River Area.[3] I gathered a list with the names of every person or firm known to be involved in each of these projects and began interviewing informants. These interviews continued (mostly in my summer vacations) for three years (1982–1985). I finally decided that new informants were giving me old information. Thus, at the end of 1985, I decided to take the end of that year as my cut-off point. I did interview beyond that time to clear up loose ends. I found local news accounts irresistible throughout the next two years, and I spoke to informants casually. But my story in this book ends with the beginning of 1986—almost exactly one year before the death of Harold Washington.

It was as I branched out from the downtown projects to examine those along the North Side that I realized that even the most knowledgeable Chicago "land-use watchers" (by now I knew that there were thousands of them) could not articulate the reasoning behind their deliberations. What they knew, even when they pooled their intelligence, was essentially a set of scattered observations enriched by daily experience. It was "only" a kind of lore or craft knowledge, and it lacked conviction unless they had had some of the same experiences. Ten really seasoned Chicago land-use observers could meet for forty-five minutes and quickly reach agreement or disagreement on the worth of some new project for the city. What would inform their decision would be 100–200 years of land-use experience. They could quote from innumerable cases and bring to bear crucial comparisons. But, essentially, they had to fall back on the claim that "we know, because we have been there."

These discussions, of course, were not without obvious conflicts and the appearance of ulterior aims. Many of the people I talked with, and almost all of those at MHPC (other than the staff), were actively engaged as investors. Most of the others I talked with were members of community organizations and often their adversaries. Yet, what impressed me was that once public discussion began one was expected to make a reasoned argument, couched largely in terms of "the public interest." By and large, they did so. Occasionally, someone simply demurred, acknowledging a conflict of interest. Others stayed away at strategic times, when their interests were overly obvious. Community leaders might overstay

3. This does not include twenty-three site changes that lay outside either the lakefront, the North River Area, and the Central Area. I examined these sites in some detail through an early search of documents but interviewed informants on only a few of them. They figure into the study primarily in the discussion of shopping malls.

and overstate, but it was to their disadvantage. They became "shrill" and less convincing for that reason.

These people were not a rough sample of Chicago's land-use investors, community watchdogs, and civic activists. By and large, they were the "more responsible" elements in the negotiation of city planning, those people who are invited to attend public meetings or, at least, those who cannot be excluded. Most were also "locals": individuals or firms who looked forward to a long stay in Chicago.

Nor was this growing list of informants in any sense the city's formal agency for planning. The MHPC is a nonprofit. The prestige of its membership gives it a credible voice in the evaluation of public land-use decisions but no direct authority. During my time on its Local Planning Committee, one of its directors became director of the Northeastern Illinois Planning Commission and another became Harold Washington's commissioner of city planning. Most of the remainder of my informants were from community organizations (nonprofits) or firms actively engaged in architecture, construction, rental management, and "rehabbing."

Yet, as I was to learn, most of Chicago's land-use planning lies outside the city's or state's formal apparatus. There is the State Street Council, the North Michigan Avenue Association, and the Central Area Committee, to mention only the most prestigious, the most powerful. Then, there is Skidmore, Owings and Merrill who authored both the Chicago 21 Plan and the 1983 Central Area Plan. There is a plethora of other firms which also attempt to set the city's land-use agenda. There are hundreds of community organizations. There are at least two major regional public agencies (NIPC and IDHA). The Chicago Department of City Planning has a staff of from 150 to 75 (it varied that much during my study). It has limited capacity for initiative and oversight. It must, however, bear the spotlight of public responsibility.

In time, I was to become familiar with informants in each of these organizational types: all the big downtown associations, the heads of most of the community organizations along the north lakefront, the larger firms, a few small firms ("rehabbers"), a small proportion of the remaining nonprofits, only the more visible politicians and some of the people with state and city responsibility for public planning. But it was the MHPC that remained my most central observation post. They seemed to possess the most detached, the most reasoned and articulate land-use strategies. They were also frank and self-confident. Perhaps it was for this reason that, after I

Methodological Appendix

told two members that I was writing a book on Chicago planning, I was not reappointed to the Local Planning Committee. I understand their apprehensions. I do not think I have hurt them. But, if they are to be frank, they must be careful. I still send in my dues.

Going to the Community

But this gets me well ahead of large parts of this study. Eleven years earlier, shortly before Morris Janowitz brought me into the deliberations of the Metropolitan Planning and Housing Council, I had moved into North Park which lay in the North River Area. The region to the south of my home was interesting because it soon became evident that it was one of the few places away from the north lakefront that was attracting considerable investment. Much of this investment was facilitated by the North River Commission. Inquiries into that organization revealed a number of patterns which were to complement what I was learning from the big, downtown projects.

First, Chicago possessed a kind of "underground" of community developers who were in some ways the mirror image of its more famous Industrial Areas Foundation organizations inspired by Saul Alinsky. Where the latter were engaged in highly visible and adversarial negotiations for public services, the former were engaged in low-profile efforts to attract new households, upgrade shopping strips, and maintain the housing stock of a self-supporting community. This network of community developers reached back, at least in the memory of some informants, to the redevelopment of Hyde Park and Lincoln Park before the word "gentrification" had been imported from London. Like the downtown land-use watchers, their learning experience was a rich lore of specific cases that could be brought into something approximating "controlled comparison." Perhaps the grossest of these comparisons was the repeated statement, "We have to avoid what happened in Uptown."

Second, like their downtown counterparts, they had to alternate between an instrumental rhetoric facilitating private investment and a moral one claiming the support of "the people." What gave this latter claim credence was the exhaustive organization of the local region into a federation of territorial groups (including the business strips) that could "speak for everyone." That claim might be challenged, but the burden of proof lay upon the skeptics. There was someone to represent everyone in this territorial configuration.

Third, it appeared that how a local region got organized depended upon who got there first, the community developers or the activists who worked within the Alinsky tradition. Extending my informants into Uptown, it became evident that the activists had entered that area during the 1960s, organizing a constituency of dependent people and polarizing the community for more than twenty years. The crucial timing for this kind of "outside intervention" (whether developers or activists) seemed to be the onset of succession.

After living in the North River Area for four years, I moved to Rogers Park. Further research in Lincoln Park, Lake View, and Edgewater had made Rogers Park the most puzzling case. Besides, my wife worked at Loyola University. We were only a short walk away.

In Lincoln Park, few of those currently active in its organizations could remember how these associations had originated, or referred only to a formal history in which grass roots heroism had seized the day to save the community from public clearance and private decay. A few elderly residents and some of those in the "developer network" did recall how the local universities and hospitals had gradually blanketed the area with territorial groups. In Lake View and Edgewater, the origin of this pattern was more available to memory although community history pivoted more nearly on the demographic differences between Edgewater and Uptown than on the actions of community entrepreneurs.

In Rogers Park, however, the polarization of its community groups was of relatively recent origin. Painstaking interviews with longtime residents did show that only a few of its organizations had ever been turf bound. But a far more revealing set of events occurred when Martin Goldsmith, with the Department of City Planning and a resident of the community, made a heroic effort to assemble all Rogers Park's community groups and work them incrementally toward a consensus on a developmental program. Despite his energy, patience, and position, nearly a year of meetings and discussions resulted in no visible movement. Even the bravest closet gentrifier could not bring himself to say that the community had to ration its number of dependent households if it were to remain viable. And the traditional community groups of home owners remained impotent in finding among their successors people who they might liken to themselves on the basis of social class rather than ethnicity. It was

Methodological Appendix

an eye-opener. Left to themselves, even "second settlement" residents could not select among their successors unless they had someone else to create a language for instrumental and moral persuasion. They were entrapped either in a language of universal acceptance or one that recognized only a complete match for themselves. Some could not openly "discriminate" on social class. Others were "tolerant" but only within ethnic boundaries.[4]

By this time (1985), I had already finalized my "sample" of 119 land-use changes in the city, eighty-nine of which were located along the north lakefront or in the North River Area. Examination of each of these cases was important because it required me to repeat in another way (often after more than a year's absence) some of the interviews I had undertaken with community developers or activists. With each site one could, so to speak, test out my arguments on the character of each community's organization by its response to specific site changes. I obtained information on each site from a minimum of three informants, often many more because some informants had been involved in several site changes. I was myself involved, though generally I took a low profile. I joined lots of groups and attended many meetings. My usual practice, however, was to try to be helpful by keeping the minutes but not take a strong position. Outside the lakefront communities and the North River Area, I did not carry out similar interviews on specific site changes.

Although I am reasonably satisfied with the adequacy of these data I do regret one omission. After I was well into these interviews, Taub et al. published their *Paths of Neighborhood Change* (1984). One of their key observations is the role that "corporate actors" play in promoting community investment. I believe they are right. Community groups do not just arise spontaneously, and much of their energy

---

4. In other words, those who are tolerant on class distinctions are intolerant on ethnic distinctions and vice versa. But the situation is more complicated than this because they also differ in which distinction they are most confident in making public. Those tolerant of ethnic distinctions are less gun-shy on class differences. Those tolerant on class distinctions are not gun-shy on ethnic differences.

Considerations of this sort might go far toward explaining Chicago's very uneven patterns of succession. There is the relatively gradual and selective process of succession among those in "adjacent" ethnic groups (e.g., Northern Europeans but also Eastern Europeans), so that neighborhood class standing remains relatively unchanged following succession. Then, there are those much more abrupt and unselective patterns of succession (e.g., between Northern and Eastern or Southern Europeans and all whites and blacks) where ethnic succession entails class succession.

can be exhausted in fending off succession unless some fairly knowl-edgeable corporate actor can direct them toward an investment program and the selective attraction of new residents. This was not obvious to me because community groups quickly forget their past, reordering it so that their emergence is more nearly the expression of spontaneous consensus. I did not completely miss the impor-tance of these corporate actors, and hints of their presence are in-cluded in Chapter 4. Another reason for my lack of emphasis on this point, however, is that some of the corporate actors I did get wind of were more equivocal or less obvious than those identified by Taub et al. Clearly, Representative Rostenkowski is extremely important to the North River Commission, although he (unlike North Park Col-lege and Swedish Covenant Hospital) is not obviously a "corporate actor." The Students for a Democratic Society played a large role in Uptown during the 1960s but with the opposite outcome. Corporate activity, then, may be fundamental to neighborhood development, but it can run in both directions. And it is complicated by the match between corporate actors and ward level political support or opposition.

Granted the complexity and equivocal character of this kind of "outside intervention," it is understandable that Chicagoans dis-trust most efforts at neighborhood improvement sponsored by anyone other than themselves. Corporate actors sometimes over-come this distrust and sometimes worsen it. But the fundamental problem seems to go beyond direct experience or that shared by rumor. Americans and Chicagoans especially have extended the electoral selection of their political leaders to the point that most of them represent very narrow constituencies. They are only a sort of official version of the special interest groups which already haunt the American imagination. Poorly paid, poorly trained, and poorly known, most local elected officials are only a scaffolding on which Chicagoans can drape their worst suspicions. The mass media would be irresponsible if it did not cater to this search for ulterior motives.

My field notes are pervaded by these suspicions and alle-gations. But you cannot just publish thousands of pages of field notes or fully satisfy yourself and your reader by repeating com-monplace allegations. Accordingly, what I have tried to do in Chapter 7 is recreate in some measure the experience of the Chicago voter. It is not quantitative sociology in the sense of measured covariation. Rather, it is an effort to give the reader some feel for the density of electoral politics, the bewildering choices and rich opportunity for intrigue.

Similarly in Chapter 8, I am trying to capture something for the reader in a way that it did not quite come to me. The "spirit of a city," its local culture, and its banalities are experienced by a field-worker almost by their omission. "Everyone knows that" is a statement of dismissal, and to ask about it too often is to raise doubts about one's regional I.Q. One cannot just sit an informant down and ask him to tell you everything that Chicagoans know so well that they do not talk about it. One must, in some way, recreate the banality of day-to-day experience, its visual density, its standard stylistic forms, and its repetitiveness. It is for this reason that I have counted a lot of things that will seem commonplace to Chicagoans but perhaps less so to outsiders. Of course, one does see many of those statues, read some of the local novelists, and, if you are on the board of the University of Chicago Press, have a sense for what researchers are avoiding and what they are attracted to. But for locals (including me), this is an overly self-conscious way of seeing something that arrives to them implicitly, as, say, in an inside joke, where you can only infer what is held to be background knowledge. In the early 1960s, for example, when Richard J. Daley was at the height of his powers, Representative Pucinski suggested him as a Democratic candidate for president of the United States. His suggestion was the source of a good deal of local merriment. No one needed to explain why. Yet, at the time Daley was probably the third or fourth most powerful politician in the country. The "unsaid" lies behind those things that are most easily understood. To convey them to outsiders, however, one must recreate a moral and cultural landscape which is more apparent to the tourist than the local who has grown up with jokes like the above.

Going beyond the Data

After a couple of years, as one moved from informants in one organization to another, information became redundant. Their arguments differed in particulars. Before Harold Washington became mayor, the public agencies were exceptionally eager to take the larger proposals of private firms and grandfather them into "dedicated" city plans. Within two years, however, the Washington regime was also caught up in the big project and the politics of urgency. What remained very similar across all informants was the double standard: one rhetoric for assessing land-use plans, and another for marketing it to different publics.

This difference extended to individual builders and developers who had no active affiliation with "planning groups."[5] Often these individuals did voice a good deal of consternation about "all this mishmash for minorities and do-gooders." What was needed in their most extreme statements was "the highest and best use." A couple did say that the city would be better off without any department of city planning, zoning, or site guidelines— "like Houston." But even they dismissed this as a pipe dream: "No one would put up with it. You have to sugarcoat it."

I do not mean to suggest by this that individual land developers are especially constrained by either their own instrumental or moral standards. If the floodgates to development were thrown open, my best guess is that it would result in a free-for-all resembling what happened in the early years of urban renewal: a scorched earth policy followed by megablock developments as large as the banks and federal government would allow. Only subsequently would "the market" pronounce its negative judgment. That is the trouble with the market. Its judgments come too late in the megadecisions of land use. In an ironic twist, many land developers have learned that they need restraint; that they tend to create Hong Kongs, rich in land values but full of emigrants. But, of course, each of them want to be free of these restraints.

What urban planning of this sort lacks is any external authority that can claim to transcend individual experience. It is not simply that members of various publics lack the experiences of seasoned observers. That will never be possible. Yet, this does not mean that these publics—blacks, the media, do-gooders, opportunists, embittered residents, the cynical, the damaged—are hopelessly resistant to informed authority.

Just about midcourse in this study, I became engaged with a number of collaborators in the production of the *Local Community Fact Book* for metropolitan Chicago. Originally developed by Ernest Burgess and Charles Newcomb in 1931, the *Fact Book* has become a standard work heavily used by community organizers, planners, city agencies, and philanthropic organizations. However modest its

5. Most, however, join some association although they may not participate beyond sending in their dues. "It can't hurt," as one of them put it to me.

statistical record, it does stand as an independent account of Chicago's community areas. Some people decide which community they live in by recourse to this volume. Some philanthropic and service providers use it as a basis for allocating resources or advocating governmental action. Most people do not understand the construction of its measurements (I do not fully understand all of them), and I know that the boundaries given for community areas are largely an artifact of Burgess, Newcomb, and Vivian Palmer's methodology.[6] Still, the *Fact Book* stands as the final arbiter of factual disputes insofar as its data can be drawn into public accounts.

The *Fact Book* seemed to me a step in the right direction although it was neither designed nor suitable for the purpose of tracking land-use decisions or public investments. Basically, it provides a fifty-year chronicle of the quality of life in Chicago's seventy-seven community areas and selected suburbs. What might serve as a far better model for urban planning are the economic indicators provided by federal agencies and routinely reported by the mass media. Even a casual reading of these news releases show that they are crucial evidence in tracking the fortunes of presidential administrations and their economic policies. The proverbial man in the street might not understand how these data are assembled, but they are nonetheless recognized "barometers" which transcend individual experience. They are not just the promotional statements of politicians or the assertions of knowledgeable lobbyists. They are economic accounts in two senses. They are running accounts to evaluate where you have been and where you might be going. They are also accountabilities that weigh on the performance of policymakers and their practice. Economists might debate their meaning and implications, but they do so within narrowed, "factual" limits. If their validity is low, their reliability is still such that standards are the same across different administrations and their policies.

This example was sufficiently intriguing that in 1987 I laid aside this manuscript for several months to do a comparative study of how these economic indicators had constrained the *Chicago Tribune's* reporting of the stockmarket crashes in 1929 and 1987. The

6. Burgess and Newcomb took authoral credit for the volume. Palmer may have done much of the work. Her subsequent work seems to describe what should have been done to create "natural areas" rather than what either she did or what Burgess and Newcomb actually did.

publication of that study is still down the road, but it convinced me that the emergence of economic indicators between 1929 and 1987 had dethroned the experienced businessman and politician as the press's authority and replaced him with people with some background in economics. Reasoning with this example in mind, I have argued that city planners cannot hope to achieve similar authority until they possess an external authority to track their performance.

Midrange Ethnography

As can be seen from this account, this was not a study that advanced from first principles to propositions and then to hypotheses and operational instrumentation. It began almost adventitiously without my full recognition, and it was punctuated by a dawning awareness that I was "onto something." The unraveling of that "something" was informed by theory, but the relationship between theory and research was ninety degrees off accepted practice. The point at which I became aroused and most eager to get more data was where existing theory is vague or where different theories confront one another. Thus, much of the data I report here is not a "representative" count from my field notes but data that I think bear on the crucial debates on urban theory and especially its application to the competitive position of central cities in the United States. It is newsworthy data, not all my data.

This will not be obvious to the general reader. I did write the first chapter first. But I did so only after most of the findings were in. The remaining chapters are a seesaw experience between data collection and interpretation. As they were written up, I would reach voids in the data and go back to fieldwork. They I would revise the chapters "to fit the data." Sometimes, I would read a theoretical work and go back and rephrase my original work. Even after there was a first draft, changes occurred. One of the reviewers wanted a more linear design in which the first chapter would forecast the findings. I made modest changes which would make it seem like I had planned the study. In the main, I agreed to say something about the entire issue in the "Methodological Appendix." By and large, I wanted the study to read like a mystery, for that is how I experienced it.

Methodological Appendix

In another respect, I did lean over backward to fulfill a descriptive responsibility which I think falls upon the ethnographer. Lots of things are worth describing more fully than necessary to satisfy contemporary theoretic claimants simply for the reason that they are reusable to other sociologists. Here Malinowski is my model. The kula ring is interesting whether or not you have a theory about it. Thus, in Chapters 2–6 I have gone to some pains to give other researchers a story that can enter the archives of urban ethnography. The generalizations I draw from these cases are modest, incremental, and only suggestive of my final conclusion.

This, then, is not your usual defense of urban ethnography. It starts adventitiously and proceeds selectively to an examination of the more contested regions of urban theory. It provides a codification of what one hopes are memorable examples. It goes back and forth between findings and interpretations, writing and data collection. It caves in to reviewers and stylistic preferences so that it seems more planful than it was. It uses the artifice of counting to recreate local experience. Worse yet, it goes beyond experience to suggest policies only dimly tried in another area.

It also embodies a moral choice which is less explicit than it ought be. I come down very much on the side of "sunrise" investments for our older cities. I am for gentrification, for more "communication-administration" functions in the enlarged Central Business District, for the upscale urban retailers, and for small-scale entrepreneurs with a new product and little need for heavy transport. I am for a twenty-four-hour downtown, urban tourism, Central Area "precincts in the sky," the popularization of high culture, the city as landscape art, and the city as an ethnic make-believe for people who have forgotten how to make their own pilaf, cannelloni, and perogi.

What, you may ask, are we going to do with all those poor people in our central cities who are already in fear of displacement? The answer, in my view, is that the alternative is still more cruel than the dangers of displacement. A single-minded redistributive policy will not work because the supply of poor people is infinitely elastic: we will get as many of them in our central cities as we make room for or support at subsistence levels. Alternatively, the scale of gentrification or general sunrise investments in our central cities is minimal, concentrated almost entirely in our CBD's and a few community areas—about 10 percent of Chicago's land area by my calculation. At that scale, gentrification and sunrise development

Methodological Appendix

hardly pose a danger. The "city as a growth machine" is a metaphor forty years too late.[7]

The prime reason for this concentration of gentrification and sunrise investment is concerted opposition to any investment program that would raise housing costs for the poor. But any private program of investment will raise costs above that of a deteriorating ghetto experiencing disinvestment. Disinvestment, however, reduces the quantity of housing stock while also raising the cost of housing in the long run by lowering its supply. Public housing will lower rental levels, but it also drives out private investment and increased abandonment in adjacent housing. Benign neglect or current patterns of public housing placement, then, are only morally satisfying to advocates of the poor, and they increase segregation.

If gentrification could be distributed more widely throughout our central cities, it would have a much more moderate effect on housing costs and could retard or reverse patterns of disinvestment and housing loss. If *all* our central city communities favored upscale investment, it would be less of a problem. And there would be more taxpayers around to contribute to transfer payments.

All this sounds too rosy, and it is. First, most investors do not want to take the profits of generalized investment but prefer to work "hot areas" where the magnitude of profits are assured for those who can obtain entry. Narrow spatial limits reduce uncertainty for investors and provide windfall returns. It is a sure thing. Selective spatial investment is a part of their mentality; it is implicit in their methodology (simple gravity models) which transfer gradient lines into bounded areas.

Second, hot spots can be singled out by political predators who can share in the spoils. Hot spots encourage high-density development where the ratio between profit and land/political costs is low. The small number of investors in hot spots is easy to organize; they contribute to political aspirants and know what they want. General investors are hard to organize, do not have to invest in political sponsorship, and look outside the central city. The only way to

7. Much as I admire Harvey Molotch's work, I believe it includes two flaws. First, it is too late. Unselective boosterism exists now only in backward areas. Even in Chicago, all investments are not good investments. Second, gut level enthusiasm for job growth swells up from the masses as well as from city magnets. Indeed, in current big city America, the main lingering support for job growth rather than, say, income growth, occurs among the poor and their advocates. Molotch's article (1976), if published in 1947, would have set a sociological record for forecasting.

Methodological Appendix

lower these advantages to a small number of local investors and political predators is to create a lot of hot spots.

One cannot do this simply by opening the floodgates to developers. The restraints that local community groups impose on them
are essential. In my view, these community groups are most effective when they organize on a territorial basis. Necessarily, this gives
homeowners and very localized businessmen a disproportionate
voice in changing land uses. Yet, they seem to be the only consumers who can anticipate a sustained market—a self-supporting
demand for central city residence and trade rather than the quick-in-
quick-out pattern that developers might embrace if left to their own
guidance. Renters and the dependent and the politically well-connected developers can hardly resist the temptations of the "free
rider."

This is not an argument against all large-scale land-use conversions. So much of Chicago (and other cities) is vacant or so lacking in
home ownership that some public authority must step in and try to
anticipate "the market." We now have a significant record of such
projects in Chicago, and there is little reason to repeat previous mis-
takes: inadequate scale, the failure to link large residential investors
with smaller ones, overreliance on subsidized housing, no provision for the use of existing structures to bridge the gap between
planned use and local trial and error.

Unfortunately, this learning experience is not self-enforcing.
Adherence to these principles will require the continued vigilance of
citywide watchdog groups, the press *and researchers*. In this case, research—my kind of research—is never just a test of theory. It is a
kind of journalism which recovers what we already know, remaking
it into contemporary language, redrawing the connection between
past experience and present examples. In this kind of journalism,
the search for some match between instrumental and moral rhetorics continues although one hopes that it does so within
narrowed, factual limits. Morris Janowitz knew this very well when
he drove me to downtown Chicago. Morris was a master at finding a
moral language for the possible rather than only the utopian. He
once told me that sociology has to be rewritten every five years. Otherwise, social amnesia makes the obvious escapable. I hope that my
venture into urban planning has recalled some of his most durable
observations on what can be both possible and moral.

BIBLIOGRAPHY

Algren, Nelson. 1951. *Chicago: City on the Make*. New York: McGraw-Hill.
_____. 1956. *A Walk on the Wild Side*. New York: Crest Books.
_____. 1960. *Who Lost an American?* New York: Macmillan.
Alinsky, Saul. 1966. *Reville for Radicals*. New York: Vintage.
Andrews, Clarence A. 1982. *Chicago in Story: A Literary History*. Iowa City, Ia.: Midwest Heritage Publishing Co.
Appelbaum, Stanley. 1980. *The Chicago World's Fair of 1893*. New York: Dover.
Asbury, Herbert. 1942. *The Gem of the Prairie*. Garden City, N.J.: Garden City.
Atlas, James. 1986. *The Great Pretender*. New York: Atheneum.
Bach, Ira J., and Mary Lackritz Gray. 1983. *A Guide to Chicago's Public Sculpture*. Chicago: University of Chicago Press.
Banfield, Edward. 1961. *Political Influence*. Glencoe, Ill.: Free Press.
Banfield, Edward, and James Q. Wilson. 1963. *City Politics*. New York: Vintage.
Barsky, Steven F. August. 1974. "Representatives of the Community: Scholars, Mass Media and Government." Ph.D. diss., Department of Sociology, University of Chicago.
Becker, Gary. 1971. *The Economics of Discrimination*. Chicago: University of Chicago Press.
Bellow, Saul. 1977. "A Kind Friend Worried About My Soul." *Jefferson Lecture*, delivered in April at the Drake Hotel, Chicago. Unpublished.
_____. 1982. *The Dean's December*. New York: Simon and Schuster.
Berry, Brian J. L. 1979. *The Open Housing Question: Race and Housing in Chicago, 1966–1976*. Cambridge, Mass.: Ballinger.
_____. 1985. "Islands of Renewal in Seas of Decay." Pp. 69–96 in *The New Urban Reality*, ed. P. Peterson. Washington, D.C.: Brookings Institute.
Berry, Brian J. L., Irving Cutler, Edwin H. Draine, Ying-cheng Kiang, Thomas R. Tocalis, and Pierre de Vise. 1976. *Chicago: Transformations of an Urban System*. Cambridge, Mass.: Ballinger.
Berry, Brian J. L., and Donald C. Dahmann. 1977. *Population Redistribution in the United States in the 1970's*. Washington, D.C.: National Academy of Sciences.
Berry, Brian J. L., and William L. Garrison. 1958. "Alternative Explanations of Urban Rank-Size Relationships." *Annals of the Association of American Geographers* 48 (March): 83–91.
Berry, Brian J. L., and Frank E. Horton. 1970. *Geographic Perspectives on Urban Systems*. Englewood Cliffs, N.J.: Prentice-Hall.

Bibliography

Berry, Brian J. L., Sandra J. Parson, and Rutherford H. Platt. 1968. *The Impact of Urban Renewal on Small Business: The Hyde Park-Kenwood Case.* Chicago: Center for Urban Studies, University of Chicago.

Birch, David L. 1970. *The Economic Future of City and Suburb.* New York: Committee for Economic Development.

Blackstone, Kevin. 1985. "Racial Violence and Harassment Escalate in Chicago Area." *Chicago Reporter* 14, no. 1 (January).

Block, Fred, and Gene Burns. 1986. "Productivity as a Social Problem." *American Sociological Review,* 51 (December): 767–780.

Block, Jean. 1978. *Hyde Park Homes.* Chicago: University of Chicago Press.

_____. 1983. *The Uses of Gothic.* Chicago: University of Chicago Press.

Bogue, Donald. n.d. *Population Projections: Chicago SMSA, Chicago City and Metropolitan Ring: 1980–2000.* Chicago: Urban, Regional and Local Data Analysis.

Bonney, Norman. 1974. "Unwelcome Strangers." Ph.D. diss., Department of Sociology, University of Chicago.

Bowden, Charles, et al. 1981. *Street Signs Chicago: Neighborhoods and Other Illusions of Big City Life.* Chicago: Chicago Review Press.

Bowley, Devereux, Jr. 1978. *The Poorhouse: Subsidized Housing in Chicago.* Carbondale: Southern Illinois University Press.

Boyer, Richard, and David Savageau. 1981. *Places Rated Almanac.* Chicago: Rand McNally.

Boylan, Ross D. 1985. "The Making of a White Ethnic Movement." Department of Sociology, University of Chicago. Unpublished paper.

Bradley, Donald S., and Mayer N. Zald. 1965. "From Commercial Elite to Political Administrator." *American Journal of Sociology* 61 (September): 153–167.

Branden, William. 1984. "Taking a Flier on a World's Fair." *Chicago* (October): 181 passim.

Brashler, William. 1976. *City Dogs.* New York: Harper and Row.

Brooks, Gwendolyn. 1983. *Mayor Harold Washington and the "I Will" City.* Chicago: Brooks Press.

Brown, David L., and John M. Wardwell, eds. 1980. *New Directions in Urban-Rural Migration: The Population Turnaround in America.* New York: Academic Press.

Bruckner, D. J. R., and Irene Macauley, eds. 1976. *Dreams in Stone: The University of Chicago.* Chicago: University of Chicago Press.

Buder, Stanley. 1967. *Pullman: An Experiment in Industrial Order and Community Planning: 1880–1930.* New York: Oxford University Press.

Bulmer, Martin. 1984. *The Chicago School of Sociology.* Chicago: University of Chicago Press.

Burg, David. 1976. *Chicago's White City of 1893.* Lexington: University of Kentucky.

Burgess, Ernest, and Charles Newcomb. 1931. *Census Data on the City of Chicago.* Chicago: University of Chicago Press.

Burnham, Daniel H., and Edward H. Bennett. 1970 (first published 1909). *Plan of Chicago.* Reprint. New York: Da Capo.

Bibliography

Cafferty, Pastora San Juan. 1986. *A Report on Civic Life in Chicago*. Chicago: Chicago Project.

Cafferty, Pastora San Juan, and William C. McCready. 1982. "The Chicago Public-Private Partnership: A Heritage of Involvement." In *Public-Private Partnerships in America*, ed. R. Fosler and R. Berger. Lexington, Mass.: Lexington Books.

Chicago Central Area Committee and the City of Chicago. 1983. *Chicago Central Area Plan*. Chicago: Chicago Central Area Committee.

Chicago Department of City Planning. 1946. *A Preliminary Comprehensive Plan*. Chicago: Chicago Department of City Planning.

_____. 1954. *Recommended Policies for Redevelopment*. Chicago: Chicago Department of City Planning.

_____. 1958. *Development Plan for the Central Area of Chicago*. Chicago: Chicago Department of City Planning.

_____. 1964. *Basic Policies for the Comprehensive Plan of Chicago*. Chicago: Chicago Department of City Planning.

Chicago Department of Development and Planning. 1966. *The Comprehensive Plan of Chicago*. Chicago: Chicago Department of Development and Planning.

_____. 1967. *The Comprehensive Plan of Chicago: Population, Economy, Land*. Chicago: Chicago Department of Development and Planning.

Chicago Economic Development Commission. 1978. *The Chicago Plan for Economic Development*. Chicago: Chicago Economic Development Commission.

Chicago Plan Commission. 1973. *Chicago 21*. Chicago: Chicago Plan Commission.

_____. 1981. *Comprehensive Plan: Goals and Policies*. Chicago: Chicago Plan Commission.

_____. 1982. *Chicago 1992: Comprehensive Plan*. Chicago: Chicago Plan Commission.

_____. n.d. *1977–1981 Capital Improvements Program*. Chicago: Chicago Plan Commission.

City of Chicago. 1984. *"Chicago Works Together" 1984 Chicago Development Plan*. Chicago.

Clark, Terry Nichols, and Lorna Crowley Ferguson. 1976. "How Many More New Yorks." *New York Affairs* 3 (Summer/Fall): 18–27.

_____. 1983. *City Money*. New York: Columbia University Press.

Condit, Carl. 1964. *The Chicago School of Architecture: A History of Commercial and Public Buildings in the Chicago Area, 1875–1925*. Chicago: University of Chicago Press.

_____. 1973. *Chicago 1910–1929: Building, Planning and Urban Technology*. Chicago: University of Chicago Press.

_____. 1974. *Chicago 1930–1970: Building, Planning and Urban Technology*. Chicago: University of Chicago Press.

Corden, Carol. 1977. *Planned Cities: New Towns in Britain and America*. Beverly Hills, Calif.: Sage Publications.

Cromie, Robert. 1982. *Chicago*. Chicago: Rand McNally.

Bibliography

Cruz, Harold. 1968. *Rebellion or Revolution*. New York: Morrow.

Dedmon, Emmett. 1981. *Fabulous Chicago: A Great City's History and People*. New York: Atheneum.

Demuth, James. 1980. *Small Town Chicago: The Comic Perspective of Finley Peter Dunne*. New York: Kennikat Press.

De Vise, Pierre. 1967. *Chicago's Widening Color Gap*. Chicago: Interuniversity Social Research Committee.

De Zutter, Hank. January 1986. *Public Housing That Works: Report on the Private, Decentralized Management of Scattered Site Units on Chicago's North Side*. Chicago: Business and Professional People for the Public Interest.

Pellow, Deborah. 1975. *Mutual Relevance of the Social and Physical Environments*. Chicago: Council for Community Services of Metropolitan Chicago.

Dreiser, Theodore. 1900. *Sister Carrie*. New York: Doubleday, Page and Co.

Duis, Perry. 1976. *Chicago: Creating New Traditions*. Chicago: Chicago Historical Society.

Duncan, Dudley, and Beverly Duncan. 1957. *The Negro Population of Chicago*. Chicago: University of Chicago Press.

Duncan, Hugh Dalziel. 1964. *The Rise of Chicago as a Literary Center from 1885 to 1920*. Totowa, N.J.: Bedminster Press.

Emmons, David. December 1986. "Community Organizing and Urban Policy: Saul Alinsky and Chicago's Citizen Action Program," Ph.D. diss., Department of Sociology, University of Chicago.

Erbe, William, Richard Glasser, Albert Hunter, John Johnstone, and Gerald Suttles. 1984. *Local Community Fact Book: Chicago Metropolitan Area*. Chicago: Chicago Review Press.

Fair, Ronald. 1970. *World of Nothing*. New York: Harper and Row.

Field, Eugene. 1900. *Sharps and Flats*. New York: Scribner's.

Firey, Walter. 1947. *Land Use in Central Boston*. Westport, Conn.: Greenwood Press.

FitzGerald, Kathleen. 1981. *Brass: Jane Byrne and the Pursuit of Power*. Chicago: Contemporary Books.

Flanagan, Maureen A. 1986. "Charter Reform in Chicago: Political Culture and Urban Progressive Reform." *Journal of Urban History* 12 (February): 109–130.

Forrest, Leon. 1977. *The Bloodworth Orphans*. New York: Random House.

———. 1983. *Two Wings to Veil My Face*. New York: Random House.

Gans, Herbert. 1962. *The Urban Villagers: Group and Class in the Life of Italian-Americans*. New York: Free Press.

Geertz, Clifford. 1980. *Negara: The Theatre State in Nineteenth Century Bali*. Princeton, N.J.: Princeton University Press.

Giancanna, Antoinette, and Thomas C. Renner. 1985. *Mafia Princess*. New York: Avon.

Gitlin, Todd, and Nanci Hollander. 1970. *Uptown: Poor Whites in Chicago*. New York: Harper Colophon Books.

Gleason, William Francis. 1970. *Daley of Chicago*. New York: Simon and Schuster.

Goode, J. Paul. 1923. "Chicago: A City of Destiny." Address at the Celebration of the Geographic Society of Chicago, Field Museum of Natural History, Chicago.

Gosnell, Harold. 1935. *Negro Politicians: The Rise of Negro Politics in Chicago*. Chicago: University of Chicago Press.

Gottfried, Alex. 1962. *Boss Cermak of Chicago*. Seattle: University of Washington Press.

Granger, Bill, and Lori Granger. 1980. *Fighting Jane: Mayor Jane Byrne and the Chicago Machine*. New York: Dial Press.

Greenstone, J. David, and Paul Peterson. 1973. *Race and Authority in Urban Politics: Community Participation in the War on Poverty*. New York: Russell Sage Foundation.

Greeley, Andrew. 1982. *Thy Brother's Wife*. New York: Warner Books.

Greer, Scott. 1965. *Urban Renewal and American Cities: The Dilemma of Democratic Intervention*. Indianapolis: Bobbs-Merrill.

Grey, Lennox Bouton. 1935. "Chicago and 'The Great American Novel': A Critical Approach to the American Epic." Ph.D. diss., Department of Sociology, University of Chicago.

Guest, Judith. 1976. *Ordinary People*. New York: Ballantine.

Guterbock, Thomas M. 1980. *Machine Politics in Transition*. Chicago: University of Chicago Press.

Harris, Neil. 1973. *Humbug! The Art of Barnum*. Chicago: University of Chicago Press.

———. 1984. "Great American Fairs and American Cities; The Role of Chicago's Columbian Exposition." In *1992 World's Fair Forum Papers: Legacies from Chicago's World's Fair: A Background for Fair Planning*. Evanston, Ill.: Center for Urban Affairs and Policy Research, Northwestern University.

Harris, Frank. 1963. *Bomb*. Chicago: University of Chicago Press.

Harris, Jerome Don. 1980. "Grass-Roots Community Organizing in the City of Chicago." Ph.D. diss., Department of Sociology, University of Illinois, Chicago.

Harwood, Edwin. 1966. "Work and Community among Newcomers: A Study of Social and Economic Adaptation." Ph.D. diss., Department of Sociology, University of Chicago.

Hauser, Philip. 1964. *Integration of the Public Schools*. Chicago: Report to Chicago Board of Education: Advisory Panel on the Integration of the Public Schools.

Hauser, Philip, and Patricia Leavey Hodge. 1968. *The Challenge of America's Metropolitan Population Outlook: 1960–1985*. New York: Praeger.

Hecht, Ben, and Charles MacArthur. 1928. *Front Page*. New York: Covici-Friede.

Hines, Thomas S. 1974. *Burnham of Chicago: Architect and Planner*. London: Oxford University Press.

Hunter, Albert J., and Gerald D. Suttles. 1972. "The Expanding Community of Limited Liability." Pp. 44–81 in *The Social Construction of Communities*. Chicago: University of Chicago Press.

Hutton, Graham. 1946. *Midwest at Noon*. Chicago: University of Chicago Press.

Bibliography

Jacobs, Jane. 1961. *The Death and Life of Great American Cities*. New York: Random House.

Jaher, Frederic Cople. 1982. *The Urban Establishment*. Urbana: University of Illinois Press.

Jones, Bryan D. 1985. *Governing Buildings and Building Government*. Tuscaloosa: University of Alabama Press.

Kahn, Melvin, and Francis J. Majors. 1984. *The Winning Ticket: The Chicago Machine and Illinois Politics*. New York: Praeger.

Karl, Barry. 1974. *Charles E. Merriam and the Study of Politics*. Chicago: University of Chicago Press.

Kazin, Alfred. 1985. "City of the Big Writers." *Chicago Tribune Sunday Magazine* (November): 24.

Kennedy, Eugene C. 1978. *Himself! The Life and Times of Mayor Richard J. Daley*. New York: Viking.

———. 1982. "Bellow Awaits Heat from Novel of 'Hard Knocks.'" *Chicago Tribune* (January 10). (a)

———. 1982. *Queen Bee*. New York: Fawcett Crest. (b)

Kogan, Herman, and Robert Cromie. 1971. *The Great Fire: Chicago 1871*. New York: Putnam's.

Kornblum, William. 1974. *Blue Collar Community*. Chicago: University of Chicago Press.

Kotter, John P., and Paul R. Lawrence. 1974. *Five Approaches to Urban Governance*. New York: Wiley.

Krasnow, Iris. 1981. "Arthur, the Magnificent." *Chicago* (April): 129 passim.

Lathrobe, Charles Joseph. 1836. *The Rambler in North America*. London: Seeley and W. Burnside.

Lehman-Haupt, Christopher. 1982. "Books of the Times." *New York Times* (January 11).

Levine, Mark L., George C. McNamee, and Daniel Greenberg. 1970. *The Tales of Hoffman*. New York: Bantam Books.

Lewis, Lloyd, and Henry Justin Smith. 1929. *Chicago: The History of Its Reputation*. New York: Harcourt Brace.

Liebling, Abbott Joseph. 1952. *Chicago: The Second City*. New York: Knopf.

Lindberg, Richard. 1985. *Chicago Ragtime: Another Look at Chicago 1880–1920*. South Bend, Ind.: Icarus Press.

Lochin, Mitchell. 1986. "Such a Deal." *Chicago Sunday Tribune Magazine* (February 2).

Lowe, David. 1978. *Lost Chicago*. Boston: Houghton Mifflin.

Lubove, Roy. 1976. *The Urban Community: Housing and Planning in the Progressive Era*. Englewood Cliffs, N.J.: Prentice-Hall.

Ludkin, Mary, and Louis H. Masotti. 1985. *Downtown Development: Chicago, 1979–1984*. Evanston Ill.: Center for Urban Affairs and Policy Research.

Lynch, Kevin. 1960. *The Image of the City*. Cambridge, Mass.: M.I.T. Press.

MacAloon, John J. 1987. "You Don't Say: There are no Spies in Sport." Unpublished paper.

McComb, David G. 1981. *Houston: A History*. Austin: University of Texas Press.

McCourt, Kathleen. 1977. *Working Class Women and Grass-Roots Politics*. Bloomington: Indiana University Press.

Macdonald, Dwight. 1970. "Introduction." Pp. xi–xxiv in *The Tales of Hoffman*, ed. M. Levine, G. McNamee, and D. Greenberg. New York: Bantam Books.

Mailer, Norman. 1968. *Miami and the Siege of Chicago*. New York: World.

Mamet, David. 1984. *Glengarry Glenn Ross*. New York: Grove Press.

Marciniak, Edward. 1981. *Reversing Urban Decline: The Winthrop-Kenmore Corridor in the Edgewater and Uptown Communities of Chicago*. Washington, D.C.: National Center for Urban Ethnic Affairs.

———. 1986. *Reclaiming the Inner City: Chicago's Near North Revitalization Confronts Cabrini-Green*. Washington, D.C.: National Center for Urban Ethnic Affairs.

Marciniak, Edward, and Nancy Jefferson. 1985. "CHA Advisory Committee Appointed by Judge Marvin E. Aspin: Final Report" (December). Chicago. Unpublished.

Mark, Norman. 1979. *Mayors, Madams and Madmen*. Chicago: Chicago Review Press.

Masotti, Louis, and Samuel Gove, eds. 1982. *After Daley*. Urbana: University of Illinois Press.

Masters, Edgar Lee. 1933. *The Tale of Chicago*. New York: Putnam's.

Mayer, Harold. 1955. *Chicago: City of Decisions*. Chicago: Geographic Society of Chicago.

Mayer, Harold, and Richard C. Wade. 1969. *Chicago: Growth of a Metropolis*. Chicago: University of Chicago Press.

Mayor's Council of Manpower and Economic Advisors. 1977. *Chicago's Economy on the Move*. Chicago: City of Chicago.

Mead, George Herbert. 1934. *The Social Psychology of George Herbert Mead*. Chicago: University of Chicago Press.

Meeker, Arthur. 1949. *Prairie Avenue*. New York: Knopf.

Menken, H. L. 1917. Untitled article. *Chicago Tribune* (October 28).

Metropolitan Housing and Planning Council. 1982. *Map 2000: Metropolitan Area Plan for the Year 2000*. Chicago: Metropolitan Housing and Planning Council.

Molotch, Harvey. 1976. "The City as a Growth Machine." *American Journal of Sociology* 82 (September): 50–65.

Muller, Chandra. 1983. "Resource Dependency in Community Based Organizations." Master's thesis, Department of Sociology, University of Chicago.

Myerson, Martin and Edward C. Banfield. 1955. *Politics, Planning and the Public Interest: The Case of Public Housing in Chicago*. Glencoe, Ill.: Free Press.

Neil, Andrew. 1980. "Chicago Through British Eyes." *The Economist* (Spring). (Republished in the *Chicago Tribune*, 6 April 1980.)

Newman, Oscar. 1973. *Defensible Space: Crime Prevention through Urban Design*. New York: Macmillan.

Nord, David Paul. 1985. "The Public Community: The Urbanization of Journalism in Chicago." *Journal of Urban History* 11 (August): 411–441.

Bibliography

Norris, Frank. 1903. *The Pit*. New York: Doubleday, Page and Co.

O'Conner, Len. 1975. *Clout: Mayor Daley and His City*. Chicago: Regnery.

———. 1977. *Requiem: The Decline and Demise of Mayor Daley and his Era*. Chicago: Contemporary Books.

Ogburn, William. 1964. *On Culture and Social Change*. Chicago: University of Chicago Press.

Palmer, Vivian. 1929. *Field Studies in Sociology: A Student's Manual*. Chicago: University of Chicago Press.

Park, Robert E. 1967. *On Social Control and Collective Behavior*. Chicago: University of Chicago Press.

Park, Robert E., Ernest Burgess, and Roderick D. McKinzie. 1967. *The City*. Chicago: University of Chicago Press.

Parton, James. 1867. "Chicago." *Atlantic Monthly* 19 (March): 325–345.

Percy, William Alexander. 1941. *Lanterns on the Levee: Recollections of a Planter's Son*. New York: Knopf.

Peterson, Paul. 1981. *City Limits*. Chicago: University of Chicago Press.

———. ed. 1985. *The New Urban Reality*. Washington, D.C.: Brookings Institute.

Pierce, Bessie Louise. 1933. *As Others See Chicago: Impressions of Visitors, 1673–1933*. Chicago: University of Chicago Press.

———. 1937, 1940, and 1957. *A History of Chicago*. 3 vols. Chicago: University of Chicago Press.

Port, Weimar. 1953. *Chicago the Pagan*. Chicago: Judy Publishing Co.

Powers, John. 1975. *Do Black Patent Leather Shoes Really Reflect up?* Chicago: Regnery.

Prager, Jeffrey. 1985. "American Political Culture and the Shifting Meaning of Race." Paper presented at the Institute for Advanced Study, Princeton, N.J., March.

Quammen, David. 1970. *To Walk the Line*. New York: Knopf.

Rakove, Milton L. 1975. *Don't Make No Waves, Don't Back No Loosers*. Bloomington: University of Indiana Press.

———. 1979. *We Don't Want Nobody Sent: An Oral History of the Daley Years*. Bloomington: University of Indiana Press.

Reilly, Bill. 1982. *Big Al's Official Guide to Chicago-ese*. Chicago: Contemporary Books.

Riedy, James L. 1981. *Chicago Sculpture*. Urbana: University of Illinois Press.

Rosen, George. 1980. *Decision-making, Chicago Style: The Genesis of the University of Illinois Campus*. Urbana: University of Illinois Press.

Rossi, Peter, and Robert A. Dentler. 1961. *The Politics of Urban Renewal: The Chicago Findings*. New York: Free Press.

Rowe, Mike. 1981. *Chicago Blues: The City and the Music*. New York: Da Capo.

Royko, Mike. 1971. *Boss: Richard J. Daley of Chicago*. New York: Dutton.

Rydell, Robert W. 1985. *All the World's a Fair*. Chicago: University of Chicago Press.

Sahlins, Marshall. 1985. *Islands of History*. Chicago: University of Chicago Press.

Sander, Richard, Joseph Bute, Jr., and Robert LeBailly. 1985. *The Future of*

Bibliography

Uptown/Edgewater: An In-Depth Look at Neighborhood Change. Chicago: Organization of the North East.

Schaaf, Barbara C. 1977. *Mr. Dooley's Chicago.* Garden City, N.Y.: Anchor Press.

Schulze, Franz. 1985. *Mies Van Der Rohe: A Critical Biography.* Chicago: University of Chicago Press.

Scott, Mel. 1969. *American City Planning since 1890.* Berkeley: University of California Press.

Shapiro, Brenda. 1981. "An Intimate Gathering in the North Loop." *Chicago* (March): 136–139.

Shapiro, Henry D. 1978. *Appalachia on Our Mind: The Southern Mountaineers in the American Consciousness, 1870–1920.* Chapel Hill: University of North Carolina Press.

Sinclair, Upton. 1906. *The Jungle.* New York: Doubleday, Page and Co.

Slim, Iceberg. 1970. *Pimp.* Fort Lauderdale, Fla.: Halloway.

Smelser, Neil. 1962. *Theory of Collective Behavior.* London: Routledge and Keegan Paul.

Smith, Carl. 1984. *Chicago and the American Literary Imagination, 1880–1920.* Chicago: University of Chicago Press.

Stead, William T. 1894. *If Christ Came to Chicago.* Chicago: Laird and Lee.

Steevens, George W. 1897. *The Land of the Dollar.* Edinburgh: Dodd, Mead and Co.

Stein, Harry. 1983. *Hoopla.* New York: Knopf.

Stern, Richard. 1980. *Packages.* New York: Coward, McCann and Geoghagan.

———. 1987. *The Position of the Body.* Evanston, Ill.: Northwestern University Press.

Sternlieb, George. 1968. *The Tenement Landlord.* New Brunswick, N.J.: Rutgers University Press.

Sternlieb, George, James W. Hughes, and Connie O. Hughes. 1982. *Demographic Trends and Economic Reality.* New Brunswick, N.J.: Center for Policy Research.

Stevens, Joe B. 1980. "The Demand for Public Goods as a Factor in the Non-metropolitan Turnaround." Pp. 115–135 in *New Directions in Urban-Rural Migration,* ed. D. Brown and J. Wardwell. New York: Academic Press.

Street, David. 1969. "Educational Change in the Mass Society." In *Innovation in Mass Education,* ed. D. Street. New York: Wiley.

Sullivan, Louis. 1956. *Autobiography of an Idea.* New York: Dover.

Suttles, Gerald D. 1968. *The Social Order of the Slum: Ethnicity and Territoriality in the Inner City.* Chicago: University of Chicago Press.

———. 1972. *The Social Construction of Communities.* Chicago: University of Chicago Press.

———. 1982. "The Contrived Community: 1970–80." *Urban Patterns: Studies in Human Ecology.* G. Theodorson, ed. University Park: University of Pennsylvania Press.

———. 1984. "The Cumulative Texture of Local Urban Culture." *American Journal of Sociology* 90 (September): 283–304.

Bibliography

Task Force of the Chicago Chapter—American Institute of Architects. 1985. *Couch Place: North Loop Theater District*. Chicago: American Institute of Architects.

Task Force on the Future of Illinois. 1980. *Illinois—The Future: Final Report*. Springfield: State of Illinois.

Taub, Richard, D. Garth Taylor, and Jan D. Dunham. 1984. *Paths of Neighborhood Change*. Chicago: University of Chicago Press.

Terkel, Studs. 1967. *Division Street: America*. New York: Pantheon.

Thompson, Wilbur. 1965. *A Preface to Urban Economics*. Baltimore: Johns Hopkins Press.

Thrasher, Frederic M. 1927. *The Gang*. Chicago: University of Chicago Press.

Towers, Robert. 1982. Review of *The Dean's December*, by Saul Bellow. *New York Times Book Review* (January 10).

Trollope, Anthony. 1862. *North America*. Philadelphia: Lippincott.

Von Hoffman, Nicholas. 1984. *Organized Crimes*. New York: Harper and Row.

Vining, Daniel. 1982. "Migration between the Core and Periphery." *Scientific American* 247 (December): 45–53.

Wade, Richard. 1959. *The Urban Frontier: The Rise of Western Cities, 1790–1830*. Cambridge, Mass.: Harvard University Press.

Walker, Daniel. 1968. *Rights in Conflict*. New York: Bantam Books.

Warner, Margaret. 1979. "The Renovation of Lincoln Park." Ph.D. diss., Committee on Human Development, University of Chicago.

Warren, Elizabeth. 1979. *Chicago's Uptown*. Chicago: Center for Urban Policy, Loyola University Press.

Warren, Elizabeth, Robert M. Aduddell, and Raymond Tatalovich. 1983. *The Impact of Subsidized Housing on Property Values*. Chicago: Center for Urban Policy, Loyola University Press.

Webb, Sidney. 1963. *Beatrice Webb's American Diary*. Madison: University of Wisconsin Press.

Weber, Marianne. 1975 (first published 1926). *Max Weber: A Biography*, trans. Harry Zorn. New York: Wiley.

Weisman, Joel, and Ralph Whitehead. 1977. "The Making of the Mayor, 1977" *Chicago* 26 (June): 123–129.

Welter, Gail Danks. 1982. *The Rogers Park Community*. Chicago: Center for Urban Studies, Loyola University Press.

Wendt, Lloyd. 1934. *Lords of the Levee*. Indianapolis: Bobbs-Merrill Co.

White, Michael J. 1984. "Racial and Ethnic Succession in Four Cities." *Urban Affairs Quarterly* 20 (December): 165–183.

Whitehead, Ralph, Jr. 1977. "Daley the Broker." *Chicago* (February).

————. 1983. "The Chicago Story: Two Dailies, a Campaign and an Earthquake." *Columbia Journalism Review* 22 (July): 25–31.

Whitnah, Donald R., ed. 1983. *Government Agencies*. Westport, Conn.: Greenwood Press.

Whyte, William Foote. 1943. *Street Corner Society: The Social Structure of an Italian Slum*. Chicago: University of Chicago Press.

Wille, Lois. 1972. *Forever Open, Clear and Free*. Chicago: Regnery.

Bibliography

Williams, Kenny J., and Bernard Duffy, 1983. *Chicago's Public Wits: A Chapter in the American Comic Spirit.* Baton Rouge: Louisiana State University.

Wilson, James Q. 1962. *The Amateur Democrat.* Chicago: University of Chicago Press.

Wilson, William Julius. 1980. *The Declining Significance of Race: Blacks and Changing America.* Chicago: University of Chicago Press.

———. 1985. "Cycles of Deprivation and the Underclass Debate." Ninth annual *Social Service Review* lecture, School of Social Service Administration, University of Chicago, May.

———. 1987. *The Truly Disadvantaged: The Inner City, the Underclass, and Public Policy.* Chicago: University of Chicago Press.

Wolfe, Tom. 1981. *From Bauhaus to Our House.* New York: Farrar Straus Giroux.

Wright, Gwendolyn. 1985. *Moralism and the Model Home: Domestic Architecture and Cultural Conflict in Chicago, 1875–1913.* Chicago: University of Chicago Press.

Yessne, Peter. 1969. *Quotations from Mayor Daley.* New York: Putnam's.

Zorbaugh, Harvey Warren. 1929. *The Gold Coast and the Slum.* Chicago: University of Chicago Press.

Zuiches, James J. 1980. "Residential Preference in Migration Theory." Pp. 163–188 in *New Directions in Urban-Rural Migration,* ed. D. Brown and J. Wardwell. New York: Academic Press.

INDEX

Advocacy groups, 92–93
Affirmative action programs, 46–47, 73, 159. *See also* Black community; Public housing
Airports, 11, 42
Algren, Nelson, 249–50
Andersonville, 88
Appalachian whites, 88n.8. *See also* White ethnics
Arabs, 46
Architecture, preservation of, 238
Arts, 240–42
Asians, 90, 105–6, 109, 116, 217, 270

Banks, 104–5, 126
Becker, Gary, 47
Bellow, Saul, 250–52, 255–59, 266
Berger, Miles, 128
Bilandic, Mayor: Chicagofest and, 234; Democratic machine and, 195–96; development projects and, 78–79, 133–34, 139–41, 147; election of, 139–40; promotion of Chicago by, 242
Biograph Theater, 243
Black community: Bellow on, 251–52, 255; "black belt" area, 52, 57; black writers, 255; Chicagofest and, 234; employment and, 41, 46; housing and, 60, 73, 159, 270. (*see also* Public housing); investment and, 42–46, 52; leaders of, 268; political power of, 267–68; population growth of, 41–42, 114; prejudices against, 46–48; public reference to, 38–41, 47–48, 217; Rogers Park and, 110; schools and, 162–67; sports support by, 234n.4;

State Street area and, 138; white advocates for, 165
Boosterism, 89, 243. *See also* Community organizations
Brickyard Mall, 79, 80
Brooks, Gwendolyn, 255
Bua, Judge, 135
Burgess, Ernest, 53, 85–86, 289–90
Burnham Park, 155, 174–86
Bush, Earl, 190
Businesses, 286–87: black communities and, 46; business associations, 30, 76, 105, 116; businessmen visibility, 208; Chicago image and, 237; shopping strips and, 76
Bus lines, 141, 142
Byrne, Jane: academicians and, 209; Cabrini-Green affair, 63–65; Chicago comparative rank and, 19, 21; Chicagofest and, 234; *Comprehensive Plan* and, 37; Dearborn Park and, 175; development projects and, 79, 83, 125–30, 134–37, 141–43; Edgewater community and, 94; promotional slogans of, 242; public housing projects and, 60–66; scandals and, 196–98; trips to other cities, 236

Cabrini-Green Homes, 61, 63–65
Carl Sandburg Village, 11, 158, 159
Carter, Harrison, 7–8
Census Bureau, 19, 21, 27
Central Area, 36–38, 52, 57–58, 76, 281
Central Area Committee, 145n.28
CHA. *See* Chicago Housing Authority